Ten   Minutes   from   Home

Beth Greenfield

Ten Minutes

HARMONY BOOKS / NEW YORK

from Home

Published in the United States by Harmony Books,
an imprint of the Crown Publishing Group,
a division of Random House, Inc., New York.
www.crownpublishing.com

Harmony Books is a registered trademark and the
Harmony Books colophon is a trademark of
Random House, Inc.

Library of Congress Cataloging-in-Publication Data
Greenfield, Beth.
Ten minutes from home/Beth Greenfield.—1st ed.
p. cm.
1. Greenfield, Beth—Mental health. 2. Traffic accident victims—United
States—Biography. 3. Traffic accidents—Psychological aspects. 4. Post-
traumatic stress disorder. 5. Authors, American—Biography. I. Title.
RC1045.P78G74 2010
362.196'85210092—dc22
[B]
                                        2009045232

ISBN 978-0-307-46205-3

Printed in the United States of America

DESIGN BY BARBARA STURMAN

10 9 8 7 6 5 4 3 2 1

First Edition

For Adam and Kristin

~

THIS book tells a true story—true in that the events actually happened, and also in that I have told it honestly, to the best of my ability. Although I cannot recall verbatim dialogue from nearly three decades ago, which is when the majority of this book takes place, I do remember many specific conversations, and have recreated them in ways that feel accurate in both word choice and in sentiment. Some minor details have been changed, unwittingly, as the years and the trauma of the time in question have simply erased various specifics from my mind. I have also changed a few names in the interest of privacy.

Ten Minutes from Home

Prologue

ALL-WOOD construction. That's what it said on the side of Grandma Ruth's coffin. I stared at that phrase while the men in Carhartt vests lowered her into the frozen ground. I stood just feet away, behind my mom, who sat in one of the white folding chairs that the folks from Bloomfield-Cooper Jewish Chapels had set out as part of the funeral package. There were just five of us—me, my parents, my mother's brother, and my partner, Kiki—and sitting felt silly to me, like something to do in a crowd. I wanted us to all be pressed up together, so I stood close behind my mother, my gloved hand on her shoulder.

At ninety-three, my grandmother had outlived her four siblings. She was long widowed and friendless, eschewing company for television and mystery novels. And our extended family was not at all close-knit. Still, it was depressing and even a bit embarrassing, when our limousine driver pulled into the cemetery, to find that our family was outnumbered by gravediggers—especially because there was another funeral about to begin, with a mob of mourners swarming the lawn of the front office, waiting to be told where to go. That burial was clearly for a young person, as the crowd consisted of sad-faced teens in black coats and boots, with teased hair and goth makeup. I wanted to know what happened—had it been drugs? a car wreck?—but there was no way to know. We continued along to Grandma's plot, right next to her husband's, my grandfather's, a man I never knew.

The day before, my mom and I had gone by my grandmother's room at the nursing home to gather up her remaining items: a store-bought quilt my mother had brought from home, a pair of worn-out slippers, a cheap blue sweatsuit that she didn't like to wear. She'd only been in that place for two weeks and, after thirty-five years of living alone in her small efficiency, despised every minute of it. I'd only seen her there a couple of times—visits that consisted of me staring at her as she sat in her wheelchair, caved in and quiet, ashamed of her predicament. She had been shutting down right in front of my eyes, and I couldn't blame her. The other residents there, almost all women, drooled and moaned and cried out about things that no one else could see. Grandma Ruth would roll her eyes and wrinkle her nose at them and look appalled, and say to us, "I don't belong here."

When we showed up at her room after she had died, I felt grounded, as if I could take care of my mother—just as I had this morning, when my mom told me she hadn't thought of getting any food for us to eat after the funeral. "What if people come by?" she had asked. I knew that no one was coming by, but I wanted my mother to feel like she'd given her mother a proper funeral day. And I knew what was expected on a post-funeral table—rye bread, egg salad, turkey, and olives. I didn't know of a good Jewish deli nearby, though, and so settled for the Italian one I remembered from childhood, Giovanni's, where my mom would buy homemade marinara sauce and dense loaves of semolina bread and balls of fresh mozzarella for us to eat on summer nights when she didn't feel like cooking. She didn't go there so much anymore, less impressed by the authentic array now that she and my father had traveled to Italy and all around Europe several times over, but the place was still there, across from the Little Silver train station, and I had fifteen minutes before I had to meet Kiki, who was coming in from our place in the city that morning. I was hasty, and didn't pay much attention to prices, just telling the cheerful woman behind the counter that I needed a platter for ten, and that it was for a funeral. I could tell that this depressed her, because it was Christmas Eve day, but she still set about her task with efficiency, checking in with me each time she arranged some more cold cuts or salad on the huge plastic plate. "This OK, hon?" she kept asking, and each time I nodded. Then I pulled out my credit card and had her load the creation, fit for a houseful of shiva sitters, into the back of my car, and when Kiki and I walked in with it my mother's eyes filled with tears of relief. "You're wonderful, Beth," she told me, and I for once felt my age, instead of like a permanent teenager, in her presence.

I had not felt that way before when there was a death. And now, in the frigid cold of the cemetery, the rabbi, a stranger hired for the task, repeated the snippets of my grandmother's character that my mom and I had told him over the phone yesterday: that she was kind and a good listener who could be a stubborn spitfire, and that she was a wonderful mother and grandmother who used to bake cookies and cakes when my mother was a girl. I watched my uncle Michael, her son, during much of this eulogy, and realized he hadn't gotten to add his own input because he'd been on a plane from California. He looked so alone and out of place, wearing jeans and sneakers under his bulky parka because his lost luggage had yet to arrive at our house. I wore my black suit—my only suit, the one I had purchased for an interview at a magazine a year earlier—and as I stood there before the rabbi I could feel the icy wind cut through the spring-weight slacks. My mom cried quietly and nodded along with the rabbi, and when he finished she read a prayer. Then the burly gravediggers positioned themselves on thin strips of AstroTurf to lower the coffin—into the perfect rectangle they had dug before our arrival—with a basic pulley system of thick canvas straps. First her head and then her feet disappeared below, and I worried that she'd shift in the box, or that she'd bang her delicate head inside. I thought how small she must have been in there, how tiny and thin, all ninety pounds of her, with her fragile arms probably folded on her chest. How I adored those arms—the silky undersides that I'd grab a piece of and rub like a Buddha's tummy, delighting in their fragility. She'd swat me away, angry, but even so I believed that she secretly liked it.

She'd never really been comfortable with touching—hugging me for only so long before pulling away, laughing and saying I was too heavy before pushing my adult head out of her lap. I'd place it there sometimes as she'd nap on our living-room sofa in an attempt to snuggle, but she never allowed it. She had actually let me touch her at Thanksgiving, just one month before, when I went to pick her up and she'd shuffled to the door, confused, sick, telling me she wasn't coming over. "I'm not up to it, Beth," she said, sighing. But when I said that I understood and headed toward the door she changed her mind. She was too weak to get dressed, so she let me help her—putting her skinny arms around my neck as she raised her bottom off her recliner to let me take down her worn and pilling pants. I saw her thighs, smooth like glassine, and her belly, flat and soft and barely wrinkled.

As I watched her go into the ground, watched my mother cry and put her hand to her face, I was struck with the incredible normalcy of this grief. This was a common grief—the kind that everyone deals with at some point. The end-of-life-cycle type of loss you don't look forward to, but expect. I didn't know I would feel so sane. I didn't know I could feel so sad, so robbed, while still knowing deep within myself that my life would go on. I knew my Grandma Ruth was going to die someday, and I dreaded it because I thought it would be like when we lost Adam—like the world was falling apart and would never be whole again.

When the funeral ended, we all slid back into the limo. "The driver said he would take us to visit Adam's grave now," my father said to me quietly. And so it was time to return to the not-so-normal. We were all quiet as we crossed the road and entered the other half of the sprawling cemetery. It had been at least ten years since I'd gone to my brother's gravesite, and I couldn't quite remember where it was. Neither could my father, though he pretended to. "Why don't you just let me run into the office and ask for the location?" I offered. My dad was stubborn. "I think I know where it is," he said, absently pressing his tongue into the lining of his cheek the way he does when he is uncertain. "I'm pretty sure I remember." It was as if I were little again, and Adam was with us, and we were doing our annual drive to Florida for Christmas break and my father couldn't remember how to get back to the highway from our motel.

"Martin! It was the other way, I'm certain of it," my mom

would say through clenched teeth. "Why can't you just pull into the Stuckey's and ask someone?"

" 'Cause I don't want to ask someone, that's why!" he'd snap, the calm excitement over our motel's breakfast buffet (with waffles!) fading fast.

Adam and I would freeze, temporarily distracted from our turf war over the backseat, forgetting, for just a moment, to worry about whose hand accidentally went over the invisible middle line into whose half. I would get a little nervous— would we be lost in the Deep South forever? Would we ever get to Grandma and Grandpa's in Miami Beach?—while Adam would ham it up, turning to me to make ridiculously distorted faces—a five-year-old class clown calming me with the whites of his eyes and the red, flaring insides of his nostrils and his wild, fishy tongue, flecked with faint toast crumbs and poking out at me, making me laugh so loud that my mom would whip her head around and cluck at us. My father wouldn't stop and ask for directions, but drive, instead, in frantic circles, cursing at the roads, blaming everyone in the whole goddamned state of Georgia for not making better goddamned signs.

But this time it was no use. We had to circle back to the office, and in I went, asking for a map, which the lady behind the counter had opened for me, pointing out the lot number of Adam's grave and circling it with blue ink. My father was embarrassed, especially since the rabbi was following in his own car. We all kept quiet. We found the row, and everything started looking familiar—the corner of the cemetery and its creepy reeds in the near distance, the elaborate headstones for folks who had been alive long enough to earn them. The ground was icy and muddy all at once, and we all got out of the limo and began to search for Adam. It was like an Easter egg hunt, but somber, all of us walking up and down rows of

dead people, eyes peeled on the ground. Even the rabbi
helped us look. I was the one to eventually spot it—a flat,
gray slab, hidden among the tall headstones. It said, simply,
ADAM R. GREENFIELD. BELOVED SON, BROTHER. 1974–1982. I
remembered the first time I saw it, when I felt both sickened
and honored by that word. BROTHER. It was for me and
me alone.

I had been with the rabbi that first time—*our* rabbi, Rabbi
Priesand, from the temple we belonged to for more than
twenty years but which my parents left by the time I had
turned thirty because, after years of being active members,
they were tired of how the place's politics overshadowed its
spirituality. The rabbi, a woman in her forties with stiff, wig-
like hair that was a bit longer than a bob and a matronly
way of dressing, offered to take me to the grave several
months after the accident, in the winter, because I'd missed
the funeral, opting to stay in the hospital even though they
would've let me leave for the afternoon. She had picked me
up in her red Chevy Chevette from the house where my mom
was taking a Japanese cooking class that day. I wondered if
the women in aprons knew where I was going, or if they
found it curious that I was going off with our rabbi, but
they never said a word while I was there.

The drive up the Garden State Parkway was long and
awkward, me humming along with the radio and talking
about junior high, answering the rabbi's questions about how
my family was getting along. "OK, I guess," I'd told her. "I
miss them so much. But I don't tell my mom because I don't
want it to make her sad. We never talk about it." When we
got to the massive graveyard the rabbi knew just where to go,
and she pulled her small car alongside the frozen ground and
past the other, larger gravestones and led me to Adam's. That's
when I saw the word, "brother," and when I started to cry. She

held me and I said, "It's not fair! It's not fair!" into her shoulder, but I was just repeating the phrase that I'd heard my mom call out so many times, her face tilted up in anger toward the sky. I didn't know whether I felt it was fair or unfair, or how I felt at all. I just knew it was an appropriate time to cry.

I returned only once with my parents, though I barely remember it. It was at the time of his first yahrzeit—the Jewish anniversary of a death—when it felt mandatory that we go and stand there and pray and cry, only I stood back from them a bit, and stayed quiet, and held in all my tears. Then, when I got my driver's license, I started going to the graveyard alone. I would sneak there, never tell my parents, pretending I was going to meet a friend, or I'd go on my way to or from college, because it was just off the highway that I had to traverse anyway.

Kristin's grave was easier to sneak off to, as it was right in Eatontown, about a five-minute drive from our house. It sat just a few hundred feet in from the road, toward the far end of the cemetery, past all of the elaborate gravestones that stood up out of the ground and formed a mini skyline in the grass. Hers, like Adam's, sat at the edge of a sea of low-key markers—the flat ones, the small and simple rectangles of polished granite laid out so closely together that they made me wonder whether the coffins were really buried underneath them at all. The first time I saw Kristin's, I remember being struck by its simplicity: a slice of light-gray stone bordered by a darker shade of gray, with a small heart carved, as if by a daydreaming teenager, into its upper right-hand corner. In its center it said KRISTIN MARY SICKEL · 1969–1982 · WE LOVE YOU.

My first time visiting it was also with the rabbi, who had taken me at my request right after going to visit Adam's. I remember crying only a bit—I think I had been tapped out—

and that I'd wanted to go mainly to see where it was, since it was so close to home, and I wanted to see if it was someplace where I might ride my bike to alone anytime I wanted. (It wasn't, as there was a highway to cross.) Her cemetery was smaller and not Jewish, and it sat, coincidentally, behind the low flat building where I believed her father worked as an engineer, separated from it by only a wide, sparse field that was ripe for being developed into a strip mall.

Once I got my driver's license and began making frequent trips to her grave, I would sit there in the prickly, dusty grass, talking to her like she'd simply been away on vacation and had missed lots of action, and I would gaze over at her father's building, wondering if he could see me from his office window and if he might be impressed that I was visiting his daughter, or if he might even come over and join me there. It never happened—I never ran into anyone at Kristin's grave—and, unlike at Jewish cemeteries, there were never any stones left behind letting me know if she'd had any recent visitors. It felt like not, like she'd been abandoned there in the quiet dirt, where the only sounds were of cars passing or pulling in slowly to deliver a hunched elderly person to visit his or her loved one, or of an occasional lawnmower at the far end of the cemetery, where the fancier patches of graves were being tended to.

The first time I went to her grave on my own I was in high school, driving my mom's boxy gray Ford sedan with the license I had received only a week before. I didn't have much time, as I'd only gotten the OK to go pick up a few things from the Pathmark. I raced through the supermarket to grab a couple of items I didn't really need—yogurt, tampons, a magazine—and then continued down the highway toward the cemetery, which was only about a mile or two farther. Something about this ability to go to Kristin's grave all on my own was thrilling, and gave me a rush of freedom that even surpassed, at that moment, the ability to drive to the house of my boyfriend, Joey, or to a party on a Saturday night. It was as if I would actually see Kristin again, like I would reconnect with her after several years apart; but my excitement faded quickly enough, when I pulled into the narrow gravel drive-way and sidled up to the row where I recalled her gravestone to be, and got out of the car and strolled until I found it—inanimate and worn looking, with a gossamer film of dusty earth, surrounded by silence. Her loss would hit me anew as I sank down to the ground to trace my finger across her name.

"Hey there," I'd say aloud. "Long time no see. I miss you." And then I'd just cry, careful not to sob in a way that would make my face and eyes look red because I didn't want my mom asking any questions.

That afternoon, after my grandmother's funeral, when I called out to everyone that I'd found the headstone, they all crept over to where I stood and looked down. My parents clung to each other. Michael stood just slightly to the side. Kiki stared at it. I hung back a bit, not ready to get as cozy with everyone as I'd been just fifteen minutes ago at Grand-ma's grave. This was different. This loss had baggage. The rabbi said a short prayer in Hebrew, and as he spoke my par-ents sobbed. Such raw grief still inside them—such different tears than for Grandma. When he was done my mother dropped to her knees, put her small, peach-colored hand on the smooth stone, and my father dropped down with her. It's like they had to collapse, letting all those old wounds in. And I, once again, closed myself off to it.

I wanted to throw myself down there with them, just like I had always wanted to do, even back then. But like then, I did the opposite. I stood erect, not crying, observing with horror and fear. Holding my breath until it was over. I imagined how

different his funeral must have been from my grandmother's—
the huge crowd of mourners, the teachers and neighbors and
temple members and relatives. How many had stood there,
graveside, half crying and half staring with curiosity, thinking,
thank God it's not us, as Adam was lowered into the ground? I
missed it, too frightened to go. But I imagined the spectacle—
his first-grade teacher and his kindergarten teacher and the
principal, the parents of all his little friends, our neighbors and
a clutch of temple folks and an array of family members. My
mom. My poor mom. I was both relieved and regretful about
missing it.

The rabbi said good-bye and drove away, and we walked
back to the limo. The driver left slowly and got back on the
highway, and we all stayed quiet for the start of the drive. But
then something lifted, and everybody breathed. And we
started talking, timidly at first. "The rabbi did a lovely job,"
my mother said. I admitted that I was hungry. My mother
said she was too. So did my father. And I realized we had
made it. We had always made it, of course. It had just never
been so clear before.

Chapter One

GRANDMA Ruth was wearing her lightweight pink slacks when we picked her up that night. I remember because the pants were the color of raspberry Junket, and for a fleeting moment I could taste the packaged custard my mom used to make when I was little.

"Hello, darling," she said to me, climbing into the back of our silver Ford Fairmont station wagon, its crimson seats warm beneath my thighs from June's late-day sun. We were headed to my annual ballet recital, and as she planted a kiss on my cheek she asked, "How's the ballerina?" I inhaled her pressed-powder scent and giggled.

Grandma's slacks were wide at the bottom, the hems brushing the tops of white, low-heeled sandals, the waist high on her short-sleeved white blouse. She always managed to pull off a cool and easygoing look, which was funny because she was not easygoing at all, but anxious and insecure, with an almost paranoid distrust of the world. She clutched her purse tightly to her chest when we were out, and lived a simple, safe life of watching television and trekking to doctor appointments and doing errands at the mall—and of spending lots of time with us, at our house. I loved that she came over frequently, for random dinners or afternoons and always for special occasions, like birthday parties and Halloween and Passover and the first night of Hanukkah.

She was a doting grandma and she loved me dearly. Only after squeezing me that night did she greet everyone else: my mom and dad, up in the front; Adam, sprawled with clownish indifference in the back hatch, barely trying to avoid the mound of my net tutu; and Kristin, my best friend, perched next to me and fanning herself with a *Teen Beat* magazine that she'd brought along for us to pore over together later that night, when we were to have a sleepover back at my house. And as we pulled away from Grandma's yellow-brick, low-income high-rise in Asbury Park—wedged between Deal Lake and the ocean in the old resort town's long-faded glory—she pressed a small cardboard box into my palm.

"For good luck," she whispered conspiratorially.

"Thanks, Grandma." It was a pair of blue heart earrings edged with gold-tone silver. I kissed her and put them in the small space of seat in between us. I would've rather worn them, but no one was allowed to wear jewelry onstage for the recital, and this was just the kind of real-ballerina rule I loved to follow as I liked to imagine that I was just as serious—and lithe and dedicated and talented—as the American Ballet Theatre dancers I liked to read about in *Dance Magazine*. This was especially true on Thursdays, when I had my after-school ballet classes at Mrs. Carroll's studio, when I would lose myself in the classical music, delight in the gritty scraping of rosin powder under my feet and watch my moving body with fascination in the huge mirrors that lined each wall. I loved the cold, musty smell of the studio, and pretended during each class that I was a famous prima ballerina, like Gelsey Kirkland or Allegra Kent, and that every plié and *rond de jambe* was perfection.

"We'll go for ice cream after the show, OK, girls?" my mom announced as we drove along the ocean towards the Long Branch church where the recital would be.

"Mmmmm, cool," Kristin said with a smile into the balmy wind that gushed through her window, making her high pony-tail flip like a happy cat's tail. She was thirteen, just a year older than me, but wiser about all the things that mattered—flirting, fashion, beauty products. I had invited her to come and watch my recital three years before, and now she came with us each year, our own little tradition. Just as my mother would be helping me with my makeup and bun each year, she'd be walking over to our place, cutting through the two neighbors' yards that separated our houses from each other, to leave her pillow and overnight bag—and, this year, a fluffy stuffed monkey—before heading out in the car with my family for the evening.

I always envied how Kristin looked, her pin-straight caramel-colored hair swept back into barrettes, or wound into a coated rubber band that left loose wisps to hug the frame of her face. She was lovely, and knew how to flirt with boys, and had an endless array of trendy clothes. That night she wore tight Jordache jeans, brown leather clogs, and a white sailor's blouse that had a wide red satin ribbon, which was tied into a loose bow just below her clavicle. I felt a stab of jealousy when she showed up at our door that night, but when she looked at me—my long red hair slicked into a tight bun, face done up by my mom in our own amateur version of stage makeup—her glossed lips formed a tiny O and then a wide smile.

"You look so pretty!" she squealed. "I can't wait to see the show." Sometimes I'd feel insecure around her, because she was cooler than me—it was possible that we would have never become friends at all if we had not first been neighbors, but she never let on. And though I sometimes secretly wondered if we were alike enough to even be friends, I only allowed myself to think about it occasionally, because I loved her so much.

The previous winter, Kristin was at our house for a sleepover, the two of us watching *The Elephant Man* on Cinemax. As we watched the movie—boring at first because it was in black-and-white, but quickly compelling in its rawness—a snowstorm began to churn up outside. We kept the backyard light on so we could watch the layers accumulate through the sliding-glass back door, and even though snow always won out with me when it came to any other competitor for my attention, this time it was actually less interesting than John Hurt's portrayal of this lumpy-headed man, with strange tufts of hair and impeccable clothing. It was so desperately sad, and near the end, after his "I am not an animal! I am a human being!" declaration, I felt my temples throb and a huge sob well up in my chest. I held it in, though, because Kristin kept laughing uncomfortably, imitating his slurred speech and trying to make light of the whole thing.

I excused myself at the end, just as the credits began to roll, and hurried into the bathroom, where I could cry and cry for the Elephant Man among the wicker towel racks and still-wrapped guest soaps and the walls covered in their blue and gold flowered wallpaper. I felt a mixture of embarrassment over my emotions and bewilderment at Kristin's lack of empathy. Eventually I pulled myself together—rinsed my face and chose one of the tiny bottles from Mom's collection of Avon perfumes, all displayed on their own hanging bamboo shelf, to dab on my wrists—and when I headed back out, found Kristin joking around with Adam, who had gotten out of bed to watch the snow.

"Who wants to go for a walk?" my father asked, standing at the edge of the laundry room, one booted foot in the kitchen, his arms already stuffed into his winter jacket, a navy knit cap already pulled down over his balding head. It was the best idea—to walk in the fresh snow, to see our old neighborhood in the dark, looking all new in its coat of white.

Kristin and I got into our snow jackets, giddy over the idea of going out at night; it was like something was finally *happening* here in our little suburban development. Mom helped Adam into his snowsuit and his sneakers, put his sneakers into plastic sandwich baggies, and his baggied feet into white rubber boots, and we were off.

My mother flicked on the side-door light, the one just outside of the laundry room, and we piled out, clumsy in our bulky coats and mittens and boots—clumsy except for Kristin, who was willowy and unencumbered in her Jordache jeans and boots with little heels, and short, snug ski jacket that cinched tightly around her middle, just above her hips. Her hair was down, exposed—"No hat?" my mom asked her, and she crinkled her nose up and said, "No! My hair!"—and when we stepped out into the triangle of light through the open door I could see the falling snowflakes sticking to the gently curling tendrils at the edge of her face, which seemed to glow in the magic of the storm.

The neighborhood was so hushed, and so were we, all five of us awed into silence. It was a light snow, the kind you could kick up into the air as if it were made out of soap flakes or grated wax and meant for the set of a TV show. It was not good for snowmen or snowballs, but perfect to traipse through. We followed my dad, with some trepidation, into the middle of the street, which glowed golden from the streetlights, and then we fell into some sort of line and started strolling down this path, covered in virgin snow, past our neighbors' quiet houses. It was thrilling to be in the road, to walk in unsafe territory, and to have it all to ourselves. And it was wonderful to be able to look into the bright interiors of people's kitchens and living rooms—to catch a glimpse of Mrs. Littman wiping down the empty dinner table, to see the eerie blue TV glow flowing down the steep front yard of the Levesques', to wave to Mr. Caviglia, who was already out sprinkling salt on the driveway, and just keep on walking, with no discernable purpose.

When we were halfway around the block and approaching Kristin's house, she shushed us all and started giggling, and whispered to me that we should try to spy on her family, and to try to see if we could catch a glimpse of her sister Tracy so that we could tell her the next day that we had seen her from out in the snow, on an adventure that she wasn't a part of. We told my parents the plan and my mom made a face like we were really naughty and said, "Oh you girls," and Adam said, "OK," and grinned, like he was finally in on something. But when we got to Kristin's house we just stood there in front of it for a minute or so, until Kristin—either guilty for plotting against Tracy or disappointed that no one seemed to notice we were there—said, "OK, let's go," and we all continued on our way, the TV shine the only thing bouncing around in the windows of Kristin's still, dark house.

Back at home, everything felt different, more a part of the world, more grown-up. I had a new perspective of our suburban development, Woodmere, and I had walked down the middle of Thornley Road and Weston Place and Sandspring Drive. Together, Kristin and I had had an adventure, and it had made up in spades for our divide earlier in the evening.

Still, she was older and much more visible to guys than I was.

"I don't know how to tell you this," she said one after-noon, the fall before the snowstorm. We were walking from her house to mine, the long way, past the four houses that sat in the curve in between our own two. Leaves and acorns popped beneath our feet on the cement sidewalk. It was not long after Kristin began junior high without me, leaving me behind, in sixth grade, and we had been hanging out at her place, me listening to tales about cute junior-high boys and gross science-class dissections, before heading to mine, where she would join us for dinner. But then she began her an-nouncement, warning me first, which made my stomach drop and my pace slow just a little. "It's about Scott," she added.

It had to be about Scott—a thirteen-year-old from our beach club who, in my eyes, was as muscular and as mature as a grown-up man. He had light brown hair that parted in the middle and feathered back on both sides of his head, a few perfectly errant strands falling into a tanned face that was warm, handsome, and a bit devilish. He had braces on his teeth and wore OP-brand surfing trunks and had a strong chest, which looked broad and proud whenever he carried his surfboard down to the ocean's edge, where he would paddle around for hours, determined to catch a massive wave, though there rarely were any. Still, every small one he caught made me suck in my breath—and Kristin too. Both of us had pain-ful crushes on him. And though he was always nice to me (and kind of had to be, since our families were friends who spent time together on the beach all summer long), it was clear that he was only truly interested in Kristin.

I felt a stab of jealousy in my gut and steadied myself for what I knew was about to come. "Just tell me," I said, wanting to get it over with.

"We kissed," she blurted, unable to contain her delight. "We made out!"

"When? Where? How was it?" I was torn between an unbearable envy and a burning curiosity; I had never known anyone to kiss a boy before, and was fascinated that this friend of mine had done it. My wonder actually outweighed any anger—especially because summer had ended, and, since none of us drove, I knew that Kristin wouldn't see Scott again until school was out and we were back at the beach club. So it would all be OK until then.

~

My stomach lurched as we pulled into the church parking lot. It was a new location for our recital, with a grander stage and audience hall than the puny one we usually danced in that was closer to home. But this building was older and creepier than that one, with so much space that it held pockets of cold in its dark corners and had the moldy smell of a basement. It was called Our Lady Star of the Sea, and though I found the name ridiculous (humiliating, actually, to say out loud), it rolled off the tongues of the other girls in my dance class— all Catholics, with a few who went to parochial school. They'd show up for ballet class in their plaid uniforms—kilts and sweaters and knee socks and crisp blue oxford shirts— and I'd be fascinated by how serious they looked before changing into their pink tights and leotards.

Mrs. Carroll ran the ballet school out of a small studio in her house—a massive white Victorian that sat on a busy corner in Eatontown and at the edge of a sprawling yard with a barn and a couple of horses. I liked to gaze out at them, watching their tails swish back and forth while I stood at the bar, gripping on too tightly as I tried to lift my pointed foot off of the high-gloss wooden floor, and hold it until the music ended and Mrs. Carroll clapped her hands and motioned for us to start on the other side.

"One, two three, *lift*, two three, *hold*, two three! Higher, Beth!" she'd call out, sometimes moving toward me to hold my leg to the height she wanted. I loved how that looked, such a gorgeous extension, but then it would drop to the floor when she let go. I wasn't such a great ballerina after all—my turnout was poor and extensions were mediocre, and I'd often forget the whole ballet posture, reverting to sticking my butt out until I caught myself in the mirror and sucked it all back in and up. But I had excellent timing and a great memory—I could see a combination once and repeat it back without cues, often earning me a place at the front of the bar.

Mrs. Carroll must have already been in her seventies then, but in impossibly waiflike, muscled shape, and with a stamina that put us to shame as she danced the whole class along with us—as well as the ones before and after—and never seemed to perspire. She wore short sweaters that knotted at the waist and tied long wraparound skirts over her leotards, and kept her near-magenta–dyed hair in neat Princess Leia side buns that never slipped out of place. She made herself up in what appeared to be garish stage makeup—bright lipstick at midday, powder so thick you could see it under the low studio lights—but she was a real grande dame and she knew it. She smoked only when she thought no one saw her, but every once in a while I arrived at my lesson early, and caught her, puffing like a toughie out in her yard as she did chores around the horses.

For our recital she usually chose a classic, like *Swan Lake* or *Giselle*, but this year she decided on a strange combo:

fragments of *Sleeping Beauty*, with costumes of long blue tutus attached to satin bodices, along with parts of the obscure *Frankenstein*, for which we had to wear long, shapeless muumuu-type outfits made of filmy orange polyester. Our costumes were always rented, so nobody's fit perfectly, and they smelled subtly musty, the tutu's netting creased in sections and the orange pieces losing stretches of their hems, trailing loose, long pieces of thread that my mom had to break off with her teeth before leaving for the church that night.

"*Swan Lake's* outfits were much better," I said to my mom backstage. She was helping me to guide the muumuu over my head without disturbing my bun or smearing my makeup.

"Oh, Beth," she said, trying not to laugh. "You'd look adorable in a paper bag."

Onstage that night I was nervous, as always, but I knew that my fans were in the audience, on my side, and it made me smile, even as I missed a turn and panicked for a moment during our *Sleeping Beauty* number, when the scratchy record playing in the wings skipped and made us giggle. But I saw my family out there in the sea of bridge chairs and, though there were white lights in my eyes, I thought everyone looked still and mesmerized and happy.

My favorite part of it all, though, was when it was over, after Mrs. Carroll had received applause and an armful of roses, after I had posed for photographs with the other dancers back-stage, when we were at Beach Plum Ice Cream on the ocean, me basking in my post-performance glory, eating my cup of coffee-chip ice cream knowing that my sleepover and late-night whispers and morning of pancakes with Kristin was still to come.

"Show me the positions again?" Kristin asked, taking a big lick from her dripping chocolate cone before holding it out to her side, readying herself for my lesson.

I loved teaching the ballet positions. "First is where your

heels are together," I told her, holding my soupy dessert in an outstretched arm as I moved to second, and then third and fourth and on to the hardest, fifth, with feet squeezed tightly together, heels to toes. My parents and grandma watched us from a nearby boardwalk bench, the three of them working their plastic spoons and waxed paper cups in a quiet rhythm, while Adam darted all around us, impish and slap-happy, globs of chocolate-chip mint in the corners of his mouth.

"Plié! Plié! Poop-ay!" he called out to the sky, laughing and leaping and skipping, melted rivulets of pastel green seeping out over the rim of his cup and down over his fingers. "Look at me! I'm a ballerina! I'm so pretty! Beth's so ugly! I mean pretty! I mean ugly!"

My parents shot him stern looks, and I tried to ignore him, just rolling my eyes to show that I heard, but that I wasn't going to get mad. He was all wound up and amusing himself, his thick head of red hair slightly shaggy and in need of a trim, the cowlicks in back sticking this way and that, holding their own in the strong breeze. Then he was singing to himself, some pop song or other, his face all tough and contorted and intense just like someone in an MTV video, ice cream dripping, staining his lips. I watched him as I held fifth, pulled my arms up on either side of my face.

"Let me try it," she said. She drew in her cocked hip, standing erect and slamming her heels together. Her hair, set free from its rubber band at some point during the recital, whipped across her face in the summer wind. She wobbled during fifth and almost spilled her ice cream and laughed really hard, which cracked us up, and we both cackled and howled in that adolescent-girl way—exaggeratedly, to let anyone who's listening know that they're not in on the joke— until my father said, "Let's go, silly girls," and we all piled into the station wagon to bring Grandma back home to Asbury.

My father pulled up to the back entrance and I kissed Grandma's cheek and she kissed mine back, getting a vague smear of frosty maroon lipstick, I knew, on my face. She told me, "That was a beautiful recital you gave," and made sure I had the earrings she had given me. They were in my dance bag, and I fished them out to show her, and then she was gone, standing slightly stooped behind the sliding glass door, smiling wide and waving good-bye, her small hand flapping up and down at the wrist instead of side to side, in the excited, exaggerated way you'd wave to a baby. I blew her a kiss.

"Only four days of school left," Kristin said after a few minutes of driving.

"I know, I can't wait!" I told her.

"Then the beach and Scott and then junior high, you and me together."

The mention of Scott made me wince, but I wasn't going to dwell on it. Not tonight. We zipped along Route 35, where there was barely another car on the road, passing gone-dark strip malls and our favorite Carvel and an old steak restaurant with its neon cow-face sign. When we passed the little furniture storefront I gazed longingly at the groovy lounge chairs in the window—huge hand sculptures with cushioned palms for seats. The early summer wind tore through the windows and through our hair, and I imagined the whole of summer— hot and salty, easy, filled with days at our beach club and late nights of cookouts, fireworks, movies—spread before us with no end, practically as wide as the ocean itself. Adam lay in the back hatch of the station wagon, humming to himself and tapping his sneaker-clad feet. My father drove on, under the amber glow of streetlights, just ten minutes from home.

Chapter Two

I T'S like I wasn't even there.

It's like I wasn't even there, but I remember.

I remember it the way that I remember movies—in a series of snippets punctuated by tiny bits of dialogue, in out-of-order snapshots that are dark and fuzzy around the edges, a series of emotions and sounds.

Sounds like my father moaning, unfathomably desperate and loud, low and insistent. Like an animal fighting off death. Like nothing I'd ever heard before or since. The sound would live in my body forever, suppressed just enough to let me forget, to let me function. But I will be able to recall it with little effort into adulthood. I will easily be able to conjure that guttural moan, hear it in my head loudly enough to make me choke up, no matter where I am or what is going on around me. It was his stranglehold on life, staggeringly vulnerable, the far-from-gentle announcement that my father was a mortal person and not just my dad.

I would learn all the details eventually—that he had been pinned beneath the steering wheel, his breath just about squeezed out of him before they cut him from the wreckage with their Jaws of Life machine and strapped him to a gurney, rushing him to the hospital and admitting him to the ICU, where it would be touch and go throughout that entire first night, and that a young man named Edward, too drunk to even walk a straight line, let alone drive one, had been partying on a North Jersey naval base before stumbling into his car and hurtling south, toward the Shore, fast and furious along Route 35, where he had lost control of his steering at the exact moment that we were about to pass him going north, and that his swerve at the Deal Road intersection had flipped his car up and over the low cement divider before dropping it onto the edge of our station wagon's roof, and that it had all happened way too fast for any of us to have seen it coming.

For the moment, though, I didn't know much beyond the fact that our car had stopped moving and that its ceiling was lower than it had been, practically grazing my head, and that the overhead light had gone on, shining down with a sickly yellow glare onto my mother, who broke the sudden stillness by flapping around in her seat, squirming from side to side and craning her neck to look at us, at the three children behind her, still stuck in her seatbelt and not thinking clearly enough to unlatch it.

"Beth? Martin? Beth! Oh my God Beth!" she was yelling, whipping her stunned, bugged-out gaze between my father and me, disoriented and panicky, unable to make a real move. My father's groaning intensified like that of a beast in a trap.

"I'm all right! I'm all right!" I told her, not knowing if it was true, ogling the car's ceiling and the way it bent in at an angle and how I could now touch it with my forehead if I were to just sit up a little straighter.

"What about Adam?!" she screamed. "What about Adam!!"

I looked toward the back hatch and saw him. He was lying on his stomach, not moving, my blue net tutu partially covering his head.

"He's fine!" I yelled, as if saying it would make it so. "He's OK!"

I saw his red hair peeking out from underneath the puff of blue.

An involuntary shiver shot through my entire body. I was wet and cold and sticky. I saw that the back of my hand was coated with blood—noticed it in the same nonchalant-observer way that I would have noticed that a new store had opened at the edge of the highway, and when I let my eyes travel up my arm and down my torso I saw that I was actually soaked with blood—my arms, my hands, my striped polished-cotton blouse. I couldn't figure out where it was coming from. I couldn't really think at all, because my father's groans were making my head swim, and I didn't know what else to do but sit in my cold, wet spot and wait.

My door flew open then, and a burst of chilly night air made me shiver again, made my teeth chatter. A man in shorts and a T-shirt had tugged the door open, and now he leaned in, put his hand on my shoulder, spoke loudly into my face.

"Are you OK!" he shouted. "Can you move!" He seemed nervous, or scared, yelling his questions like statements, holding his arms out to me.

I didn't know who he was or when he had arrived there, in the middle of the road, but he seemed so nice, and going with him seemed better than sitting under the harsh overhead light, listening helplessly as my father gasped for air. My feet were bare because I had kicked off my navy Dr. Scholl's during the ride so I went to slip them on but I couldn't get the right one on because it was suddenly too small. I kept trying, jamming my toes into that little space between the wood and the leather, but it was like it had been switched, when I wasn't looking, with a child's shoe. I glanced down to find out what the trouble was and gasped when I saw it: a foot that was huge and round and purple. It must have hurt, too, but I didn't feel it yet.

"My foot's really swollen," I told the man, though I didn't quite believe it was mine. He looked down at it, yelled, "Put your arms around my neck!"

I was about to do it, because I just had to get out of there, until I remembered Kristin. I turned to my left to see if she would come along too, but she was lying on her side, legs dangling off the seat, face covered with hair that was slick with deep red blood, thick with sparkling shards of broken glass. I turned back away.

"OK," I told the man, wrapping my sticky arms around his warm neck, leaning on him heavily as I hopped over to a nearby curb and sat down with a thud. A crowd of people had gathered all around me. They were unfamiliar, all blank stares and wide eyes, faces glowing red and eerie from the lights of an ambulance that sat there, its motor whirring, its back doors open, bright interior white and clean and waiting.

"I think I'm going to be sick."

It was my mom, speaking to no one in particular. I didn't know where she had come from, but there she was, sitting on the curb next to me, crying and sucking in her breath and talking fast, like a crazy person.

A woman in an orange jacket, an EMT, materialized with a little square plastic bucket, held it in front of my mom's face, chin height, and my mom vomited into it again and again. It was mesmerizing. I had never seen her throw up before.

"That's your nerves," the EMT told her calmly, rubbing her back. "Just nerves."

But when the woman looked up and saw me, bloodied and shivering, she looked alarmed. She placed the bucket into my mother's hands, signaled for a man in an EMT jacket to take her place and squatted in front of me, her face close to mine. Her cold hands prodded my neck, flew along my arms, up the front and back of my shirt, her eyes wild and confused. I was compliant, though I didn't know what she was looking for.

"Where does it hurt?" she asked me. "Where are you bleeding from?"

"My foot's swollen." That's all I knew for sure.

"Let's get some ice on her and splint this," she told another guy, gently touching the heel of my foot. But still she poked at me, her face stony with worry.

"Where's all the blood from, sweetie?" she kept asking, her voice more panicky each time. "Where are you bleeding?"

Oh, that! I thought. *It's not mine, silly!*

"It's my friend's," I told her.

I was so calm, so matter-of-fact, that her eyes got rounder and she sort of froze for a second. My head felt fizzy, and I missed what she said, distracted by the loud buzz of machinery over by our car. I glanced at it and saw sparks flying. I didn't ask any questions.

~

The last time I was so close to an ambulance was when Adam had to get stitches under his eye. One minute he had been running around and around the perimeter of the house, laughing and breathlessly singing a Police song, trying to rile me as I sat practicing Mozart's "Turkish March" at the piano.

"*Don't* stand," he half sang, half shouted, "don't stand, don't stand so close to me!"

Next minute he was down on the floor, next to the iron railing that edged the living room, crumpled and screaming, face streaming with blood. Mom appeared in an instant, her floral, snap-front apron cockeyed on her body, a dish towel thrown over her shoulder.

"What happened, Beth?" she yelled to me. "Where did he hurt himself?"

How should I have known? She looked to me to be the older sister that I was. But I was terrible in those kinds of moments. Passive and terrified, I froze at the piano as she held Adam in her lap. He was shrieking, my mother's fingers poking around in his mouth, getting streaked with blood and feeling for its source until she found what she thought were broken teeth but quickly realized were just half-chewed pretzels, the pieces soggy, white, and salty, that Adam had been chomping on as he ran in circles. Then she swiped at his face with her towel and found the two gashes, both just an inch below his eye.

"Go call an ambulance, Beth!" she cried.

My instinct was to hide under the piano bench, clamp my palms over my ears. But she was glaring at me with fear and worry, relying on me, and so I dashed blindly into the kitchen, stood face-to-face with the dial of the white wall phone. But I only lifted up the receiver for a moment before hanging it back up, too afraid—of *what* I didn't know—to actually dial the 542-0100 number I'd known by heart since kindergarten (and which was right in front of my eyes, in the form of a square, fluorescent-green Emergency! sticker that my mom had plastered on the side of the phone).

"What are you doing?" My mom had come into the kitchen to see if I had dialed, found me just standing there instead.

"I don't want to call!" I started to cry, creating a cacophony with Adam's loud whimpers in the other room.

"Forget it, Beth, I'll do it!" she snapped. "Go and sit with your brother right now!"

We switched places, her half-screeching into the phone and me on the floor with him, much more at ease, holding his head and dabbing at the blood and telling him, "It's OK. Don't cry." I sat there with him until the ambulance came, and once they were loaded in my mom sent me over to Kristin's to wait with her family until they got home.

I made my way over in the dark, taking the shortcut alongside the Cichettis' and the Naomolis' property lines and hearing the crunch of dead, fallen oak leaves under my sneakers. I could look up and see the almost-full moon peeking through the trees and floating in the cloudless sky when I emerged in Kristin's backyard, beside her playhouse and her above-ground pool, which was covered with a thick tarp that had a shallow puddle filled with withered leaves at one end. I saw the blue TV-light glow from there and went toward it, standing at the sliding-glass back door and watching, for just a moment, the entire family—Mr. and Mrs. Sickel, Tracy, and Kristin, who was curled up on the couch's ottoman with their orange cat, Tabby—as they gazed intently at the TV screen. Then I rapped lightly on the door, and Kristin jumped up to let me in.

"Is Adam OK?" she asked, tossing a handful of popcorn into her mouth. I nodded. Kristin was already in her pajamas—a short nightshirt with a fading Donny Osmond iron-on and a pair of thick tube socks that she had pulled up tight to her knees—and her hair was in a high and hasty ponytail. Everyone waved.

"Come on in and watch 'The Making of *Star Wars*' with us!" Mrs. Sickel said.

I joined them on the couch and ate some popcorn. But I could barely concentrate until my mom rang the doorbell to take me home, and I saw Adam in the car—drowsy, bandaged, and bruised, but OK.

I thought of that night—its scariness, albeit brief and minor—for just an instant as the ambulance flew over the road toward the hospital, and I lay back feeling weightless and free, reveling in the speed at which we moved. But then all I could do was worry that we had left everyone else behind—Adam, Kristin, and my dad, all still back at the car. Inside this flying spaceship it was just me with my mom, who kept asking me over and over again if I was all right.

I kept telling her yes, just to quiet her, and I tried to focus on what I could see whizzing by the window above my head: the neon Charlie's Bar sign, traffic lights both red and green, the glow of closed-for-the-night strip malls, an oddly beautiful flash of the moon. My mom was directing everyone, telling the drivers over and over again to take us to the area's better hospital—"Monmouth Medical! Not Jersey Shore!"— and she threw up some more and smoothed the hair over my forehead and spoke to me in a desperately frightened voice that I'd never heard before. I stayed still and silent and tried not to look at her.

We were there in a flash, at the hospital where I was born and where I'd not been since—except for when I was about eight and my father had had a hernia operation and came to the window of his room to wave down to me where I stood, in the parking lot, as close to the world of sick and half-dead people as my mother would allow. I had been clutching a half-eaten Big Wheel as I waved back, bursting with relief to see that he was smiling, but just as happy to get back into the car to finish my snack, its chocolate slowly melting into its thin foil wrapper. Now I was loaded out of the ambulance and wheeled right inside, into the emergency room, where I felt the blast of air conditioning hit my damp skin.

I half expected to see my father waiting for us with Adam and Kristin, but instead I saw a near-empty waiting room and a girl about my age with her dad, lingering near the admissions counter. She had long brown hair hanging loosely and wore a white halter dress that exposed her tanned shoulders. I imagined her to be there waiting for her mom, standing there anxiously with her dad to find out information, when in I flew, bloodied and strange, still in stage makeup, my bun falling out of place. She stared at me, and I felt ashamed because I knew I looked like a mess, but I was past her in an instant, pushed down a long hallway until my gurney was positioned in a small space surrounded on all sides by grayish, mint-green curtains.

My mother walked alongside me the whole time, crying and asking questions and muttering "Oh my God, oh my God, oh my God," breathing fast and hard and keeping a cold, shaky hand on my shoulder. When we got to my room some staff people convinced her to get onto a stretcher next to mine, which she did, but instead of lying down she sat up on it, moving from her knees to her butt to her knees in a frantic, anxious dance.

"Where's my husband? Is my son OK?" she asked the few nurses who had begun to crowd into our little section. "Did someone call Kristin's parents? Do you need a phone number? Who hit us? *Who hit us?*" And then, in between all of it she'd cry out, "Beth? Beth!" and I'd answer, "I'm here, Mom! I'm fine!" and she'd say, "Oh thank you, God," and then keep on asking her questions, though I didn't hear anyone giving her any answers.

Then in walked a doctor—white coat, stethoscope, grim look. He came over to me to examine my foot.

"How's it feeling there?" he asked, pressing four thick fingers gently into the sides and top of my foot. "Painful, right?"

"Uh-huh."

"Looks like quite a break you've got there. We'll take some X-rays and wait until the swelling goes down before we put it in a cast—probably tomorrow morning."

"OK." I had always secretly envied my friends who had broken bones and gotten casts, which they'd wear like super-cool accessories, adorned with brightly colored signatures and doodles from everyone in class. Joanne got one after falling off her bike and breaking her arm. Jeff got one all the way up past his knee after a skiing wipeout. But I'd wanted to get my broken bone through one of those benign ways—not like this.

"Your husband had to be cut out of the car." The doctor had moved on to my mom, just a few feet away from me, to the edge of her stretcher, where she finally lay back. He spoke softly, but with a strong resolve, so that he could be both soothing and believed. "He was trapped behind the steering wheel, and he's got some broken ribs, a fractured shoulder, a punctured lung."

"Oh my God!" she was crying again. "Where is he?"

"He's on his way here, and it looks like he'll be OK."

I breathed out.

Then he said that Kristin's parents had been called and I wondered again where she was. My mom was crying, and though I was on my back I could see her if I turned my head all the way to the left, could see she was holding her face in her hands. She kept asking about Adam, and the doctor took a deep breath. I could see him in full view, standing at the foot of her bed.

"Mrs. Greenfield," he said to her. "I am so very, very sorry," he said. "But I have to tell you that your son," he said, "is gone."

"No! No! No! No! No!" My mother screamed and wailed, sat up straight on her stretcher like a corpse popping out of the earth at the end of a horror movie. They pulled a curtain around her then, and some nurses closed in all around me— one smoothing my hair, another squeezing my hand, another wrapping her beefy arms around me.

I felt as if I must have misheard, as if there was a definition of "gone" that I wasn't aware of, as if that doctor was a fool and didn't even know who Adam was and was talking to the wrong mother, and there would be a hopeful follow-up statement to what he had said any minute.

But all he said was, "We tried to save him, but he just didn't make it. I am so, so very sorry."

I folded inward then, sobbing from somewhere so deep inside that I wasn't even aware it had begun. I felt myself slipping far, far away from my mom and from the nurses, barely feeling their skin on mine, my head buzzing with snow, like on a TV with no reception, wiping out all that was happening around me.

The nurse who hugged me was fat and warm, and I sobbed into her soft and massive perfumed breasts, inhaling her scent and trying mightily to disappear. The nurses told me, "Let it out." They said, "Beth, we're so sorry," and "OK, sweetie. Everything will be OK." I barely heard them, though, and could think of only one thing to ask: "Can you give me something to make me go to sleep?" I asked them over and over again. "Can't you please give me something that will make me go to sleep?"

The nurses seemed confused by my request, barely acknowledging it and continuing on with their clichéd comforts. But I knew there was something that people could get to disappear from moments like these because I'd seen it on *General Hospital*, which I watched every day after school. Whatever the drug was, it was a shot, and it was pulled out every time a woman wound up in the hospital after a traumatic situation—hurricane, kidnapping, plane crash, attack by a madman, whatever—and it would soothe her into a peaceful unconsciousness as someone stood over her, holding her hand and whispering, "That's it, hush now. Just go to sleep." That's just what I wanted.

Instead I got a couple of Tylenols with codeine and a plastic cup of water, and a gentle, blond nurse who helped me out of my striped blouse and red polished-cotton Sassoon pants. She used small, sharp scissors to cut them up from the cuff along the inseam so they could slip over my hugely swollen foot. I cringed when she did it because I had picked out the pants just a week before at the mall, at Alexander's, and Mom had said OK because they were on sale and because they were not too tight and because I'd needed a special outfit to wear for my recital night. Now they were ruined, stained with wide patches of blood, the right leg cut and shredded.

"I don't see where this blood is coming from," the nurse said, looking frustrated and worried as she examined my legs and belly.

I told her calmly, just like I did the EMT, "It's not mine. It's Kristin's." It's like I either didn't know what I was saying— *blood*, that it was her *blood*—or that I felt perversely lucky because I had this part of her on me.

The nurse didn't ask any more questions then, and was quiet as she used a warm cloth to rub the blood, thick and sticky, off of my skin, squeezing crimson water into a small sink over and over again. I shivered in the air-conditioning as she helped me into a light blue hospital gown that tied at the back. Then she handed me another cup of water.

"Swish gulps around in your mouth and then spit into this," she told me, putting a small bedpan on my lap. "We need to get that shattered glass out of your braces."

"I have glass in my braces?" I couldn't feel a thing.

"Yes, honey. From the car windows."

"Do you have a mirror? I want to see."

She left the room for a minute to get one, small and square, in a plastic frame, and when she returned and handed it to me I sat up and stared at myself. I looked strange—glassy-eyed and puffy faced from crying, stage makeup still evident with streaks of blush and eye shadow, which was smeary, and the smooth bun in my hair shifted down to one side of my head. I plucked bobby pins out of my hair, handing them to the nurse and letting my hair go free, and grimaced into the mirror to look at my teeth and their braces, seeing, sure enough, white powder packed into the metal bands.

"It doesn't even look like glass," I said. "Weird."

"It's kind of pulverized," she explained. "Must have been quite an impact."

I did the water swishing and spitting thing until it looked pretty clear, and then the curtain around my mother opened up and I saw that she looked calmer—or drugged or defeated—and was sitting in a wheelchair. She was being taken away, and held an outstretched arm toward me and cried, "I'm sorry, Beth, I'm so sorry!" Her hair was rumpled and her face was sanguine and twisted, and she looked like a distraught stranger. And then she was gone.

Then began a parade of people—a blond woman in a white lab coat who wheeled in an EKG machine, hooking me up to it for a few minutes; a nurse who transferred me briefly to the ice-cold X-ray room, where I lay still and scared until they told me they were through; a new doctor who took a look at my foot, lightly prodding and tapping it and making me cry in pain; some of the nurses who had been there when the doctor said that Adam was gone.

In between, I was left alone for short spurts, during which I lay still and obsessively counted the squares of the speckled drop ceiling above me—ten across and six down, making it a nice even sixty—and when I stopped counting I just listened to the sounds of the emergency room around me. I heard people talking with doctors, all hidden behind their own curtains. One person was throwing up loudly, another moaned.

"It's awful, the constipation!" said another. "I haven't gone in days and it hurts!"

We were supposed to go on a family trip to Niagara Falls in a few days, right after school let out for the summer, and I realized with a profound disappointment that we wouldn't be going now. Then I noticed thick rings of dried blood under my nails and sucked on my fingers, which tasted metallic.

"Beth?" I'd closed my eyes for a minute, opened them when I heard my name.

"What are you doing here?" I asked, sitting up.

It was the rabbi from our temple, right there, standing in the space where the curtains parted. She was with two other women from the temple, Mrs. Brandwene and Mrs. Tuchband, who were, I would eventually learn, members of the official Emergency Support Committee. It must have been past midnight, and they looked weary and red-eyed, the rabbi's usually-stiff bobbed hair slightly mussed up and her petite frame clothed haphazardly in sweatpants and a polo shirt—a strange departure from the formal pantsuits and A-line skirts and royal-blue rabbinical robes I was used to seeing her in.

"I'm here to see you and your family," she said, smiling faintly. "How are you doing?"

I couldn't get past the fact that she was awake so late, and that she was here, so fast, visiting me in her sweatpants.

"I've been counting the tiles on the ceiling to give my mind something to think about," I told them.

"Don't do that, sweetie," Mrs. Tuchband said. "You'll hurt your eyes."

They came toward me and stood around me, placed their hands on my shoulders, my forehead, the small of my back. The rabbi leaned in and gave me a hug.

"The doctor said that Adam is dead," I told them, fishing for the truth.

Everyone was quiet. The rabbi closed her eyes for just a second and then looked right into mine. "Yes," she told me, her voice quiet and hoarse. "I'm so very sorry."

I thought that there was a chance she hadn't gotten it right, so I moved on. "Where's my mom?" I asked.

"She's with your dad."

"Where's Kristin?"

"She's with her parents," she said.

I was glad to have the company, but felt weird about it too, like I had to entertain them. "I broke my foot," I told them.

"Does it hurt very badly?" Mrs. Brandwene asked.

"Yes, it kills!" And then, "Do you think they could give me something to make me sleep?"

They gave me the same perplexed looks that the nurses had, and I felt hopeless.

"Just lie back," Mrs. Tuchband said. "I bet you'll fall asleep all on your own."

But it wasn't about sleeping, I wanted to tell them. It wasn't about being tired. Still, I lay back down, let her pet my head and closed my eyes. But I only saw twisted metal and splotches of blood and Adam's hair peeking out from underneath the blue tutu, and so I opened them, saw my hacked-up pants and the bedpan that I had spat into and my purple foot packed in ice, then closed them again.

Chapter Three

THEY brought me up to the adolescent ward called BBR2 sometime that night, when it seemed that the entire rest of the hospital was asleep. I can't remember who wheeled my stretcher, but I know that I was more relieved than scared to be whisked, alone, out of the emergency room, into a huge, empty elevator and down a soothingly dim hallway into a dark and peaceful room. It got me away from the madness, away from my mom.

"My foot hurts really bad," I told someone, a nurse, and she was sweet and said, "I know, it'll get better," but that wasn't helpful, so I told her again and again—because the pain was searing, enough to make me sweaty and nauseous—until she went away and then returned with some pills, which I gulped down, hoping they'd not only numb the pain but make me unconscious, too.

I got the bed by the door, though the one near the window was empty, and I lay in it alone for a while, I'm not sure how long, waiting for the drug to wash over me, closing my eyes but not quite sleeping, thinking about the recital and the ice cream and the sleepover that didn't happen—Kristin's pillow and stuffed monkey at home in my bedroom.

"Hello, dear."

An elderly woman, pudgy and uniformed, like a nurse, roused me, but her voice was indifferent—not sweet like the others' had been.

"Hello."

"How are we this evening?"

I was confused by the question. What could possibly be my answer? She didn't wait for it.

"I just need to ask you some intake questions," she said, plopping into a clunky bedside chair and sighing as she retrieved a pen from behind her ear. She started with my name, my address, and I answered her suspiciously, wondering why I, instead of my parents, was answering such things.

"Date of birth?" she continued.

"April twentieth, 1970."

"Do you have any brothers or sisters?"

I searched her face for irony, ignorance—a clue, perhaps, that I did have a brother indeed—and I winced as my foot pain groaned back to life. I told her, mainly to see if it was true (because perhaps it wasn't true after all if she could ask such a thing), "They said my brother died."

"Oh, yes, dear," she said, no apologies. "Besides him." Her pen sat poised above her clipboard.

"No," I told her, stunned. I barely heard the rest of the questions, though I must have answered, because she wrote things down and nodded her head at me and then she was off, and as she left the room I asked her to please bring me more pills, because my foot was on fire, and because I was way too awake.

Nobody came with the pills, but people came in and out of the room to examine and prod at my foot, take it on and off ice, get the swelling down so it would be ready for a cast the next morning. And then I had a visitor—my cousin Susan, who lived in South Jersey and who we usually only saw at Thanksgiving. She was my mom's first cousin, one of three sisters in their thirties, and I adored her.

"Hi, Bethie," she said, rushing into my room from the hallway with a nervous, bewildered energy, as if she were being chased.

I had to blink a few times before her presence registered with me. How did she get here so quickly? How did she know? It made it worse in a way, having Susan here, so out of context—a sure sign that this was all real, and that it was a very big deal.

"Susan? What are you doing here?" was all I could say. She stood over me, put her face close to mine, and I saw that the tiny freckles around her eyes were stained with running, clotted black mascara. I had never seen her cry before.

"They called me. Mom gave them my number as next of kin," she said. "Oh, Bethie, Bethie. I'm so sorry. How does your foot feel?"

"It hurts a lot," I told her. "Where is everyone?"

"Mommy and Daddy are together," she said. "You'll see them soon."

"And Kristin?"

Her eyes watered, and she said, "With her parents."

So that left Adam. But neither of us mentioned him.

She blew her nose and sat on the edge of my bed. It must have been three in the morning by then—a time I'd never before been awake to see—and I couldn't help but doze off, fitfully.

When I woke up Susan was gone. In her place was Mrs. Tuchband, standing over me and putting her soft, spicily perfumed hand on my cheek. She was about my mom's height, five feet tall, and had hair just like hers—chestnut brown and chopped into a short, feathery 'do. She was pretty, with warm eyes that crinkled in the corners when she smiled. It felt odd, having this practical stranger be there with me, taking care of me like a mom, but I was so happy to have her that I wanted to cry.

"Try to sleep, Beth," she said, her voice thick with worry and exhaustion.

"How? My foot hurts so bad," I told her.

I moaned out loud for the rest of the night, and she settled into another chunky wooden chair, like the one the intake nurse had sat in, this one across the room near the empty bed, under the window. I could see her only faintly in the darkness, her form like a shadow through the filtered light of the hallway and the mottled veil of pain in my head.

"Try to imagine," Mrs. Tuchband suggested, "That the pain is really an itch. Try to concentrate really hard on that."

I tried, though it was a struggle to focus, and though I was convinced that such a trick would never work.

"I can remember sitting in hospital rooms with my Ellen, after all of her knee surgeries," she told me. "And it would hurt so much and I would say to her, 'Turn that pain into an itch!'"

"Did it work?" I asked, momentarily distracted by the mention of her daughter, who was eighteen and so hip and so beautiful—a singer who would come around to all the Sunday school classrooms with her guitar, teaching "Dayanu" or "Eli Eli," the downy curls of her strawberry-blond hair resting on her arms. Her voice was mesmerizing—husky and sweet and soft and immense all at once. I always sang my best when she was there because I wanted her to notice me.

"It *would* work!" Mrs. Tuchband said. "Let's make it work for you. Did you turn the pain into an itch yet?"

"Yes," I lied.

"Good. Now concentrate really hard and move the itch to your pinkie finger, and scratch it! Scratch it hard until it goes away!"

I scratched at my left pinkie until my fingernails left red streaks, but all the while I was still moaning, too, and tears leaked out of my eyes. There was no itch, only pain, and in between the scratching and trying to imagine I kept returning to just one thought: Adam is dead. Adam is dead. Adam is dead.

How could it be true? Dead was for movies—horror movies, like *Friday the 13th* and *The Blob* and *Dracula*, which I'd watch with Adam on rainy Saturday afternoons, shielding my eyes from the gory parts while screaming with delight. It couldn't be true.

I finally fell asleep, my nails still desperately digging into my pinkie.

~

When I opened my eyes again, Mrs. Tuchband was still there, across the room, hunched and asleep in her chair just beneath the window, where the blue glow of dawn was seeping in. I slowly pieced together where I was, remembered the sound of the roof crashing in and the sight of Adam on his stomach, motionless beneath my tutu, and then the news, delivered by the doctor whose face I could not picture.

"Do you want me to call for more pain medication?" Mrs. Tuchband was awake then, sitting up and rubbing her face and slowly standing, her hair stuck straight up like a feather on the side that had been pressed into the back of the chair. "You were moaning," she explained, coming closer to my bed. "You were moaning about your foot."

I had temporarily forgotten about my foot, but now that, too, came back to me. I felt the searing pain and looked down to try and see it but it was splinted and wrapped elaborately, with just my toes, purple and swollen as raw sausages, peeking through the top. "Yes. It hurts so bad," I said groggily. "What time is it?"

"Five thirty. You rest now, and I'll go and find a nurse."

It was the time of morning that I wasn't accustomed to seeing face-to-face, but always sideways, the almost imperceptible light slipping in through the crack between my bedroom windows and their heavy shades just as my father was leaving for work. I was nudged awake by the sound of the heavy garage door going up, its squeaky metal wheels grinding in their tracks as he lifted it by hand to step out onto the driveway and then close it behind him before easing into his Pinto, turning the motor over and letting it warm for a minute or so before backing out of the driveway and heading off for the twenty-minute drive to Toms River High School North, where he wore a button-down shirt and tie every single day of his thirty-year tenure as an American history teacher there. "I can't *stand* that some of these new, younger teachers don't wear ties," he'd say. "You've *got*. To *look*. *Professional*."

I would picture him leaving, moving through the chilly darkness of our house all alone, eating cereal at the kitchen table, reading the paper, putting on his shoes and his coat and heading out into the day before the sun even officially broke through the sky, and I would feel a twinge of sadness about it all before falling back into my deep sleep, only to have to get up myself an hour later. For the longest time, in a tradition that would continue until high school, my mom would be my gentle alarm clock. She'd come into my room fresh out of her own bed, still warm and rumpled in her nightgown, and climb under the covers with me, whispering, "Beth. Time to get up," and I would groan and tell her "Noooo," and she'd lay there with me for five or ten minutes and then try again, this time with a bit more urgency in her voice. "Beth," she'd say, "come on. You're going to be late. What do you want for breakfast?"

"Oatmeal," I'd tell her. Or "Rice Krispies" or "Pop-Tarts." And she'd go and get it all ready for me, but not until I was sitting up and focused on getting to the shower, and she was pretty certain that I wouldn't fall back asleep and make myself late.

I had hoped that some sort of normalcy would return at daybreak, but it didn't seem likely as I lay there alone, surveying the hospital room in the morning light. Next to me, along the wall where Mrs. Tuchband had slept, the other bed was still empty. A drab gray curtain hung between it and me, blocking my view of its pillows, and also in between us was a narrow table on wheels with a yellow plastic pitcher and the small white bedpan that I had peed into the night before. A television, mounted high on the wall in front of me, was off.

"OK, sweetheart, she's on her way." Mrs. Tuchband had returned, pouring some water from the pitcher into a plastic cup and standing beside my bed with it in her hand. I barely knew her, and yet here she was, the only one holding vigil. She'd lost Mrs. Brandwene somewhere along the way, as well as the rabbi, who had gone to see my father in the ICU.

"Good morning!" A chirpy nurse entered the room, palming a miniature, pleated Dixie cup. "This is Tylenol with codeine. It's not quite time for it, but since you're really in pain I'll give it to you early." She smiled at me and then at Mrs. Tuchband, dropping the pills into my hand. I swallowed them with the water and then lay back into the pillows, feeling exhausted.

"Sleep, dear. I'm going to need to get home," Mrs. Tuchband said. "But your cousin Susan is on her way up. And Mom will be in here soon. They're letting her share a room with you. Isn't that nice?" I nodded, and then faded away.

I slept hard, dreamed of nothing and woke up gradually sometime later, the ruckus at the next bed registering only as a distant din at first, bringing me up out of my drugged slumber in a way that felt like bursting to the surface of the pool at the beach club after attempting to swim the entire length under water. And only when my head finally popped out completely did I realize that it was Mom's voice at the center of the commotion.

"If only we hadn't stopped at that gas station! If only we had left the ice cream place five minutes earlier!" Her words came out like whines and groans, broken up by hoarse sobs and waves of childlike weeping. "Oh why did we have to take that route home? It's not fair! It's not fair! If only I hadn't let him sit in the back hatch! If only if only if only . . ."

"Please take this, Mrs. Greenfield. Please, it will help you."

"I don't want any drugs! I want my son!"

"It's just a little something. It will calm you. Please, Mrs. Greenfield."

She was quiet for a moment and then began crying again. "But we were almost home," she said pleadingly. And then she yelled it, as if saying it was what made her realize it in the first place. "We were almost home!!"

I listened with the distanced fascination of someone watching a trauma scene on *Marcus Welby, M.D.*, but with less empathy and more shock. It unhinged me to hear my mom losing it like that; scared me like nothing else ever had before.

One of the nurses—there were about three clustered around her bed, plus a doctor and the rabbi and my cousin Susan—saw that I was awake and yanked the curtain between our beds, blocking the whole scene from my view. But my mom caught the move and shifted her frantic attention to me, so I closed my eyes and tried to pretend I was still asleep.

"Beth? Are you awake, Beth?"

"Mrs. Greenfield, please, let her . . ."

"Oh my Beth!" I snuck a peek and there she was, at my bedside, a wreck, the back of her hospital gown flapping around, her eyes terribly hard and glassy. "Oh Beth I'm so sorry! So sorry!" She dove at me with a desperate lunge, leaned over me and pulled me into her chest, pressing her cheek against mine and stroking the top of my head. "This isn't fair for you. This isn't right . . ." She spoke dramatically and continuously into me, and I recoiled with each word, each new squeeze, going stiff and emotionless beneath her. I couldn't cry, couldn't look at her, couldn't bear to be in the room. I felt compelled to let her know that I was fine so she would leave me alone, though, and so, bereft of any other ideas of how to do so, I smiled at her. It was maniacal looking, I'm sure, the way I looked right at her and forced up the corners of my mouth—not my eyes, not my cheeks—into a big, toothy grin that was pure mechanics, total desperation. My mother paused when she saw my face, pulled her arms away and dropped them to her sides.

"Are you OK, Beth?" she asked, confused.

"I'm fine!"

"You can talk to me. You know that, don't you? You can talk to me. You can cry, let it out."

"I'm fine." I was, in a way. I was completely numb. Couldn't have cried if I tried.

She looked even sadder then—alone, as if her last shred

of support had gone, abandoned her. Like she was the
crazy one for grieving so hard. A tiny drop of me melted inside, regretting the way I had smiled and signaled a standoff.
But just a drop. I couldn't help it; she was on her own. And so
was I.

Chapter Four

S HE'D always been prone to hysterics. Lightning storms
made my mother as panicky as I'd imagined an eight-on-
the-Richter-scale earthquake might have. Talking on the
phone during them was prohibited, as was standing in front
of windows.

"The safest place to be in a lightning storm is on a couch
or a bed, because of its mattress," she'd say, "or in a car, because of its rubber tires." She'd remind us of this if we happened to be in the car when the storm broke out—which
happened often in the summer, when we would have just
fled the beach, hurriedly tossing the blanket and chairs and
sun umbrella into our locker and hopping, sandy feet and
all, into the car because of black clouds and the beginning
of rain. Thunder would rumble the sky on our way home,
thrilling both Adam and me, but then a white-hot bolt would
dart ferociously in the distance and we'd glance nervously at

Mom—steeling ourselves not for the storm, but for her reaction to it.

"Oh boy," she'd say. "Oh cripes. Here we go. You guys OK?" We were, of course. She wasn't. Then would come the downpour and all bets would be off. "Oh boy. I'm pulling over," she'd say, fear sounding like indignant anger. "I can't see a thing and I'm pulling over. Sorry, folks!"

And there we'd sit, on the side of Ocean or Sycamore Avenue or Route 36, sheets of rain rushing across the windows like we were in a car wash, Mom giving a running commentary about how she was doing the right thing by waiting, and how all the drivers zipping by were idiots, and how it didn't matter if we missed the movie or got home a little bit later. "At least we'll get there in one piece," she'd say.

She was nervous when it came to us, too.

One summer I remember playing in the shallow end of our beach club's outdoor pool, loving the sensation of my lanky, five-year-old body slicing through the chlorinated coolness. I was playing "gymnastics" with Melissa, using one of the shiny black lane lines as a balance beam on which to do underwater handstands and cartwheels, and as my head popped out of the water near the end of a particularly graceful move, I heard Mom's unmistakably shrill panic voice pierce through the thick afternoon air.

"Adam! Where is it! Adam! Open your mouth!" She was yelling, and the other mothers lounging around the pool were looking at her. I stopped playing, dipped my head back in the water to smooth out my hair, and peered toward her. When I had first entered the water she had been stretched out on a chaise lounge wearing her blue flowered bikini and watching me, with Adam, who was seven months old, propped peacefully between her legs as he played with the dial of our little transistor radio. But now they both looked unhinged—my mom jumping to her feet dramatically, grabbing both the radio and my brother. Some of the other kids in the pool—including Melissa, who by now was just standing in place, consternation etched in her forehead—stopped what they were doing and looked back and forth between me and my family.

"Where's the battery, Adam? Open your mouth! Oh my God, oh my God . . ." My mom was losing it, Adam was hysterical and suddenly I realized that I should have probably been scared too. So I lifted myself out of the pool and padded over, dripping wet and sprouting goose bumps from the cool wind that the ocean had whipped up. I glanced toward Billy, the afternoon lifeguard, who wore only a tiny red Speedo and a whistle on a string, and saw he was watching us with concern, trying to figure out if he should dash over and help.

"Mom!" I called. "What happened? What's wrong with Adam?"

"Beth! We need an ambulance! He swallowed the battery!" For evidence she held up the radio, its battery slot empty. She clutched at Adam, who was red and squirming, and tossed the radio down onto the chaise lounge before trying to pry his mouth open to look inside. He writhed and resisted, and by now the two of them were making enough noise to prompt Billy to hustle over. I was torn between utter mortification and a queasy fear that Adam would die of battery poisoning at any moment.

"Billy! Oh Billy! I don't know how I didn't see him do it!" my mom cried. "He puts everything in his mouth these days! I should have known better!"

And only then, as Billy took Adam into his tan, ropy arms and began rapping firmly on his chubby pink back, did I see it: the battery, which glinted like a silver coin on the cement pool deck, right next to our bottle of Sundown Sunscreen and my mom's shiny pink can of Tab. I snapped it up and held it high in the air, as if raising a flag to signal victory.

"Mom!" I shouted, my voice quavering with the rush of tears that was about to begin. "Look!"

~

She had always been nervous and overprotective, even before we adopted Adam, but when he came along it was all the more noticeable—and all the more intense—as he gave her more of a reason to worry than I ever did. I was a cautious child. I looked both ways each time I crossed our rarely traf-ficked street and I pumped the brakes on my bicycle to tem-per the speed as I coasted down a hill. I'd never broken a bone or fallen on my head, and I rarely even skinned a knee. But Adam had a daring streak that caused my mom distress. He liked to race his bike around the neighborhood and jump from the top of the jungle gym and run headlong into the crush of ocean waves. When he was three my mother rushed him to his first hospital visit after he had sat quietly at the far edge of our backyard and pushed a small pebble high up into his right nostril.

"I put a pebble in my nose," he announced to Mom. She was stirring onions and garlic in a pan, getting ready to throw in the eggplant and zucchini for our ratatouille dinner on that early summer evening. I had just come in from a long after-noon of collecting more than thirty helpless peeper frogs in our plastic baby pool. I'd added blades of grass and fuschia azalea blossoms and shallow puddles of water from the hose to help the creatures feel at home, and I was excited about my plan to release them all at once, in a hopping mass, right after dinner. But Adam, who stood calmly in the kitchen as he re-ported his actions, his bare feet shedding fresh dirt onto my mom's shiny yellow linoleum floor, easily distracted me.

"You did *what* with a pebble?" Her anxious tone rose up like the whistle on a tea kettle—always an alarming, irritating surprise. My heart sank. Here we go, I thought.

People ask me now if my mother got even more overprotective after the accident, and they're surprised when I tell them that I am not so sure. I actually think that it might have been worse before—before she really knew what she was trying to protect us from, and before the worst had come and snatched one of us and shown her that there was nothing she could do. She could rely on rules beforehand: Don't swim right after you eat; look both ways before you cross the street; don't eat apples collected on Halloween before cutting them open and checking for razorblades.

"But Mom, *Mrs. Landaur* made those candy apples," I'd remind her each year as she'd pluck one from each of our pillowcases, which sagged with Hershey's Miniatures and lollipops and Tootsie Rolls that Adam and I would have collected on our rounds through the neighborhood.

"Beth, I don't care. You never know," my mom would say, and she'd take those fat, gorgeous, ruby-red treats and tear off the perfect squares of wax paper and pull a plastic-handled steak knife out of the kitchen drawer. Then she'd hack, with focused swipes, into each beautiful apple until it fell into imperfect chunks. I'd watch its white flesh brown quickly under the cracked, glasslike shards of its shell, and I'd imagine how wonderful it would be if just once I could bite into its hard, sticky side like I knew everyone else did.

Another rule: "If a stranger comes up to you after school and tells you, 'I'm a friend of your mother's, and she sent me to pick you up and take you home,' then run away and tell a teacher right away." This never happened, though I used to wonder about it a lot once she warned us. I'd wonder, if my mom hadn't warned me, would I have believed the person and gone along for the ride? And even with the warning, would I be too shy to refuse? Sometimes I got scared on our walk to or from elementary school—a ten-minute journey on white sidewalks that took us past nine neighbors' houses and the tennis courts and sledding hill of the schoolyard. A strange car would slip by sometimes, and I'd think, Will this be it?

One time there was an announcement made on the loudspeaker at school, just before the ringing of the final bell. "Attention, students: Walkers, please remain in the classroom after school today to await instructions." No one but bus riders was allowed to leave. The parking lot slowly filled with mothers in cars. They had been called, we found out later, because a strange man had "exposed himself" to Robin Bryant as she walked to school, late, that very morning. She had reported it, and a squad car came and picked her up and drove her around the neighborhood, in the hopes of having her point out the flasher. But he was long gone—or hiding out in the bushes. And no one was taking any chances.

"Hop in, Beth," my mom commanded, nervously, through her window. She'd come in our station wagon—a gold Hornet that my dad had purchased at the lot for a big discount because the previous owner had returned it, practically new, after getting the ceiling reupholstered in a classic green-and-tan Gucci pattern for his wife, who hated it. I loved the dizzying pattern of face-to-face Gs, which my dad liked to joke stood for "Greenfield," and I gazed up at them after slipping into the backseat next to Adam, who was in his car seat. "What's going on?" I asked.

"There was a strange man in the neighborhood this morning," she said, angry and distracted. It's how she got when she was scared. "A real pervert. He exposed himself to Robin Bryant."

I thought of Robin—older and cool, in sixth grade and with perfectly feathered hair. A few years later she would become one of our favorite babysitters and teach us how to do the Hustle on the sea of green-gray carpeting in our usually-off-limits living room—the same living room she'd come to sit shiva in with her mom after the accident, acting distant and uncomfortable, and not quite able to look at me. Even then I would remember her as The Girl Who Was Flashed—just as I must have already become, to her, The Girl Who Survived the Accident.

Chapter Five

I WAS four years old when they brought Adam home.

"Sometimes women have babies that they are too young to take care of," my mother had explained to me, before that day, about where he would come from. She explained to me about adoption as we lay in my bedroom, sprawled together on the fluffy pink and red shag carpet that I loved to burrow into, its strands like the hair of a creature that would be on *Sesame Street*. "You will be the big sister!" she told me. "He is going to love you so much."

They'd wanted me to have a sibling so badly. But my mom had had fertility problems, had spent years traveling to see specialists in the city to get hormone shots, miscarrying over and over again before finally having me at thirty-one. So after a few years with just me, when doctors said it was unlikely that she'd get pregnant again, they'd registered with a Jewish adoption agency, writing a letter to the prospective birth mother about me, their redheaded daughter, and what a great big sister I would be.

"That's what did it," my mother would tell me years later. "When her son came out with red hair, she remembered reading about yours. It seemed like a match that was meant to be."

There were frequent visits to a lawyer's office before Adam arrived, and I'd often go along, sinking into a deep leather chair in the corner of his vast office and staring at his massive print of Andrew Wyeth's *Christina's World* as my parents' legalese chatter faded into a distant hum. I'd sit there, content, getting lost in the scene of this ragged woman trying to crawl toward home, making up stories about whom she was trying so desperately to reach.

I'd see the original painting years later, during freshman year in college, strolling through the Wadsworth Atheneum in Hartford, recognizing it in a way that had made me gasp. It was famous, of course, but in that moment I'd remembered it only from the lawyer's office. I bought a print of it to hang in my dorm room, and when I got back to campus I stuck it up hastily right on the tan cinder-block wall above my bottom bunk bed. I used that Smurf-blue Fun-Tak, pressed into the back of each corner, and kept it up for that entire year. No one but me knew that it was a shrine to Adam, to his beginning.

His hair actually looked brown to me the first time I saw him, but I didn't say anything. I glimpsed the startling mass of it as I stood with Grandma Ruth in the front door, pressing my nose against the heavy storm window and watching as my mom carried him, a tiny bundle, out of the gold Hornet and into the house.

It was a crisp, clear December day, and he was wrapped tightly in a plaid wool blanket. He had pink skin and a pudgy, aggravated face, and when my mom brought him inside and sat with him in the white rocking chair in his bedroom, she unpeeled his wound-up layers to reveal fat sausage arms and legs. We all gathered in there to admire him, my dad on a chair and me on his lap and my grandmother hovering in the doorway, Adam sucking a bottle of formula in my mother's arms. After he had eaten I got to hold him. I sat in the rocking chair and my mother handed him over very gently, instructing me on where to place my hands and how to cradle his floppy head. I was so happy to have him, to have him be my tiny baby brother, to have someone to watch out for.

His hair soon lightened into a copper clear as mine. People would look at him in the mall or in the Pathmark, a fat little Buddha in a stroller, and note the resemblance. "You look so much alike!" they'd say, smiling at me. "Two redheads!"

This was my favorite part, because the resemblance was such an unlikely one, and sometimes, unable to help myself, I'd blurt out, "But he's adopted! Isn't that amazing?" Then they would look more closely and wrinkle their brows and glance nervously at my mother, who would glare at me. I knew it was too much information for strangers, but sometimes I gave it up anyway, so proud that Adam looked like me that I in some way believed he was my creation. I simply wanted credit.

I never knew anything different—adopted, not adopted. I only knew he was my brother, and that he called me "Beffie," and that he was funny, goofy, clever. By the time he was six he liked Sting and the Police, especially *Zenyatta Mondatta*, and he had a good singing voice and great rhythm. He loved *Star Wars* and collected the little figurines, along with Matchbox cars. He idolized me and believed anything I told him; I had this doll, a Fisher-Price girl named "My Friend Mandy," and I used to tell him that she could talk. I'd have her say things to Adam, ventriloquist-style, and if he doubted it was her I'd ridicule him into believing. Then when he lost his first tooth I instructed him to put it under the pillow so the tooth fairy could collect it, and I said I had an idea about how he would find out if she was real. We got our mom's tape recorder—one of those old-fashioned decks that lay long on the table—and we set it up and pressed RECORD and left it by the side of his bed. After he'd fallen asleep I crept in and took it and brought it into the kitchen, where I recorded the sound our china dinner bell made when I shook it—very delicate and fairylike, I thought. I returned it to his bedside, and in the morning he listened with excitement, clutching the few dollar bills that had been left in place of his tooth.

He had terrible dust and mold allergies, and often he'd start out the day with dark circles under his eyes. He had slightly sallow skin and his thick head of red hair had strands that stood up in back, and during his last summer he wore these swim trunks that were bright red and made of some type of plastic, so they would puff up around him when he first stepped into the ocean or pool, and when he got out only the white lining would be wet, and it would drip down the insides of his thighs.

He used to hit his head against the pillow every night before he fell asleep. I knew because I could hear him, just on the other side of the wall from me, and sometimes the steady rhythm soothed me, too. I told my mom when I first heard it, and she went in to try and figure out what was wrong. The pediatrician told her it was OK, just a way that some kids comfort themselves, and I rolled my eyes, thought, Why does he do all these weird things? Later, after he was gone, I realized that there was something nice about it, something reliable and self-sufficient and special.

Some relatives didn't understand the adoption concept— didn't understand that he was my parents' child, same as me.

After he was gone, my great aunt Mildred said, "At least he was only adopted," and my mom never forgave her.

My mother would have to call the adoption agency to tell them what happened, though she and my father would never know if the information had been passed on to the birth mother. "I worry that his mother will show up at our door one day, wondering what happened to him," my father will confess to me more than two decades later. "I think about that all the time." I myself would often try to imagine the woman, by then in her twenties and possibly raising a new child of her own—one that she had felt ready to keep. I'd wonder if she had been full of regret about giving Adam away, and if she'd thought of him daily. I'd wonder if she'd ever find out what happened, and if she'd have to mourn the child she never knew all over again, and if she'd blame us for not taking good enough care of him for her. I would fantasize about tracking her down and meeting her, about holding her close to me and looking into her eyes, searching for Adam in her face and in her voice and in her skin and in her hair. I would apologize to her, tell her everything she wanted to know about her son, make sure she understood how we loved him. But somehow it would not have seemed right to make her see me, to give her a person to blame—to let her see that I was still here and that I was not hers.

Chapter Six

I SPENT several days in the hospital, the first two imagining Kristin in her own room just down the hall from me, her mother there at her side. I pictured her sleeping, then sitting up in bed, perhaps with a broken arm or bruised forehead, watching the mounted TV and receiving visitors that included everyone but me because I was already too upset, everyone must have thought, and because my foot was broken, or because it was just too difficult for the nurses to arrange a visit, though none of those reasons made much sense to me. Sometimes I heard her laughing—her screechy thirteen-year-old-girl laugh that fluttered between a honk and a breathy exhale, which would often tear out of her as she clutched her taut belly and dramatically flipped her head forward and back, her fine brown hair flying wildly. I thought I heard that melodious sound at least two or three times, but only mentioned it once.

It was after waking to a peaceful second morning. My mother's side of the room was empty, so I knew she had already gone down to the ICU to sit with my father, and a thin but definite stream of sunlight poured in through the window by her bed. I could hear a faint hubbub of activity from the nurses' station, which was just outside my room. And then I heard the laugh, like a heart-stopping bar of music. It was Kristin, no doubt about it, coming from somewhere far down at the end of the hall. My heart beat faster and I grabbed for the little white contraption that hung by a wire off the metal bed railings and I pressed it as hard as I could.

Marie, my favorite nurse on the floor, appeared in the doorway in her purple scrubs, still on duty from the night before. "Good morning, Beth," she said. "What do you need, sweetie?" She had her long puff of frizzy brown hair pulled messily into a large tortoiseshell barrette. Her eyes were soft and caring behind slightly tinted glasses—huge square ones with dramatically sloping arms.

"I just heard Kristin! You know, my friend? Who I was telling you about? I just heard her laughing and I was wondering if I could see her. Is her room down the hall?" I was already trying to sit up and smooth my hair, my eyes searching the room's perimeter for something cute that I could throw over my hospital gown.

"Hmm, I'm not sure," she said. Something changed in her face and she turned her back to me, picking up empty cups and smoothing the blanket on my mother's empty bed with odd attention to detail. "It's very early still. Why don't I braid your hair and help you wash up for breakfast?"

People had been evasive on the subject of Kristin since I'd arrived, my mother especially. Though I was beginning to get the sense that her family was angry with mine for putting their daughter in harm's way, and that perhaps they just wanted to be left alone. I hoped that we'd still be friends, and that I would see her as soon as we got home, but I didn't want to wait until then to see her, and wanted to at least stand in her doorway and wave, to lay my eyes on her and see for sure that she was OK.

Marie came over to my bed and looked at me closely. "How *are* you?" she asked. "Your mom is very worried about you. She's with your dad now, in the ICU."

"I'm all right," I said, looking into her warm, brown eyes. I wanted to crawl inside of them. "Sad, I guess."

She put her hands on my shoulders and gave me a squeeze. "You're a very strong girl," she told me. "You are going to be all right." Then she slowly turned me around, so that I was sitting sideways in the bed, and grabbed my brush off the side table and started pulling it through my hair, which felt impossibly tangled and greasy. But I let her yank at it, and work it into a braid, because I basked in her presence, in feeling the tips of her tan fingers graze across my scalp and the nape of my neck. I had never felt so starved for attention, and it surprised me, but didn't deter my quest for it.

"Oh, look who's here," she said brightly, and I looked over from the TV, which was broadcasting a game show with the sound turned off, to find an impossibly perky woman who was about Marie's age—tall and brittle-thin, with well-bronzed skin and a blond bob, wearing jeans and a T-shirt and a plastic name tag rather than the usual nurse's or tech's uniform.

The woman gave me an exaggerated grin and waved. "Hello! I'm Nini! I organize social activities on the floor. We'll be showing a movie down the hall later, and I wanted to invite you to join us!"

She seemed to know who I was already—a phenomenon that I'd not quite caught on to yet. I assumed I was anonymous, just a girl in a hospital with lots of visitors and a foot in a cast. But I must have been the subject of some discussion out in those mysterious halls, which were corridors I never stepped into, and which I pictured in fuzzy, nonspecific ways as a sedate, sad, ever-complicated maze of wings with too many patients to even keep track of. But when I would finally be wheeled out into them later in the week—both times to be brought directly into the elevator, to be taken first to physical therapy and then again to visit my dad in the ICU—the hallway was bright, too bright, suffused with a false cheer that gave me a pit in my stomach. Nini was from this foreign, frightful world, trying to get me excited about a movie, which seemed absurd. I looked at her with a mix of curiosity and disdain, and saw her react as a thought flew into her head, making her even more animated than she'd been.

"Oh! I almost forgot! There's someone I'd really love you to meet," she said. "She's about your age and lives not far from you. Let me go grab her. Her name is Kristin."

My heart leapt with joy and I whipped around toward Marie. "Finally!" I said, my voice squeaking with excitement. "Wait till she sees that we already know each other!" But Marie's face did not beam back at me, and she grabbed my wrist and held it like she was trying to tell me something, but all she said was, "No. Beth. It's actually not . . ." But before I could register what she was saying, a slight, blond girl in a hospital gown floated into my room. She seemed to be pals with Nini, who was behind her, smiling.

"Beth, this is Kristin," Nini told me, her hand on the girl's bony shoulder, the girl smiling and a bit too exuberant, rising up and down in a sort of nervously frantic series of half-executed ballet pliés while holding her hands on her hips. "Hi!" she said. "Nini says you do ballet too! Are you coming to the movie later?"

I was too stunned to speak, and instead just peered at her closely, thinking, No, you are definitely not Kristin.

"I'm anorexic," she said, puckering up her mouth and sort of rolling her eyes in Nini's direction. This fascinated me—I had just seen *The Best Little Girl in the World* on TV a few weeks before—and it explained her delicate frame. But it distracted me for only a moment. "What are you in for?" she asked.

I had yet to bounce back from the mistaken identity, and now she wanted me to recount what had happened. "A car accident," I said blankly, and then motioned to my cast, and the scatter of now-melted cold packs that littered the end of the bed. "I broke my foot." I felt tears coming on, and wanted her to go. I could not have felt less of a desire to bond with this girl—this wrong Kristin—who was not my friend.

"Well it's a good thing nothing worse happened!" she said sweetly.

"I think we need to let Beth get some rest now," Marie cut in, placing a warm hand on my shoulder and shooting Nini a look that I didn't quite understand.

"OK, but try to come later!" Kristin said, before flitting out the door.

When I looked at Marie she had watery eyes. "I'm so sorry about that, Beth," she told me, removing her glasses to wipe them clean with the underside of her lavender sweater. "I'm sorry about the mix-up. Why don't you rest, and I'll come back later." She leaned over and gave me a hug and then she was gone.

I wondered why no one explained the confusing situation to me, and what it was all about, and why no one would tell me where my Kristin was. I decided to be patient, and then drifted off into a light sleep.

I woke up sometime later and opened my eyes to see my mom coming into the room. She was in a wheelchair, being pushed by a nurse I didn't recognize, wearing one of her own nightshirts from home and holding a balled-up tissue in her hand. "Hi, baby," she said when I opened my eyes, on the verge of crying when she said it. "How are you?"

An itchy anxiety crept over me, and then I felt myself close off from her completely, felt my face go red and tingly in front of this unfamiliar nurse, found myself wishing she'd just *stop it already*, let me go back to being here, quiet, on my own, because her coming into the room like this was a stark reminder that something serious was going on, and that things were not, and would never be, the same. But she only pushed herself closer to me, until she was so close that her knees were pressing into the side of my bed. Her hair was unwashed and matted against one side of her head, and she looked drained and nervous, plucking at the tissue ball until it was just a shredded, filmy pile in her lap.

"I need to tell you something, Beth," she said, a pleading look in her eyes. "I need to tell you something very difficult."

I don't remember if I knew what it was going to be, although I really don't think that I did. I thought maybe it would be something about my father, that he was going to have to stay in the hospital for a long time, or maybe something even more benign, like "I love you," or "I'm sorry."

But instead she said this: "It's about Kristin. Kristin . . . didn't, um . . . make it. Kristin didn't make it, Beth. I'm sorry. I'm so sorry!" And then she was sobbing, her crumpled face buried in her hand, even before I had a chance to start.

I didn't quite comprehend it at first—*didn't make it*—and I looked to the nurse, who had been joined by another from my floor. They were both leaning against the wall, looking like they'd prefer to climb through it but remained where they were, apparently to provide some sort of emotional support.

"The viewing is tonight, Beth," my mom continued, enunciating each word like a radio host, her eyes wide to keep her from crying again. "And the funeral is in a couple of days. Oh, I didn't want to have to tell you this!"

I felt as if someone had thrown a very heavy blanket over me and was holding it down over my head, and I heard the din of the mysterious hallway—beeping monitors and call buttons and ringing telephones and soft conversation and even some laughter—and I got lost in it, let it carry me out of there, away from my mom, away from the news that I couldn't seem to take in beyond what it meant, factually, that it wasn't Kristin's laugh I had heard after all, and that the other Kristin, the bubbly, annoying anorexic, was the only one on the floor after all.

~

Marie will tell me about the Kristin secret more than a decade later, when we randomly and unexpectedly run into each other in a Manhattan pet shop. I will be in my twenties, working for a local city council member, on my way from the office to a community meeting about an egregious landlord, to be held in a nearby church, and on the way there I will duck into a random pet store, planning to pick up a catnip treat for my new and beloved black cat named Luther. I will walk into the store, directly to the back, where the toy display hovered to the right of the purchase counter, trying not to interrupt the saleslady at the register and the lone customer, in the midst of a friendly conversation. But when I walk in between them I will steal a look at the customer—a beautiful, warm-eyed brunette in jeans and a sweater—and know in an instant that it is Marie. She will also know right away that it's me. We'll embrace, long and tight, piquing the curiosity of the woman working in the pet store, but not explaining beyond,

"We knew each other another life ago. In New Jersey." We will exchange numbers, scarcely able to keep from crying, and go out to dinner a few days later, to an old-school Italian place in Chelsea, where she lived, where we ran into each other in the first place. I will drink too much wine and dig into a plate of manicotti and obsess over the past with her—pump her for the details of what she remembered, hear about the plan among my mom and the other nurses to keep Kristin's death from me because I'd had enough grief to deal with over Adam, because I was too young to handle the truth, because everyone thought it would be best to give me a little bit of breathing room between news of each death. But Marie was against it, she'll explain. She was against it but in the minority, and so she had to evade my questions and sometimes even lie, look me in the face and tell me we'd see Kristin later even though we wouldn't, even though she died that night in the car—how could she not have, with all of that blood?—and that, on the very first night when I asked for her and was told that her parents were with her, they probably were. But they would have been there to identify her body. I will relive it all that night, looking into those same warm, brown eyes and the edges of her frizzy hair, which will have been tamed and updated with product, and twisted into a bun, and she will explain to me that she left nursing shortly after that time because it was too painful, much to do with me, and my family, and my grief, and the lying over Kristin.

Chapter Seven

M Y third morning in the hospital was the morning of Adam's funeral. I sat in bed waiting to leave, wearing a purple sundress that Grandma Lil had brought me from home, my unwashed hair brushed and braided by Marie.

Marie had spent extra time with me in my room the night before, when I'd shown her my poetry and told her all about Kristin, prompted into a crying jag by watching a broadcast of the *Miss Teen USA Pageant*, on which a plain and pretty blond girl sang the sappy theme from *Ice Castles*, which Kristin and I had loved.

"We were going to be in junior high together starting in the fall," I told Marie. She wore smears of lavender eye shadow across each lid, and had her wild puff of brown hair pulled back on each side with matching violet combs. Marie was the kind of pretty woman whom I trusted instantly—the type I felt I loved after receiving only a few minutes of her attention, because it seemed as if she really saw me, as if she understood me, and because she was so lovely to look at.

"I'm so sorry, sweetie," she said, sitting on the edge of my bed and pulling me to her, letting me press my tear streaked face into her clavicle, which smelled very faintly of flowery perfume. My mother was out of the room, visiting my father in the ICU, and I was so relieved. "Kristin was lucky to have a friend like you."

That had made me cry harder. "I'm just going to miss her so much!" I told her. "I just can't believe I'm never going to see her again!"

"I know," she told me, stroking my hair and bringing her face so close to mine that I could see her eyes begin to well up with tears. "I know."

She came around again early in the morning, just before her shift ended, to help me with my braids. "Your hair is such a beautiful color," she had said, doting on me because I had told her I felt like a mess, and then gently yanking out tangles with my fat pink comb as she sat at the edge of my bed.

"I feel so gross," I'd told her.

"Oh, Beth," she'd said, smiling, her full lips shiny with gloss. "You look pretty."

Then my cousin Susan and her sister Eileen came by, dressed in somber gray suits and handing me a waxy white bag holding a chocolate glazed doughnut. As I gobbled it down, two policemen stepped into the room, hovering at the foot of my bed.

"Miss Beth Greenfield?" asked one.

"Yes?" I thought for an instant that I may have been in trouble, even though it seemed absurd. Susan put her hand on my shoulder.

"Uh, we're just here to take an accident report—to get

your account of what happened. Mind if we ask you a few questions?"

"No." I was nervous, though. I had never seen cops so close-up before, and I was transfixed by the guns that bulged in their worn leather hip holsters. They wore light blue, short-sleeved shirts and dark pants and clunky shoes, and one pulled a long, fat pad of paper out of his back pocket. They asked me my full name, the names of everyone in the car and where we had all been sitting, and what type of injuries I had.

"Where were you coming from?"

"My ballet recital," I said.

"And who was driving?"

"My father," I said quietly.

"Do you know whose fault it was?" the one taking notes asked.

"Not his!"

"No, no," he said. "The other driver. He was drunk."

They said they were finished then, and that I had done a good job, and Eileen ushered them out of there quickly while Susan stood at my bedside and pulled my head into her hip.

"It was a drunk driver?" I asked her, my head buzzing from the news.

"Yes, Bethie."

I had heard of drunk drivers before—seen public service announcements on TV about them, the weight of the issue never quite sinking in. It had always seemed so irrelevant.

Soon Marie came back in to bring me a square plastic bin filled with warm soapy water, and Susan and Eileen stepped out while she helped me take a sponge bath. I was mostly quiet as she wrung out a white cloth and handed it to me over and over again so I could swipe at my face, my neck, my armpits. I was thinking about the drunk driver, wondering if he had gotten hurt too, and if he felt sorry about what he had done.

"All done, Beth," she said, after helping me slip into my dress.

Then Marie had to go home, leaving me waiting in the bed, missing her, of all people, waiting for the funeral, not believing that it would truly take place. But soon the curtains, still pulled around my bed, parted, and Uncle Michael, who had arrived the night before from Arizona, stepped in.

"Hey, kiddo," he said. "Howya doin'?"

He was wearing gray pants and an ill-fitting blue suit jacket and his head was slightly bowed. His thick, jet-black hair was combed in a way that made him look like a kid who had been forced to look presentable.

Usually Michael didn't look so serious. He was Mom's happy-go-lucky younger brother. Before he moved out West he liked to play ABBA on the eight-track in his '65 butter-yellow Mustang. The car had a spray of small holes in the rusted-through floor in the back, and whenever I rode with him I could peer through them and see the road moving blurry-fast beneath us, which both thrilled and terrified me. He smoked Marlboros, a pack a day, dated a pretty, pudgy Puerto Rican girl named Candy, and had lived in a big house near the ocean with a group of other single guys, dropping in to have dinner with us once a month or so and driving my mother crazy with his liberal, fired-up political proclamations. But right then, there in my hospital room in his suit jacket, he was more composed and adult than I'd ever seen him before.

"I'm fine," I said, shrugging.

"Beth, you know you don't have to come to the funeral if you don't want to, right?" He looked into my eyes, pressed his lips together, put a hand gently on my shoulder.

"No," I told him. "I don't know that." My mom had, in fact, told me that morning that I didn't have to go, but I didn't want to discuss it with her at all, and had shunned her attempt to let me get out of it. With Michael, it was as if a door had been cracked open, and there was air flooding through. I took a deep breath.

"I'm telling you that you do not have to go," he said. "No one would think anything bad about you if you stayed here."

I sat with the idea of it for a minute or so, wondering what would be right, wishing I could check with my mom before making a decision. But I didn't know where she was. I imagined seeing Adam's coffin lowered into the ground, my mom wailing and throwing herself toward the hole in the earth, me crying in front of everyone we'd ever known. It didn't seem right for me to skip it. I wasn't a baby, after all. But the idea of going made my head hurt, made my chest tighten with fear. I made a snap decision.

"I'll stay," I told him, very quietly.

"You'll stay here? You don't want to go?"

"Right," I said. "I don't want to go."

He seemed pleased with himself for being the one to give me the out, and that I had trusted him enough to take him up on it. "OK," he said. "OK. Then you don't have to, kiddo. I'll tell your mom, don't worry. And I'll come see you right after it's over."

He kissed my forehead and hurried off, and I was immediately regretful. But also relieved. I was mostly happy to have a break from my mother, who had been in the next bed over and waking me several times a day with her wails, creating scenes that caused groups of nurses to scurry in and pull the curtains around her, probably giving her shots or pills or something that quieted her into a slurring, sleepy, clingy thing. I'd had enough of her for the moment, though I couldn't tell anyone, of course, because it would have just sounded so awful.

When I was certain my mother had left the premises, I slithered out of my clothes and into my stale hospital gown. I was stuck on my back because of my foot, which sat aching in its fresh plaster cast, floating over the crisp white bed sheets like a separate being, my purple toes now resembling fat earthworms. My calf itched, and I dug my fingers under the top rim of plaster, which just grazed the bottom of my kneecap, scratching the little part of skin that I could reach. I thought about my mom at the funeral, about Adam in a child-size coffin, my father stuck in his bed in the ICU. I didn't cry, though. Instead I pushed it all away, all the bad thoughts, and started enjoying my solitude. I played with the buttons that moved my bed up and down, settling into a new, more reclined position, and stared at the phone. I wished that it would ring, or that I had someone to call. Then I flipped on the TV and found *Days of Our Lives*, half over, and I didn't even care. I must have fallen asleep right away.

By four that afternoon I was getting post-funeral visitors— visitors that surprised me because of how out of context they were, like my art and music teachers from grammar school, former teachers from fifth and third grades. My principal, Mr. Addeo, came in while I was asleep and left me a note, with a bouquet of pink carnations, and then later, just before dinner, my cousin Susan came and brought me a hot fudge sundae from a nearby ice cream parlor. I loved having the visitors all to myself, loved being the center of attention, the minor celebrity that everyone wanted to please. But I was ashamed to like it too—ashamed to enjoy anything for even a second, knowing how much had been lost.

When the rabbi came, she told me about the funeral, and how big it was, how lovely. "It was really OK that you weren't there," she said, noticing how I looked down and away when she told me about all the people who had shown up, how I mashed my lips together and turned crimson when she talked about everyone's generosity.

"I taped it for you," she added, "so that you can listen to it whenever you're ready."

I would ask her to bring the recording over to our house about a week later, and she would show up just after dinner one night and go with me into my room and sit calmly with me on my bed, press Play on the same flat black tape recorder I had used to record the tooth-fairy bell. Though it was of poor quality, I could hear various people crying and gasping and blowing their noses in the background. I heard my mother several times. Her cry was unmistakable—tight and desperate and chilling, like a cat in a cage, on its way to the vet. I wondered who all those people were, how many lives a seven-year-old could have possibly touched.

Then I heard the rabbi's voice, telling everyone, "Many of us are angry with God right now. We're wondering, How could God have let this happen?" And she'd tell them this: that God did not control us all like puppets on strings, but that he created people with the ability to make choices for themselves.

"The man who killed Adam and Kristin made a choice to get drunk that night," I heard her say, "and made a choice to then get into his car."

It would end soon, and the din of mourners would rise until there was nothing to listen to, and the rabbi pressed Stop and made it all come to a halt.

"But where are they now?" I asked her. "Where do Jews believe that Adam and Kristin are now?"

"Judaism teaches that when a person you love dies," she explained, placing one of her small hands over her heart, "They live on forever inside of those who love them."

I pictured my insides, contained, inanimate—simple heart and lungs and bones—and understood that truly, they were nowhere. Just gone.

~

My mother returned from Adam's funeral in the late afternoon. She looked utterly destroyed—like in a cartoon, when a bomb explodes in front of a character's face and it winds up looking singed and bewildered, hair blown back and eyebrows burned off, eyes wide and glazed. It was how she seemed to me then, shuffling over to her bed—barely acknowledging me—like she'd just survived a siege, or a full-scale war, and I thought, *Bring my mother back. Or get me out of here.*

Chapter Eight

THE morning they told me I would finally be able to visit my dad was, I suppose everyone thought, going to feel like a joyous reunion. It had been three days since we had all entered the hospital, and three days that I'd not seen my father, who was on another floor in another wing in the intensive care unit, trying to pull through having a collapsed lung and damaged shoulder and broken ribs and a bruised heart—which had always sounded to me like some sort of schmaltzy metaphor but was in fact a physical injury, and probably the worst of all to recover from. My mom went down to see him every day, leaving me alone or with visitors for hours at a time that were always such pure relief for me, free of her crying and carrying on about "what if" and her constant attempts to get me to tell her how I was feeling.

"Beth, you're going to get to see your father today!" said a nurse whom I cannot remember now, but who spent part of her morning helping me wash myself with a washcloth and brushing my hair and checking that I'd finished breakfast and then helping me tie the back of my hospital gown securely, so it wouldn't flop open as I moved about. I was fine to be excluded from the ICU visits, afraid of what I'd see there, of what my father would look like, of what I would be expected to say to him. But no one else understood that, and instead assumed I'd be desperate to get to him.

It was decided that I'd be taken down after lunch, and so after my primping, I was left alone to doze off and await my soggy, open-faced turkey sandwich, all to be followed by the ICU field trip. My mom was already down there, and returned to our room just before I was to go, giving me time alone with him, which I was worried about. What would I possibly say?

"Good morning, my sweet Beth," my mother said, stepping tentatively into our room. I noticed that this was how she walked now—gingerly, with both fear and effort, as if she could not possibly handle what would next fly into her path. She wore a hospital gown and navy-blue sweatpants and her glasses, and she kept smoothing her hair across her head with a stiff right hand in a new sort of tic that disturbed me. "Your Poppy is looking forward to seeing you," she told me. "He loves you so much and he wants you to see that he's OK. Just don't be scared by all the wires, OK? They're just helping him breathe and giving him medicine. He's going to be OK."

I hadn't given much thought to what he'd look like, that there'd be wires or tubes or other medical things, and then I dreaded the visit even more. But I had to go. My mom kissed my forehead and I closed my eyes, trying to disappear as she did it, and then her eyes welled up and she continued her shuffling sort of sleepwalk over to her side of the room and crawled into bed, whimpering softly to herself. I couldn't comfort her, and I didn't want to. So I just stayed put, flicking through channels like nothing was going on.

I must have dozed off then, awaking as the nurse who would take me downstairs approached me slowly, pushing an empty wheelchair. I looked to my right and saw that my mom was asleep on her bed, a small lump breathing rapidly, her hands curled like a child's to her chest.

"Is it time to go?" I asked.

"If you're ready, sure," she said. "Let's go see your dad."

She helped me down from my high, sweaty bed and into the wheelchair, and adjusted the footrest so that it cradled my heavy plaster cast, which had been applied sometime during my first day in the hospital by a handsome, dark-haired young doctor with chocolate-brown eyes. Susan and Eileen had been there, holding my hands and patting my forehead as he and a nurse dipped wide strips of gauze in the bowl of milky plaster before placing them around the cottony splints on either side of my calf and my foot. After he left we marveled about how handsome he had been, my cousins mock fighting over him, and when he came back the next day to check on the swelling I reddened and grinned, forgetting, for just a moment, all that had happened.

When the nurse pushed me into the hallway the air felt so different on my face—breezy, almost, and discordantly fresh, when compared to the staleness of my room, which had quickly become my small world. We passed by other rooms, and I peered in, catching blurred glimpses of kids my age, some lying in bed, others standing in their rooms, which were filled with parents or friends who looked crisp and brightly colored and slightly uncomfortable and so clearly from the outside world. The hallway was abuzz with nurses and some other kids who wandered around in hospital gowns, some with teenage attitudes that created a surreal sort of school-hall scene.

We got onto a massive elevator that stopped on every floor, picking up and depositing doctors and techs, nervous visitors clutching flowers, and sad ones wiping at their eyes. I wanted so badly to know everyone's story. We got off in the lobby, not far from the double glass doors of the main entrance, which opened and closed and blew warm summer Jersey Shore air into my face. It was sunny outside, and people were going about their business out there in the world, and it made me feel withered and gray and that there'd be way too much to face once we left here, and as if I wanted the nurse to turn around and take me back up to my fetid cocoon. But we continued on, through an uphill corridor to the new wing of the hospital, where we rode yet another huge elevator, this time with a nurse and an elderly woman on a stretcher, which felt invasive and strange.

We were let out, finally, at the intensive care unit. The lights were low and it was eerily quiet, with no clutches of visitors milling about, and just a couple of mellow nurses at the desk, which was set up like a control station, encircled by about a dozen dark rooms, each filled with still, half-dead patients. My father was among them.

"OK, Beth, so I'm going to bring you into your dad's room now, and then I'll leave you alone with him," said the nurse, speaking gently, as if she realized how tentative I felt. "I'll come back for you in fifteen minutes or so. He needs his rest, and shouldn't be visiting for too long." The pit in my stomach spread rapidly, until I thought I couldn't breathe, but I managed to suck in a deep breath and blow it out quickly enough to dissipate the stars I had begun to see.

She wheeled me into one of the dark rooms, and there

was my father, although at first I didn't recognize him. He looked impossibly small and powerless, shrunken, and both too young and too old all at once. He had tubes in his nose, in his arms, in his legs, and monitors attached to his furry chest, which peeked out of his hospital gown in a way that felt indecent, just like the flash of his thigh that had slipped out from under the sheet. The room smelled of his sweat and his sadness, and when I looked at his eyes they seemed the only truly alive part of him—alert and shiny pinpricks of light and shock and fear.

"Hello, Bethie," he whispered in a gravelly, struggling voice. Without even realizing it, I had begun to cry. I always tried not to cry in front of my father, but there was no option. It just came, like a flood.

"I'm sorry," he said, in such a weak voice it was staggering. "I didn't see the car. I didn't see it . . ." He closed his eyes and began whimpering, and I was amazed that he thought it was his fault. It had never crossed my mind—they said it was a drunk driver, so what was he supposed to have done?—and when I realized then the weight of guilt he must have felt I cried even harder.

"It's not your fault, Poppy," I told him, holding the sob in my chest. "It wasn't your fault. No one thinks that." I couldn't recall ever having comforted my own father before, and it felt both adult, which was strengthening, and too difficult, which was dizzying. I reached for his closest hand, which looked withered, and which had a small bruise at the site where a needle was attached. It felt warm to the touch, and so weak, in a way I would have never imagined him capable of being, and when I stroked it with my own I saw tears run down his cheeks. It terrified me.

This was a scene out of a film. This could not have been happening to me. This was like the eleven o'clock movie, the tragic touches—tubes in his nose, girl in wheelchair, grown man crying, expressions of guilt—added in for dramatic effect. I thought of all the ways I could dissipate the situation, all the silly things I could tell him—about all the teachers who had come to visit me so far, how the nurses had taken a shine to me and brushed and French braided my hair, how Marie had sat with me the other night, reading my poetry.

"My teachers came to visit me," I began. "Mrs. Zipperson brought me ice cream."

He opened his mouth for a moment and looked like he was about to make a joke, which was his normal response to things, and which I would have been overjoyed to hear, no matter how corny. But instead he just took a belabored breath and raised his eyebrows and gave me this look, as if to say, "Can you believe this?"

~

My father often got scolded by my mom, usually for being too lenient, or for laughing when Adam and I misbehaved and tried to distract them from punishing us by clowning around, which my father often fell for, because he was largely a child, which exasperated my mom. He never cooked or cleaned—aside from taking out the garbage, which was his major household task, or vacuuming, begrudgingly, when instructed by my mom to do so before we had company. His jobs were man jobs—mowing and fertilizing the lawn and trimming the hedges, tarring the driveway in the spring, raking leaves and hauling them to the curb, shoveling the driveway after snowstorms, planting rows of trees along the edge of our property by digging shallow holes in the dirt and carefully placing in the burlap wrapped balls of roots before covering them back up with fresh earth while we watched with wonder as he transformed our yard.

But he was, like so many fathers, the fun, funny, pushover parent. When I was six he taught me how to ride my blue bike with the flowered white basket, removing the training wheels, gripping the back of my seat and running alongside of me down our street. The first time he let go I fell to the side, crashing on top of him, but he just brushed off his knees and stood up, said, "That's OK! I'm OK!" and made sure I didn't have any scrapes. I didn't, so we did it again, and this time when he let go I kept riding; it was like flying along Thornley Road, like using a superpower I never knew was tucked away inside of me. He was so proud that he leapt up and down and pumped his fist in the air and yelled, "All right! All right! Good job!"

When I was three he started teaching me how to swim, getting in the pool with me and holding my hands as I floated on my stomach, facing him, kicking my feet as forcefully as I could as he led me around the shallow end, getting me to stick my face in the water to learn how to breathe and blow. Eventually he brought me—along with Kristin—to the beach club for swim-team practice on weekday mornings, and he'd cheer loudly from the sidelines when we had meets, leaping and clapping and chuckling with joy whenever I won a ribbon. I marveled right back at him during adult-swim hour at the beach club; he was often the first one in, adjusting his goggles and taking over a lane and swimming with smoothness and strength for a full mile without ever stopping to rest, the wisps of his comb-over floating to the wrong side of his bald spot and hanging stuck to the side of his head like a Hasidic man's *pais* when he finally finished, standing at the shallow end of the pool to catch his breath before climbing out over the cement edge.

He joked with us all the time—told silly stories and made faces and noises and ridiculous moves, spoke in his own made-up gibberish that made us, as well as Mom, laugh. When I cried as a kid he would wipe my tears with a warm, hammy finger, and then lift it to his tongue as if sampling a fine broth. "Needs more salt," he'd say. "Definitely needs just a little more salt." And I would laugh and sniffle and forget to keep crying.

But sometimes he was forgetful, childish, and distracted— like when he threw tantrums for losing his car keys, or not being able to find the ketchup or the milk or the Swiss cheese in the refrigerator because my mother had "hid it" from him. Sometimes—and here is the unspeakable—he drove a bit erratically, easily prone to road rage. He'd been known to speed up to pass "jerks," and to yell insults, too, his face a violet ball of inexplicable furor. His most egregious error, though, came almost a year before the accident, at temple, on the morning of Yom Kippur. We had arrived a bit late to services, and my father pulled into the synagogue's horseshoe driveway and stopped at the edge of the brick walkway, so he could let us off and then go park the car at the far edge of the parking lot.

"All right, kids, let's hustle. I don't want to wind up way in the back," my mom said, grabbing her purse and a sweater for the air-conditioning and sliding out of the passenger seat of the new Fairmont. It still smelled like fresh new car, and I got a full whiff of it when she slammed her door. "Martin, please hurry," she said through the still-open window. "I'll keep an eye out for you, so you can find us in there."

"All right, all right! Get out so I can get going!" he said, impatiently. He wore navy slacks and a brown blazer and a silk tie with maroon and navy diagonal stripes that hung elegantly—not heavily, like his wool teacher ties—on his light blue dress shirt. On his lap was the slate-blue velvet pouch that he cherished, which had a delicate zipper and held his yarmulke and white silk *tallis*, and which he had since his Bar Mitzvah.

I climbed out of the backseat on the passenger side, careful not to wrinkle my dark denim prairie skirt or let my plaid blouse become untucked from my waist. I delighted in the click that my wedge-heel sandals made on the brick walk and flipped my long, freshly washed hair behind one shoulder, already beginning to look around for Matthew, my current crush. I left the door open behind me for Adam, and stood with my mom waiting for him to emerge. He began to climb out, his light blue dress shirt already half falling out of the waistband of his navy slacks, but as he put one foot down on the tar of the driveway and still had one on the floor of the car's backseat, my dad, without first checking behind him, began to pull away, and Adam fell to the ground.

"Martin!" my mother screamed. "Martin! Stop! What's wrong with you!" She ran to Adam, who had begun to cry, and pulled him up, holding him tightly to her chest. "You didn't even look!" The car had not gotten far—maybe a foot—and my father slammed on the brakes, causing the still open car door to swing back and forth. He shook his head but said nothing, put the car in park and jumped out of his seat. I just stood there, frozen and ready for a scene, as several dressed-up families I did not know filed past us, heads down, making beelines for the front door. When they opened it I could hear the first whiny notes of the organ, signaling the start of the service.

"What happened? Is he OK?" My father looked ashen, and when he jumped out of the car his velvet pouch fell to the driveway. He left it there for the moment, and ran to Adam and my mother.

"What happened? You weren't paying attention, that's

what happened!" my mother yelled at him, lunging forward while hugging Adam tightly, putting her lips to his forehead as he screamed out of fear into her chest.

"I thought he was out of the car!" he said. "I thought he was out of the car! Hey, Adam, you're OK. Aren't you, buddy? Poppy's sorry." My father appeared to be so crushed it was difficult to look at him, and my mom didn't make it any easier.

"You didn't even look first before pulling away!" she yelled. "How could you not have looked first?" Adam continued to wail, and my father took him into his arms to soothe him, saying, "Poppy's sorry," over and over again. I stepped into the driveway to pick up his velvet pouch and close the car door so that a stream of latecomers could get by. Finally Adam stopped crying, and my father went to park the car, but my mother had a hard time letting it go, and we would spend the first several years without Adam remembering that moment each time we pulled into the temple driveway—never discussing it, but feeling the car get heavy with silence, my parents glassy-eyed and sighing, anytime my dad dropped Mom and Grandma and me out at the front door.

"I didn't mean to drive away so early," my dad said just once, a few years later, in the tiniest of voices, staring off into the distance. "I thought he'd gotten out of the car."

"I know, Martin," my mom said to him then. "I know."

~

I thought that nothing could touch my father—not really touch him, beyond hurt feelings or scolding from my mom or annoyance from a fellow driver. I didn't think he could get crushed behind a steering wheel and almost die, and make noises that would haunt me forever. It was strange not being able to embrace him, just having to sit there with my heavy cast, touch his warm, still hand, feel the heat of the room and the weight of his stare until the nurse returned to wheel me away. I told him I loved him as I left, and he cried there in his bed, but I couldn't do anything more.

Chapter Nine

KRISTIN'S funeral was two days later, my fifth day in the hospital. The day I was being released. This time I was a bit more determined to make it—partially out of guilt for missing Adam's, partially because I wanted to see everyone who would be there, though I didn't want to see her coffin lowered into the ground. Again I wore my purple sundress, waited in bed to be picked up, hair braided by Marie. This time I would leave my room for good.

"Hi there, Beth. How are you feeling?" It was Mrs. Lieberman, our friend from the beach club and mother of Scott, the object of my and Kristin's crush. I liked her a lot, loved when we sat near her on the beach, when they stayed down late with us for a barbecue and she would talk to me like I was an adult, sitting there in her striped canvas beach chair in her one-piece suit until the sun went down, waiting as long as she could to pull on her sweats. Her hair was a short stack of brown curls that moved in one soft wave with the breeze, and she smiled at me with her wide brown eyes, even when she wasn't smiling. When my mother had told me the night before that Mrs. Lieberman would be picking me up and taking me to the funeral and then home, so my mom could be with my dad in the ICU, it was just another thing to make me inappropriately happy.

"I'm OK," I told her. "Ready to go, I guess."

"Scott's with me," she said. "He's waiting in the hallway."

I couldn't believe she had brought him. I wondered how I looked, and I got the same fluttery feeling in my chest that I always got when he was around, and felt a bit shaky as Mrs. Lieberman helped me into a waiting wheelchair with a nurse who had stopped in to help us. When we entered the hallway and I saw him he was extra kind to me, and he offered to hold my small bag and my crutches.

"Sorry about what happened," he said, looking down at his feet when he spoke. His hair wasn't as in place as it usually was, and I noticed a small pimple, red and angry, on his jaw. I was too humiliated to really look at him, or to have him look at me. I tried to get beyond worrying about my attraction to him, which seemed unimportant now. I knew he had liked Kristin better anyway, and I wondered if he missed her. I wondered if we would bond over losing her.

We couldn't leave right away because there was a holdup at the discharge station.

"We're going to miss the funeral!" I said, near tears, wondering how I would live with myself if I missed both. Mrs. Lieberman seemed calm.

"We'll be fine, dear," she said. "Don't worry."

The outside air was shockingly salty and fresh, the sunshine warm liquid on my face. Scott stood with me, still in my wheelchair, while his mom went to pull the car around. It

was so awkward, me unwashed and squinty-eyed and damaged, my heavy cast dangling an inch above the ground because the leg holder had been missing and I had wanted to
get out of there before they could find one. Scott just stood
there silently, clutching my bag at his belly as if it were
a football, gnawing at his bottom lip and glancing at me
only once, as if sneaking a peek at something he wasn't allowed to see.

He rode up front with his mom in their wide boat of a
station wagon, and I sat sideways in the back, my cast straight
out in front of me on the hot vinyl seat, staring out of my
window at familiar places—the Long Branch train station, my
friend Maria's house, Mrs. Carroll's ballet studio, the ShopRite
where my mom sometimes bought groceries—as if I'd never
seen them before. When we turned onto the short dead end
where the funeral home was, it was lined with cars, and
people had just begun to stream out of the building into the
sun.

"Looks like we might have missed it, Beth," Mrs. Lieberman said softly. I felt a stab of shame and sadness as she pulled
her car alongside the curb near the home and turned the en-
gine off. Most of the mourners were Kristin's age, wearing
dresses or shirts with ties, crying and wiping their forearms
across their eyes, leaning into their mothers for support. I
wondered if anyone noticed that I hadn't been there, and if
there had been this many people at Adam's funeral. Most of
the kids were unfamiliar, probably from the junior high, but I
recognized Tricia, one of Kristin's good friends from school
who also belonged to the beach club. The three of us had
hung out a few times, and I liked her well enough, though she
was too bubbly and prissy, in my opinion. Kristin had mostly
kept us separate.

"Oh, Beth, how are you?" she asked grimly, seeing me

through the rolled-down window and coming toward the car. "When did you get out of the hospital?"

"Just now," I told her. "That's why we're late."

"It was really sad," she said, and then continued crying into a crumpled up pink tissue she had in her hand. She wore mascara, and it was making little black pools below her eyes. Her bouncy brown hair was shellacked into a cotton candy–like puff, and she wore a tasteful gray dress with sandals. Her mother, who looked exactly like her, only tanner and older, stood behind her with a hand on her daughter's shoulder. She was crying too.

"Beth, I hope you are feeling better soon," her mom said to me. "It is good to see you." Then she put her arm around Tricia and steered her away.

Mrs. Lieberman reached into the backseat and put her hand on my cast. "Don't feel guilty," she told me. "We tried our best." I just stared at the back of Scott's head, which bowed a little when she spoke. And then she started the car and we drove on, toward my house. I was completely numb. (I will ask my mom two decades later why I missed the funeral altogether and she'll say she doesn't remember—but she will have a feeling that she delayed our leaving on purpose, because she said she could tell that I didn't truly want to be there anyway.)

When we turned onto my street, things looked completely strange—the neat rows of split-level colonials and long ranch houses, like ours, all fronted by neat squares of manicured lawn. It was the middle of a workday and the last week of school before summer break, and so the neighborhood was quiet and still, with no cars left in driveways and no people out and about. My first thought when I saw our house was that it looked scruffier than I'd remembered—its sad brown surface and rust-colored shutters faded and worn and in need of a paint job, especially in the harsh glare of the bright June sun.

"Here we are, Beth," said Mrs. Leiberman. "Home sweet home. I bet it'll feel good to sleep in your own bed tonight." She turned toward the backseat when she said this, with sweaty bunches of curls sticking to her forehead, and her black linen shirt twisting around her arm as she strained to see me behind her. And though she was smiling, I caught something else in her round eyes—fear, or sadness, or empathy. She had to have known that I was not looking forward to being in this house, empty and damaged. But I played along.

"Yeah," I said. "Let's go in."

Scott got out of the front seat and opened my door for me. I thought about how this would have made me swoon under normal circumstances, but suddenly I didn't much care. Nothing about this moment was normal—walking on crutches up our narrow driveway, being home on a day when I should have been at school, knowing that neither of my parents would be in the house to greet me and realizing that Adam wouldn't be in there, either, that he'd never be in there again. I stopped for a moment, let it all wash over me, and then felt Mrs. Lieberman's hand on the small of my back and continued up the paved walkway, between the two bright-pink azalea bushes, and up the one small step onto our front porch. Grandma Lil, wearing a blue house dress, appeared in the doorway and gasped when she saw me.

"My Beth! Come inside!" she said, pushing the screen door open and squeezing me with such intensity it nearly knocked me over. Then she stepped out of the way so I could maneuver myself through the door. She welcomed in Scott and his mother, thanked them, asked them if we had made it to the funeral. They spoke quietly in the doorway while I took in the new look of home.

The dining room table—a heavy round slab of oak that we only used on special occasions, like dinner parties or Passover seders, for which my mom made it larger with a middle leaf before covering it with a thin, foam padding and then a marigold-colored tablecloth—was uncharacteristically in use. Its bare surface was covered with massive fruit baskets, the careful arrangements of pears, apples, and bananas still shrink-wrapped in shiny, colored cellophane. I inched closer on my crutches to read the cards, but they were all the same—"We're so sorry," and "With deepest sympathy," with names of temple families and neighbors—and so I moved on to the kitchen. It was empty, but looked as though it had recently hosted a party, with white foam cups of cold coffee, brewed in the old plug-in percolator, scattered around a half-eaten platter of cold cuts out on the table, and dirty paper plates placed next to it in an orderly stack.

"Beth, dear, how about a sandwich?" Grandma Lil called from the other room. "There's roast beef and turkey left, and delicious rye bread."

I wasn't hungry, but opened both the side-by-side fridge and freezer doors to have a look, out of habit. The refrigerator was packed to the gills as usual—fruit and leftovers and milk and grapefruit juice and yogurts—and the freezer, usually reserved for half gallons of ice cream and cans of frozen O.J., was bursting too, mostly with unfamiliar, hand-wrapped blocks of meals from neighbors, labeled LASAGNA, MEAT LOAF, CHICKEN CASSEROLE on pieces of masking tape in my grandmother's stretched-out, angular handwriting.

Tucked back on the bottom shelf, though, I saw something that made me dizzy for a second: a half-eaten ice pop—the kind you make from orange juice in smooth plastic Tupperware molds—laying on a small, round dish. It was Adam's. I knew it instantly. We had been eating them just a week ago, after school, when we had to leave suddenly so Mom could get me to ballet class in time. She wouldn't let us take our ice pops in the car because she was afraid they'd drip, so I wolfed mine down in two bites and Adam decided to save his for when we returned. But he wound up forgetting all about it. I reached down and touched it lightly, and thought of eating it, of putting my mouth on the small bite mark that he had left behind, of getting just a little bit of Adam inside of me. Then I thought it should be saved, that maybe there'd be a scientist somewhere who could collect the Adam cells that still clung to the frozen juice, put them in a petri dish and bring him back. Clone him. I stood there daydreaming in the icy-cold air, thinking that if it could be done on *The Bionic Woman*, perhaps it could be done for real. I didn't know if it was really so ridiculous or not, so I left it in the freezer, moving it farther back and out of sight, so that it wouldn't get thrown away. Then I thought of my mom saying, "Don't keep the door open like that!" and I closed it, shivering a bit from the cold that gusted into my face. I heard only snatches of what Grandma Lil and Mrs. Lieberman were talking about in the living room, where they'd sat down together.

". . . the punctured lung . . ."

". . . almost died . . ."

". . . when they told her parents . . ."

I wondered where Scott was—sitting there listening? waiting in the hot car?—and if I should be entertaining him. But I decided to ignore him for a while.

I approached Adam's room, feeling physically ill. I was half expecting to see him in there, alive and happy, wondering what all the fuss was about. Instead I saw Grandpa Norman, whose back was to the door as he crouched on his knees on the flat blue and maroon speckled carpeting before a large pile of Adam's clothing. I saw his gold baseball T-shirt with the *Star Wars* iron-on, his three pairs of white-kneed jeans, the white swim trunks with the blue racing stripe and the red ones with the white drawstring.

I stopped for a moment to try to figure out what was going on when it hit me that Grandpa was putting the clothing into empty supermarket paper bags, and that he must have been preparing to give it all away. I leaned all my weight on my left foot and pressed my head lightly into the doorjamb, taking in the lingering Adam scent, and made a creak, startling my grandfather. He turned around slowly, seeming weighted or drugged, and his face didn't light up as it always had when he'd catch sight of me, whether in the Miami airport as I was first stepping off the plane or in their tiny kitchen, where I'd be standing for several minutes, fixing a bowl of just-because-we're-on-vacation Frosted Flakes before he'd look up from his half of grapefruit and spread-out *Miami Herald* and realize that I was awake, and that I had joined him.

"Hey, you," he said, his voice quieter and huskier than usual. "Whatchya doin'?"

Grandpa Norman presented himself as gruff. He never said much and acted grumpy a lot of the time. But he softened when we visited, always affectionate with me and with Adam, holding our hands and hugging us so tightly. He was as sweet with Grandma as he was annoyed, and when he'd drink a little scotch after dinner his face would get red and he'd laugh long and loud and joyously, and we'd scramble onto his lap, and he would tell us we were good kids, and I knew that meant that he loved us.

"I just got home from the hospital. Mrs. Lieberman drove me," I told him. "What are *you* doing?"

"Just cleaning up for your mama," he said, rising up toward me, grabbing me hard and planting a kiss on my cheek before returning to his task, putting his back to me once again.

Cleaning up.

Before my parents brought Adam home, his room had been the office. It was where my father sat at his fat, wooden, glass-topped desk, grading the papers of his high school students, sometimes late into the night, after dreading it aloud for much of the day. He used red pencils to make his marks, and to write big A's or B's or D's across the tops of the pages, and to point in the air when explaining to me what he was grading, what the assignment was and how the kids had done.

"Unbelievable!" he'd sometimes declare, stomping out of the office and into the den, where I would be watching TV with Mom.

"These kids don't know how to spell! Look at this, Deb," he'd say, thrusting a paper in her face as she sat with me watching *Little House on the Prairie*. "How can you make it to high school and not know how to spell 'people'?"

But for Adam's arrival they had turned the office into a nursery, with the same wooden crib and white rocking chair that I had slept in and been nursed in. There was a changing table in the corner, and sometimes on Saturday mornings I would get out of bed before my parents to find Adam awake and I would take him out of his crib and hoist him onto the table and change his diaper, singing him songs that I would make up as I went along. When he was almost three they moved his crib and his changing table into the attic and bought him a bed, although Mom was nervous about it at first and so outfitted it with a metal side rail that kept him from rolling out at night.

I thought about him banging his head against the pillow each night to lull himself to sleep. There was something so soothingly rhythmic about it—the rocking and banging, the sound of his head thumping the pillow and the bed smacking the wall and the squeak of the bedsprings, all of which I could hear in my bed, just on the other side of the wall from his. I liked having proof that he was there.

After Adam was gone, after Grandpa gathered up the clothes, it would remain Adam's room, although empty of his belongings, for just a few months, with Mom going in there to sit on the bed and cry, me listening to her from my room, where I'd be frozen with fear. I'd never join her, or even go and peek to see if she was all right, but instead I would stay on my own bed and sob along with her. I would sneak into his room sometimes too, but only when I'd know that Mom was sleeping or out of the house, and that there was no way she'd walk in on me and discover me, hunched in front of Adam's closet, breathing in the huge puff of his scent that spilled out when I pulled open the door, shuffling silently through his stack of records and board games and books, hoping that somehow he might rematerialize among all of his things—that I might conjure him up, at least for a moment, just by jostling his spirit.

But at that point, just home from the hospital and standing in the doorway as Grandpa Norman turned back to his task of sorting clothing, I had yet to even step over the threshold into Adam's room. It was something I knew I'd have to do alone.

I turned toward the living room, where I heard Scott and his mom getting ready to go. "Thanks for taking me home," I told them.

"Of course, Beth," Mrs. Lieberman said. Then she gave me a big hug and put her hand on my head, let it linger there for a moment. "You take care of yourself, and of your mom. We'll see you back at the beach soon." All that week, I had begun to sense deep meaning in people's basic words. "Take care" meant "What happened to you is unspeakable, so I don't know what to say."

"Take care of Mom" meant, "I know she's a mess. Don't do anything to make it worse." In general, people stuck to their clichés. They let me figure out the rest.

"Later," Scott said, nodding in my direction. "Feel better."

Grandma Lil saw them to the door and then wrapped her arms around me. When she let go I saw that her eyes were wet with tears, and that her lip quivered as she tried to hold herself together.

"That's my granddaughter," she said, gripping each arm. "That's my Beth." She held my face between the palms of her hands, soft and warm, vaguely scented with lemony hand cream and tuna salad, and leaned in to stamp a juicy kiss just under my left eye. I closed it and smiled, thinking of all the times she'd put her lips to my cheeks, so relieved she was there to do it then.

Chapter Ten

I WOKE up the next morning and realized, with sinking disappointment, that it was the last day of sixth grade. I'd so wanted to be there—to say goodbye to my friends for the summer, and to my hugely pregnant teacher, Mrs. Hamilton, and to simply savor my last day in the elementary school before moving on to the junior high in the fall. I had always loved last days of school—sitting in a stifling classroom, backs of thighs sticking to plastic seats, HAVE A GREAT SUMMER! written on the chalkboard in a teacher's curly script, no work of any kind being done and everyone perfectly OK with it. I loved savoring that last drop of structure, knowing that summer's lovely laziness was stretched out before us.

"Can't I just go to the last day?" I'd asked my mom the night before, my first night back in my bed.

"No, Beth," she'd said, shaking her head and closing her eyes in that way she did when something was completely non-negotiable, which was often. "It's not appropriate. And not necessary."

I knew it was true. But I didn't want to miss anything.

The next morning, my mother had answered the phone to find that it was Mrs. Hamilton herself, who had called to say that she and a couple of other teachers would like to come by after school for a visit. "To check in on her," she had said, "and to bring her some things that might cheer her up."

The prospect of having Mrs. Hamilton come to my house had both thrilled and unnerved me, and I thought of the last time we'd had a teacher over for a visit, when I was in kindergarten, and Mrs. Chakrin had come over for lunch. It was back when people did such things, and when I was young enough so that blurring the lines between teacher and Mom's friend didn't seem so strange. My mom had made a ham-and-cheese quiche and glasses of fresh iced tea, and I had sat at the kitchen table as close as I could get to Mrs. Chakrin, on whom I'd had a fierce schoolgirl crush, without actually touching her. Today's visit would be different.

When I heard a car door slam I peered out of my bedroom window, through the red blooming branches of the cork-bark bush. They had come from the school in one car, driving the three big blocks through our suburban development, along the two streets that I had followed every school day since kindergarten. Mrs. Hamilton's belly looked as if it had grown since just last week, and she held both hands behind her, pressed into the small of her back, as she lumbered up our driveway. She was with Miss Geer, the music teacher, who clutched a large manila folder under one arm and made a clip-clop sound on our driveway with her high heels, and with Mr. Addeo, the school principal, who fastened the top button of his suit jacket and shook out his pants legs, one quick shake to the left, one to the right, before joining Mrs. Hamilton in the short walk to our front door. I couldn't believe they were making a personal house call. It made me feel very important, a bit nervous and, suddenly, quite shy. I didn't want to act too happy to see them, for fear they'd think I wasn't sad. But I didn't want to act sad, either.

When the doorbell rang, Grandma Lil stayed in the kitchen and let me answer it. I hustled to it on my crutches, smiling a little too wide when I saw the trio, so out of context there on my front porch.

"Hi there, sweetie," Mrs. Hamilton said as I pushed the screen door open for them to step through. "How are you doing?" I told her fine, not knowing what else to say, let her soothing baby voice wash over me. She now held one hand under her belly, and when she stepped into the house she swayed a bit, and Mr. Addeo took hold of her elbow.

"It's getting harder and harder to get around!" Mrs. Hamilton had a Dorothy Hamill haircut and shiny braces on her teeth, and when she smiled I saw that she'd gotten new tiny rubber bands that stretched tightly up and down in the back corners of her jaw. They made her sound, when she spoke, like she had wads of gum stuffed into the sides of her mouth.

Mr. Addeo and Miss Geer each chuckled along with her, but just a little, and it was only right then that I realized that they all must have been a bit nervous too.

As we stood in the foyer, just inside of the door, they each doled out awkward hugs to me. I'd begun to grow accustomed to hugging teachers, something I'd never come close to doing before my week in the hospital. My grandmother appeared then—in lieu of my mom, who was back at the hospital visiting my dad—just to say a quick hello and offer iced tea or juice, which everyone refused, before scurrying back into the den to join random temple members and cousins who sat dismantling fruit baskets while speaking in hushed, dark tones.

"So, well, we can all just sit here," I said, stepping into the rarely used living room. It was basically where I practiced the piano and lay on the carpet listening to records on my parents' new stereo, and where they entertained adult visitors on occasion, chatting and laughing and sipping cups of coffee long after Adam and I had gone to bed. But right then I felt it was appropriate to use it for my own guests. Besides, it felt like it was hanging on the farthest edge of our house, which, deeper in, had an over-burdened, sad, and murky air—too intimate a space to share with teachers.

Mr. Addeo cleared his throat. "So, Beth. We're not only here to visit with you, to pay our respects to you, but also to present you with the many awards that you won this afternoon," he said, his lips curled into a tight, proud smile. I had forgotten, until that moment, that it had not only been the last day of classes, but the day of a special awards ceremony that was held in the echo-filled all-purpose room. "And you have certainly earned quite a stack of them!"

Mr. Addeo was a burly Italian man with silvering, kinky-curly black hair, who smelled of a blend of musky aftershave and stale cigarettes. He always wore a suit and tie, and had a presence so feared that he could bring the high-pitched buzz of our packed lunchtime cafeteria to a silent halt just by stepping his polished shoes onto the edge of the shiny floor and standing there for a few seconds. One kid would catch sight of him, and then another, and then there'd be fierce whispering, "Mr. Addeo! Shhhh! It's Mr. Addeo!" followed by utter quiet. Since I never got in trouble I didn't know him particularly well, though he did know me by name, and would state it, matter-of-factly, accompanied by a friendly nod whenever we happened to pass each other in the hallways.

Besides that, I didn't think he knew much about me—or Adam—and so was surprised to see him quoted in the newspaper story about the accident. I had found the front page on the kitchen table just that morning and trembled when I saw it, thinking Grandma Lil must have left it out there by mistake. Before she could realize it, though, I grabbed it and hurried with it into my room, where I could close the door and read every word slowly and carefully. The story—TWO YOUNGSTERS DIE AS ANOTHER AUTO JUMPS A DIVIDER—was on the front page of the *Asbury Park Press*, sandwiched between SHELLING ERUPTS SOUTH OF BEIRUT and MERCHANTS HOPE FOR MORE SUN, which had a photo of two girls about my age in their bathing suits, wet and laughing as they made their way out of the ocean. I stared into their eyes, procrastinating, before forcing my gaze to settle on the photos that ran along with the accident story: two small ones, one each of Adam and Kristin. I recognized Adam's as his most recent school portrait, his blue sweater pulled neatly down over a collared shirt, thick red hair a bit unruly around his part, but I had never seen that particular shot of Kristin before: her face smiling, taken straight on, hair pulled back, sparkling gold earrings. Only after studying every detail of her—the white open collar resting on a pink cardigan, barrettes in her hair—did I begin reading.

> *Two children involved in a car crash while returning home from a piano recital were among three Monmouth County people killed accidently [sic] over the weekend.*
>
> *The youngsters, Adam Greenfield, 7, and Kristin M. Sickel, 13, both of Eatontown, died after a car jumped a divider and landed on top of the auto they were riding in at Route 35 and Deal Road in Ocean Township late Saturday night.*

Young Greenfield and Miss Sickel were pronounced dead at
12:02 a.m. yesterday at Monmouth Medical Center, Long
Branch.

Arrested and charged with two counts of death by auto is
Edward J. Pahule of Milwaukee.

Pahule, based at the Earle Naval Weapons Station,
Middletown Township, also faces a charge of drunk driving.

I hadn't known any of these details—the time of death,
the name of the driver—and had to breathe extra deeply to
capture air in my lungs as I learned them then, from the local
newspaper, just like everybody else in town. And I found myself feeling unreasonably annoyed that it said we had been at
my piano, rather than ballet, recital. But mostly, reading the
story—which I must have done three times, very slowly, before returning it to its haphazard spot on the kitchen table—
made it cruelly real. And it gave me plenty more horrifying
images to have tucked away in my mind.

After the story covered the basics—including those of an
unrelated death, of a twenty-eight-year-old man who drowned
in his parents' pool, which felt disrespectful to both accidents,
I thought—there were many quotes about Kristin from junior
high school friends I didn't know and from John Collins, the
school music teacher and choir director whom Kristin had
talked about frequently. He said that Kristin "was a beautiful youngster who could relate to adults with maturity beyond her years. It's a loss that can't be replaced." Someone
named Casey Reynolds said that she "had a lot of school
spirit" and "loved going to parties." I read the quotes over and
over, jealous of the life she'd had at junior high that had not
included me, disturbed that I didn't get to give any of my own
quotes about her.

Mr. Addeo recalled Kristin to be "an extremely talented

girl." And then he was quoted about Adam, and our family. "He loved coming to school, his mom and dad, his sister," it said. "He was a happy and bright little boy."

Had Adam really loved going to school? I supposed he liked it, though I guess I hadn't ever really asked him. And his saying that Adam loved us was, I guess, a sweet assumption. Happy and bright I would give him. I didn't dare ask him about what he had said as he sat there, suit slacks hiked up above his black dress socks, shiny shoes pressed into our carpet, cologne scent filling the air of our living room. He settled onto the couch with Miss Geer.

She was the most sullen of the three visitors, balanced quietly at the edge of the soft cushions, hands in her lap. Her blond bob was pulled back on the sides with combs, and she wore a festive yellow sundress and a long white cardigan, and white high-heeled sandals. She was the music teacher, and she went around from classroom to classroom pushing her wheeled cart, which contained a record player and small percussion instruments like tambourines and triangles, and battered hardcover music books for sing-alongs of "Michael, Row Your Boat Ashore" or "This Land Is Your Land" or "There's a Hole in the Bucket." I adored Miss Geer, who conducted the band and taught everyone their instrument lessons in her tiny windowless office, where I would squeeze in with three other clarinetists for a half an hour every Tuesday afternoon, trying in vain to get through "The Star-Spangled Banner" or "Greensleeves" without blowing any squeaks.

"We all missed you at today's ceremony," Mrs. Hamilton said, settling into my favorite little fancy chair, with a thick fat cadet blue cushion upholstered in a pattern of vines, at the perimeter of the living room. "Especially since you won so many awards! You got a huge applause anytime your name was announced." My teacher looked and sounded like a kid, a pregnant one, especially with her hugely round glasses that dwarfed her already tiny face. Her belly sat like a beach ball in her lap.

Mr. Addeo proceeded to announce each of my prizes with put-on pomp and circumstance, as if he were back at the ceremony. Mrs. Hamilton and Miss Geer clapped after each announcement.

"And now, in the category of Musical Excellence . . ." he said.

"And now, in the category of Outstanding Academic Achievement . . .

"And now, for the Physical Education Presidential Award . . ."

After I had about six of the oak-tag certificates, each with a fancy blue-ribbon border, stacked neatly on my lap, he said, "And, finally, for the award of Perfect Attendance . . ."

"Wait, what? But it wasn't perfect," I interjected. "I missed the last three days."

"These last days don't count," Mr. Addeo said, his eyes soft and earnest. "They were out of your control."

The reality that I'd blown my chances of perfect attendance that year had entered my mind while I was still in the hospital, stuck in the adjustable bed and staring at *Days of Our Lives* on the mounted television, which made me realize that it was the middle of the afternoon on a Tuesday, and that everyone else was in school. I was missing the last few days of sixth grade, after showing up every day for the entire year. I had become fixated on getting the perfect attendance certificate.

Now I just felt like a cheat, as if I'd been given a pity award, and I felt my face burn. Still, I could tell they had made their decision, and so I placed the questionable certificate on top of the others, and held onto them tightly with both hands.

"And I have something from the students who love and miss you," Mrs. Hamilton said, pulling a thick brown envelope out of her tote bag and presenting it to me like it was the best prize of all. "Cards, from all of your classmates!"

The packet of cards bulged, and I grabbed hold of it and held it on my lap, desperately curious, all of a sudden, to see what my sixth-grade classmates would possibly be able to say to someone whose brother had just been killed. I was slightly startled to think about the fact that everyone knew about our tragedy, that people must have discussed my loss at school, in my absence. I wondered what the conversations had been like, and if they had known about the accident before arriving at school that morning, told about it by parents who had read it in the *Asbury Park Press*, or if Mrs. Hamilton—or even Mr. Addeo—had been the one to break the news.

Soon my visitors left, after doling out hugs that were more comfortable the second time around, and I went to my bedroom and dropped the packet onto the pink and yellow flowered comforter that stretched across the top of my twin bed. My room was at the end of the hall, with one window that looked out over the flat rectangle of front lawn and another that faced the side yard, with its tangle of dormant rose bushes poking out of a layer of wood chips, a pair of birch trees and a hedge of forsythias that edged the driveway of our next-door neighbors, the Littmans. When we were younger Mara and Alyson used to come calling for me by coming up to the side of our house.

"Beth!" they would shout up into my bedroom window. "Can you come outside?" and I would open the window and stick my head out and say, "I'll be right there!" and feel grown-up and important, having an exchange that was just in my room, and not at the front door, under the gaze of my parents. Sometimes I'd toss items down to where they stood on the lawn—colored sticks of chalk for writing on the drive-way, a few messy-haired Barbies, bottles of nail polish—before heading out to join them in one of our yards.

I sat on the edge of my bed and held the envelope from Mrs. Hamilton on my lap, pinching open the bendable gold clasp to extract the neat stack of cards, each made from a sheet of white construction paper that was folded once in half. I breathed deeply as I read through them, blushing each time I got to another name—Scott Taylor, the friendless, pink-faced fat boy who wore thick glasses and wheezed his way through every gym class, drew a hospital in red crayon and wrote GET WELL SOON OR ELSE!; my artistic neighbor, Joanne Tannenbaum, who had been my best friend until we grew apart in the second grade, wrote BETH, WE MISS YOU . . . THIS MUCH! and made a cutout of herself that popped out of the card's center when you opened it. Jenny Mamos wrote GET WELL SOON but in place of the word "well" drew a little picture of one, pail and all; David O'Brien drew a picture of me with pink hair and wrote WHAT DO YOU GET WHEN YOU CROSS A SMART GIRL WITH A PRETTY GIRL? YOU GET BETH!; and Pam Cody drew a picture of me in a hospital bed, getting a shot in my naked butt from a grim-faced nurse.

My heart sank as it became apparent that not one of the twenty cards would mention Adam. Only Mrs. Hamilton's short cursive letter—stuck in the big envelope among the stack of cards—hinted at anything more than physical pain. "Knowing you, I hope you'll express the feelings you feel now by writing," she wrote in her perfect, bubble script. "You'll be surprised how much relief it will bring you."

I realized that my four broken metatarsal bones—just like my father's busted ribs and punctured lung—had provided people with something concrete to talk about. "How's your foot?" everyone could ask, instead of, "How's your grief?" I could go for checkups with the orthopedist, Dad could do his breathing exercises in the den. We could focus on our bodies, do follow-up X-rays and give everyone tangible things to focus on, things that would actually mend. It was deceiving, the physical healing, as it held no consequence, really. It offered no larger relief—just normal breathing, movement, my cast eventually being cut off to reveal a pale and atrophied calf covered with a new coat of white-blond fur.

Still, as I read and reread the cards I was repeatedly startled by their omissions, ashamed that I'd expected anything different. I sat there for a while, staring at the pile, until Grandma Lil rapped lightly on the door to tell me that it was time for dinner. I went to join her and whomever else was still hanging around, vaguely hopeful that there hadn't been any loss after all.

Chapter Eleven

S HE and Grandpa Norman left a week later. Grandma
Lil cried freely while holding me against the stiff cones
of her bra, which strained beneath the stretchy polyester of
her sleeveless T-shirt, and Grandpa Norman was mostly
silent, eyes tearing up just slightly as he said, in a scratchy,
constricted voice, "Take care, kiddo. Love you." Mom had
said her good-byes inside, though I could see her lingering, a
slouched and quiet silhouette just inside the front screen
door.

It had been a relief to have them in our house for the
week—Grandma making her signature treats, blintzes and
rice pudding, and hosting the streams of visitors who had
come to bring casseroles or flowers or to simply sit for a half
an hour on our low brown couch, making small talk with me
or with Grandma, sipping coffee that she had brewed in our
old olive-green metal percolator.

Grandma had made sure everything happened smoothly, while Grandpa stayed behind the scenes, clearing out Adam's room and comforting Mom when no one else was with her. But mostly they had filled in the physical space left by Adam and kept the creeping grief monster at bay and made sure all the banalities of our household chugged along—dishwashing, laundering, phone answering, remembering to turn the lights on when night would fall. They were a buffer between my mom and me, and went on daily visits to see my father, who had remained in the ICU until transferring onto a regular floor two nights before they left.

As I watched Grandma and Grandpa's rental car disappear at the end of Thornley Road, I remembered complaining to my mom once, when I was younger, about Grandma Lil's kisses. She had long, crooked teeth that glimmered with the metal of fillings and bridges, and wore thick, gritty lipsticks in garish reds and corals that left a coat of colored slime on my cheeks.

"They're too wet and slobbery," I whined, "and she gets lipstick all over my face. I don't want her to kiss me!" I was about six, and we were on an airplane, Eastern Airlines, getting ready to touch down in Miami, where Dad's parents would surely already be waiting at the arrival gate.

Mom looked at me sternly when I told her this and said to me: "Beth. Listen to me. Your grandma waits all year for us to visit at Christmastime. She loves you very much, and if she wants to give you wet kisses when she sees you for the first time at the airport, then you are going to let her. Do you hear me? It won't kill you."

I nodded glumly and never complained again, and when we landed that night and walked the short stretch from the airplane to the boarding area, there they were, grinning and calling out our names and harnessing so much excitable energy between them that I couldn't help but smile too, and then run into their arms, letting them both go crazy with kisses and hugs.

"I get so worried that you don't love me as much as your Grandma Ruth," Grandma Lil would tell me every December, when we'd spend our winter-break week visiting Miami Beach. "I'm so far away and she's right there, and I worry that we won't be as close!"

It made me uncomfortable, having to reassure her so. "I love you both the same," I would say, unable to imagine how that wouldn't be the truth. "And I miss you so much when I'm away."

Then her eyes would tear and she would look so grateful, say, "Really?" and wrap me in her arms—and kiss me, wetly, right on my face, just as she had done on our driveway that steamy July morning before driving away with Grandpa, before leaving me alone with Mom and our grief.

When their car turned off of our street and toward the highway I stood there for a few minutes, looking around at our neighborhood, which was still and humid and quiet on this weekday morning, when adults were at work and kids were at camp. It was just more emptiness, more absence. I tried to take a deep breath but could only draw a shallow, panicky one—something I found would happen on a daily basis now, though I would ignore it, and the lightheadedness that followed, until months passed and I could finally begin to suck air all the way into my lungs again. Until then, I'd fake it—take a series of shallow breaths until I felt the dizziness subside—which I did that morning on the driveway. Then I turned toward my mother, who was still there, lurking in the foyer. When I got back inside, she pulled me toward her and cried into my hair.

"Oh, Beth," she whimpered. "Oh, Beth, I'm so sorry! I'm

so sorry, Beth." I let her hold me but I gave her nothing back, just stood there, ossified, and took it for as long as I could stand it, and then I pulled away, refusing even to meet her desperate gaze. There was so much I thought about saying to her—

> *It's not your fault.*
> *I miss him so much.*
> *Why did this have to happen?*
> *Stop crying, please!*
> *I feel the same as you.*
> *At least you still have me.*
> *I love you.*

There was so much I thought about saying but just did not—could not—because of some overwhelming mixture of anger and fear. It's like she was a stranger, someone I wasn't sure I could trust. But at the same time she was me, my reflection—where did I end and she begin?—and she was expressing every emotion I thought I might be feeling before I could even be sure. I didn't want to fight her for it, so I relinquished my sadness to her before it even took hold of me.

I headed to my bedroom so I could hide, figure out a strategy. I wound up sitting on my bed for a while and just thinking, mainly about how it seemed I had forgotten how to feel. I was numb, mostly, and vaguely sad, but I knew I was supposed to be distraught. I knew it was what people expected because I heard them when they came by to sit shiva—"Beth seems just fine," they'd say, puzzled, concerned. So I wondered if I could re-teach myself emotion, maybe by secretly acting out scenes of grief or sorrow, just as I'd seen them on my soaps, pretending that a camera was trained on my every move.

I tried it out that afternoon and, with my door shut and locked, stared and stared at a photo of myself and Adam, both of us leaning against a palm tree on the beach in Miami not quite a year before. I was in a purple bikini, trying to look sultry and wise though still eleven; Adam was six, spindly and knobby-kneed and squinting into the sun, his white swim trunks ballooning over his skinny middle. I looked hard at the image, told myself "You will never, ever see him again!" until, finally, I cried.

The grief didn't start out big but I corralled it there, and then it felt so huge that I feared I couldn't contain it. I eased myself off my bed, limped across the room and opened my sliding closet door. I reached in to grab a hunk of clothes, lifted them by their white plastic hangers in one thick, tangled mass and hauled them onto my fuzzy red and pink shag carpet. I did that over and over again until there was not a stitch of clothing left hanging, all while moaning and whimpering quietly so my mother, out in the kitchen and talking and crying into the phone to someone, wouldn't hear me. Then there was nothing left to do but be as over-the-top as Monica Quartermaine would have been on *General Hospital*: I threw myself right onto the pile of cotton jumpers and velour sweaters and terrycloth halter tops and I cried all over everything, until my tears wet my arms and my hair and the top of the mountain of clothes. I was dizzy, but more awake, and I sat alone in my mess for a long time before numbly hanging each item, one by one, back in the closet. Somewhere in my head I called, "Scene."

Grandma Ruth showed up that afternoon to take over for Grandma Lil, and she provided a stark contrast: thin and delicate, with a subdued style that prevented her from wearing anything flashy and from speaking too loudly, and she exhibited a wide-eyed, childlike surprise about everything from

Chinese food to touch-tone telephones. She had married a man eighteen years her senior when she was just twenty-one years old, and when he died, just a year after I was born, she could neither drive a car nor balance a checkbook, exuding a girlish quality that would remain until the day she died.

Still, at our house she pulsed with a strong and in-charge energy that I had never felt from her before. She was going to spend a few nights with us—something new, since she was fussy about her sleeping arrangements, from the firmness of the bed to the quiet of the room to the brightness of the read-ing lights. She cherished her privacy. But this seemed to count as a special enough occasion for her to make an excep-tion, and I watched with a bit of amazement as she set her small blue-gray valise just inside the edge of Adam's room.

"How about some tuna fish, Beth?" she asked, tying Mom's yellow flowered apron around her waist and washing her hands, up to her elbows, in the kitchen sink.

"OK," I called from the couch, where I was still belly up in front of the soaps.

I had yet to see Grandma Ruth cry over Adam, which kind of surprised me—though I'd never seen her cry about anything before, not even her husband, Aaron, whom she'd worshiped, who installed commercial air-conditioning sys-tems for a living and read poetry and played classical piano and was a dreamer, my mom always said, just like me. Since his death my grandmother had sat in front of the television, peeling starchy McIntosh apples into a paper towel spread across her lap, reading mystery novels in her chair by the window, bundled up on warm spring days.

It would take another twenty years for me to see her tears, in fact, as her usual reaction to any mention of Adam or of the accident would be to hold her head and shake it back and forth slowly, *tssk-tsssking* before quietly slipping out of the room. It would be when I was in my twenties, home visiting from New York, with Grandma over for dinner. After eating, I'd feel nostalgic, and slip into the living room to play some piano and to dredge up all my 33 LP record albums, like Marie Osmond's *Paper Roses* and Helen Reddy's *I Don't Know How to Love Him* and Debby Boone's *You Light Up My Life*. I put that song on, really loudly, and called Grandma into the living room because of how it used to be our song when I was about seven. That's when she had taken me to see the movie, and I had loved the theme song because it was in an easy key to sing along with, and I would sing it to her like she was my first true love.

So when I put the record on that night, she came bounding into the living room, hands clasped together and held to her chest. She gestured to herself in a coy way as if to say, "Me? Is this something you are doing all for little old me?" Then she came in slowly and sat down on the embroidered seat cushions of the living-room couch as I sang along for her, and she put her head in her hands—a dramatic gesture I'd only ever seen her do in jest. But when she didn't look up after a few seconds, I realized she meant it. She was weeping into her hands, shaking her head in embarrassment, not wanting me to see her red, watery eyes.

It was the first time I ever saw my grandmother cry in my whole life, and when I asked her what was wrong, if I should turn it off, she said no. So I sat next to her on the couch and asked her why she was crying, and all she could say was, "Because I love you." I sat next to her for the rest of the song, holding her all the way around like I would've held a lover, and felt her tiny frame in my arms, her bony shoulders and her thin spine and the fragile part of her neck where her skull met her backbone and I knew why she was crying, and why I was crying and why Mom was hovering around the corner in the hallway crying, obscuring herself from her mother but allowing me to see. There was just too much to recount, to dwell on, to sob over together, but I knew the meaning of her measured grief, her little eruption that couldn't be helped after years of holding it in.

~

I drifted into a light sleep on the couch sometime after *General Hospital* ended and awoke at dusk, with Grandma Ruth gently coaxing me to the kitchen table for a square of the reheated lasagna that a neighbor had brought by earlier in the week. When she served it, it was still a little bit cold in its center, though I didn't say anything.

Later, our neighbor Mrs. Fritz brought a chicken casserole and the mom of my other best friend, Elizabeth—with whom I would ride bikes and romp on the playground, rather than focus on fashion and boys, like with Kristin—brought a chocolate cake. They spent about a half an hour visiting, both of them together, speaking in muted tones to my mom, who sat with them in the dimly lit living room in the front of the house while I dove into more television—a movie on Cinemax this time, *Resurrection*, in which the husband of Ellen Burstyn's character dies in a fiery car accident.

"We're so sorry," Mrs. Fritz said, poking her head into the den, Elizabeth's mom right behind her, nodding, lips pressed tightly together into a straight line.

"Thank you," I told them, barely turning away from the TV screen. It was the part where she was coming back to life, and I was transfixed.

It was incongruous having all of these strangers in our house. Until Adam died, the most interacting I had ever done with my suburban neighbors—besides those who were my friends—was when I was a ten-year-old selling Girl Scout Cookies door-to-door. I'd put on my flimsy green uniform, grab a disposable pen and the shiny stiff order form that had bright pictures of the Thin Mints and Peanut Butter Tagalongs, and head from house to house. Each time I approached one—ranch, colonial, split level—it was with trepidation and excitement, as I was stepping over the invisible barrier that began where the sidewalk met the property line.

But things changed after the accident. Suddenly fathers I had only waved to from our passing station wagon, mothers I had only said five words to when playing with their daughters in the backyard, older siblings of pals I had only stared at in awe from afar—suddenly they were all in my home. They sat on my couch and at the kitchen table, bringing carnation-heavy floral arrangements and fruit baskets and baked goods, looking at me with pity and curiosity, asking, "How are you coming along?" Dads would pat my head or clap me on the back and moms would cry and pull me close to them. Their children would stand near me a bit wide-eyed, and only when they were left alone with me so that their parents could go and comfort my weeping mother would they make stilted conversation, giving me a bit of news about the end of school or telling me about a particular TV show, fidgeting nervously with the cuff of their shorts or lint in their pockets, unsure of how to speak to me now that I had become someone new.

After Elizabeth's mom and Mrs. Fritz had gone my mom and grandmother came in to sit with me, sinking beside me on the couch.

"Why don't you get some sleep, Bethie," my mom said, with a clarity and sweetness that I hadn't heard in her since before all of this. She sounded like her old self—someone I missed desperately—and I felt suddenly and unexpectedly warm toward her as I leaned my head into her shoulder. She stroked my hair.

"The movie's almost over," I told her in a sleepy voice. "It's really good. This woman died for a second and then came back to life after a car accident."

My mom exhaled heavily, with a sad sigh, and I was instantly sorry, thinking I'd really set her off now. But she held it together, and I clicked off the TV, my head still buzzing in the unfamiliar silence that remained. The movie was on every night this week, I reasoned. I could watch the end tomorrow.

"OK," I told her. "I'm going to sleep." I leaned over my grandmother, whose tiny body was tucked into one end of the sofa, and kissed her cheek. It was so dewy and smooth, without a single wrinkle, and smelled of pressed powder and apples.

My mom followed me past Adam's room, where the door was shut tight, and down the short carpeted hallway to my room, which felt cave-like from the air-conditioning that had been seeping in all day, before my mom turned it off and opened all the windows, insisting on letting in some real air. "I feel all cooped up in here," she'd said. Rick Springfield stared down at us from a glossy poster I'd gotten at the mall, at Oriental Pearl. The envelope of cards from my classmates sat in the middle of my bed, on the bedspread my mother still smoothed in her daily stupor. My room felt both terrifically comforting and horrifyingly depressing, mocking me with proof of my once ho-hum life here.

"Your grandma's been a real help," my mom said, turning down the bed for me as I wriggled out of my terrycloth jumper and into a thick gray extra-large Rick Springfield T-shirt that Melissa had bought for me at the concert I was supposed to have attended with her the week before. "Just like Grandma and Grandpa were before they left." /

"I miss them," I told her.

"I know you do," she said. "It'll be hard to get back to normal here, without all these extra people around."

We were conversing like normal, like we understood each other. I knew it wouldn't last long. So I ended it.

"Anyway, good night," I said.

"Good night, my Beth. I love you."

She left, and my mind began racing immediately. All I could see were images from the night of the accident: blood soaked through my shirt and dried into the wrinkles of my knuckles and below the whites of my fingernails; the roof of the car bent and twisted and almost touching the top of my head; my dad trapped and screaming in the front seat, barely visible from beneath the dashboard—and then bodies, just indiscriminate bodies littered on the ground all around me, like how Jonestown looked on the cover of *Time* magazine, death piled everywhere I turned. I sat up in bed and pulled my knees to my chest and squeezed my eyes shut. When I opened them I saw that a shaft of moonlight had splashed across the tufts of my hot-pink shag carpeting, and that the shape it formed was not beautiful, but horrific—like one of those outlines of a dead body that police mark with tape in the street at the scene of a murder. I squeezed my eyes closed again and waited for it to disappear, but when I looked again it was there still, brighter and whiter and more gruesome than before.

I imagined Adam's body lying within the stain of light, buried beneath the puff of my tutu, just a flash of copper hair peeking out from the baby-blue netting. And then I slipped out of my bed and out of my room, not sure what I would do.

When I opened my bedroom door I heard the muffled television in the den—a show with canned laughter, which surprised me—and the very faint sound of my mom talking with my grandma. I contemplated going back into my room like nothing had happened—they sounded normal out there, without a care in the world—but I knew I just couldn't do it. I plodded down the hall and into the den, squinting in the light. My mom lay on the couch, her head in her mom's lap. I had never before witnessed such intimacy between them.

"Beth? What is it?" My mom sensed me in the room before I spoke and sat up.

"I can't sleep."

"Come sit with us."

"Yes, Beth darling, come here," Grandma Ruth added, gesturing with an outstretched arm for me to join them.

"The moonlight looks like a dead body," I said. And then I started to cry.

"Where? What do you mean, a dead body?" my mother's voice shifted back to post-accident. Not soothing anymore.

"Like a dead body! Like when the police draw around the body with chalk or tape! It's like somebody died in there!" I was beyond my own control then, hallucinating or having a panic attack, not sure where any of this was coming from, or what any of it had to do with the accident, or reality in general. I wept freely in front of both of them, unable to do any differently.

My mother jumped up and held me, as I stood brittle and silent. Grandma remained on the couch, shaking her head slowly and clicking her tongue, her hands clasped before her in anxious prayer. Then my mom led me back into the bedroom to investigate the flash of light. It disappeared beneath the artificial light from the hallway when we opened the door, and I wanted to just forget the whole thing.

"It's fine now," I pleaded. "I'm OK. The light is gone. It's OK now. I can go to sleep." I regretted letting my guard down, tried desperately to pull it back up.

"I'll lie with you for a while, Beth," my mom said. "Come on. Let's both get into your bed."

I slipped under my thin yellow blanket and turned away to face the wall, closing my eyes. I felt her lingering there, lying at the edge of my bed, for some time, but I breathed shallowly and tried not to move a muscle until I felt her sniffle and sigh and then rise from my bed, walking slowly out of my room and closing the door behind her.

Chapter Twelve

THE day my father returned home from the hospital is mainly a blur in my memory, but I know that he squashed my bizarre happy act—the one that I tossed in my mom's face every time she glared at me with lonely desperation—with the sickening sadness in his eyes. I saw it the second he slipped in through the front door, after I had watched him step gingerly up the driveway, my mom buzzing nervously at his side. I took note of the way he looked hollowed-out and filled back in with some sort of bulked-up version of himself, like the relish-clogged stuffing of a deviled egg, and saw that his left arm was hanging a bit lower than his right, looking heavy and apelike, his hand curled into his hip, as if he'd had a stroke. I opened the front screen door for him and stepped aside and out onto the porch in my pink halter-top romper and bare feet, said, "Hi, Poppy. Welcome home." He strained to give me a smile, but I could barely detect it, which made my stomach drop, because it meant that I alone could not make him happy.

We all avoided each other in the house once he was there—or maybe I just avoided them. Though we'd all been through the same experience, though we all missed Adam and our pre-accident existence, we did not bond with or take comfort in one another. Instead we floated through the halls or holed up in rooms as three separate and marooned entities. My mother's universe was their bedroom, where she napped in darkness, heavy shades remaining down throughout the day, the pea-green wool carpet rushing around her like a moat that we rarely waded through. And while she had been so dedicated to visiting my father while he was still in the hospital, her attitude toward him shifted once he got home—she was impatient with him when he didn't express his grief as freely, annoyed if he wanted to carry on as if everything were the same.

My father joined the New Jersey Task Force on Drunk Driving, leaving the house on frequent evenings to attend meetings, which he told us about in gratingly loud and fired-up detail when he returned.

"We're just going to put these scumbags away!" he'd report. "They want to suck down the booze and then get in their cars? Fine. No problem. We'll let 'em rot in jail, that's all."

"Is that going to bring him back?" my mother would ask him, stonefaced, causing my father to sigh and look at the floor. "Then I don't want to hear it!"

When he was at home he took refuge in the den, in his La-Z-Boy chair, where he would pretend to read the paper as usual but where he often just sat, staring into the middle distance toward the kitchen, the newspaper draped like a blanket over his knees. It's also where he did his physical therapy exercises—blowing as powerfully as he could into a clear tube, trying to make the plastic marble float higher in its silo than it had the day before, gently raising and lowering his arm out sideways to get it into a ninety-degree angle with his side. He'd stand there flapping in the early dusk, the spicy orange sunset and fading heat and joyous hum of summer sealed outside, right in the neighborhood, but worlds away.

While I was busy avoiding everyone, I craved connection. For this, I would keep an eye out for tangible acknowledgments of the accident, watching out my bedroom window for the mail's arrival and trying to act casual—like it was just dumb luck that I went out at the perfect time every day, hopping into the humid morning to grab the fat stack of envelopes that awaited us in the black metal mailbox that stood on its post at the end of the driveway. Condolence cards poured in throughout the summer and then slowed to a trickle that lasted well into the fall, and I opened any that were addressed "Greenfield Family," obsessing over them as if they held the most fascinating prose and relishing the idea that we were on people's minds and not just here in this hollow house, mourning and searching.

I lived to see what people had written next to the YOU ARE IN OUR THOUGHTS AND PRAYERS already printed inside. Each message was both a reminder of the reality, which allowed me to soak it in on yet a deeper level and wallow in it, as well as a lifeline, reminding me that someone out there was still thinking about me, and feeling sympathetic, even if the flow of visitors had decreased and then stopped altogether, leaving me alone with my parents and the sad, thick grief that drifted through every corner of our house like a thick, humid fog.

The majority of the envelopes had just my parents' names on them, though, and I would study the return addresses to see if I knew the family that sent it, and in either case I would hover near my mom as she opened them, sighing and sniffling, and then I'd sneak long looks at them when she got distracted by the telephone or the doorbell or a random memory that seized her and forced her to wander, lost, out of the room.

Every once in a while there would be one for me, just for me, and I would bring it into my bedroom where I could tear it open in private, studying the card itself—was it funny? blank inside? a real adult sympathy card offering up a prayer or cliché in a tight, cursive font?—to try and ascertain what the sender was really trying to say. One was a get-well card that had a shiny color photo of a cocker spaniel in a basket of red roses on its cover. It came from one of our babysitters, Karin Erickson, who wrote, "Please be strong so you can get better and I promise I'll come to see you real soon." I don't know what intrigued me more—the idea that the accident was such a real fact that my babysitters knew about it, or that Karin had thought enough about me to purchase the card, write something inside, and stamp it and stick it in the mail. I stared at it, astounded by the acknowledgment of my loss.

The only type of mail that was better than a pile of condolence cards was the monthly temple newsletter, which held all kinds of keys to who was thinking about us through the list of contributions to the Greenfield Education Fund. My parents had worked with the rabbi to set it up—a fund to help pay for a new video player and television for the Sunday school, to which people could make contributions in Adam's memory. I knew the page that held the list of new gifts and I would turn directly to it after stealthily snagging the newsletter from the pile of mail and bringing it into my bedroom to read before sneaking it back into the pile for my parents to find. All that summer it was the fund that received the most donations—given by at least ten families a month, from those we were closest with to those I knew only from annual Yom Kippur services, or because one of their kids was in my Hebrew school class.

Temple turned out to be my saving grace, even before the accident. I was no religious zealot, but while other kids my age had complained about it bitterly—about boring Sunday school and Hebrew school classes, and about having to dress up for services, which were dull and endless and like a punishment—I somehow loved it all. I adored the rituals—the melancholy music, the gold-padded pews and matching sanctuary carpet, the royal blue *Gates of Prayer* books that closed with a wonderful thud after we sang the last strains of "Adon Olam." I loved the silver eternal light, which dangled from a glimmering chain just above where the rabbi stood.

Rabbi Sally Jane Priesand—named almost the same as my favorite Judy Blume character in *Starring Sally J. Friedman as Herself*—was the very first woman rabbi ever ordained, and I was enamored with her. She was gawky and socially awkward, and when she sang along with the cantor you could hear her joyous, tone-deaf voice echoing against the farthest wall in the sanctuary. She was kind to me, and encouraging, and would be a caring teacher when I studied for my Bat Mitzvah. And though I couldn't yet comprehend the entirety of her sermons—too political and liberal and pro-Palestine for my father's taste—I always took away enough to find them beautiful and wise.

But mostly my feeling toward Monmouth Reform Temple, with its sterile modern architecture and quirky congregation of suburbanites, was a terribly selfish love. It's because there,

I always had a willing audience. And walking into the lobby was like being received.

"Such a beautiful young lady," Mr. Rosen would say, after kissing me hello and grazing my cheek with his thick, scratchy beard.

"What a lovely voice you have," Cantor Suzanne would tell me.

"Gorgeous hair color!" Mrs. Tuchband would exclaim, and then joke, "What dye number should I ask for at the beauty salon?"

Inside it was a race to say hello to as many people as possible before the organ began the hymn that would signal the start of the service. There were friends from Sunday school and friends of Mom's shrouded in clouds of soapy perfume and hairspray. They would kiss me roughly and leave lipstick prints on my cheek, and then wipe it right off, even harder, with their thumbs, though I didn't mind if the stains lingered.

After the accident, the temple became even more important. I regarded my appearances there, which became more frequent, as a series of shows, or performances, this time about pity-based attentions that I craved, constantly. I got it there, anytime, now that absolutely everyone knew us. The mob of people who greeted us personally had doubled, maybe tripled, and I felt like something of a celebrity—a sad, injured one, but a celebrity nonetheless. My mom could not give me sympathy, though she tried, so I accepted it hungrily from every other mother I could find.

"Beth, darling," Mrs. Fink would say to me. "How's it going today." She, like the others, would say it like a statement, kind of like, Here we go again with the routine, I know it's not going well, I'm going to ask anyway, but it's more like I'm telling you that I know it's not good, and that's OK. She'd squeeze me so tight I'd not be able to breathe for a second. I adored being hidden, if only for a moment, from the world, in her large breasts. "How's Mom." We all knew how Mom was: not good, barely holding on, a wreck. "Oh, she's all right," I'd say, and we would smile at each other, subtly, lips pressed together and eyes shiny with sadness and worry.

"Hi, Beth honey," I'd get from Mrs. Miller, who had short, chic hair and a keen fashion sense and a daughter just a few years older than me whom I'd always admired from afar.

"How's Mommy," Mrs. Koslow would ask. She was an older woman than my mother and had a high-pitched voice and birdlike, graceful hands. She would place one on each of my shoulders and peer at me over her glasses and add, "And how are *you*," which was harder to answer. "Fine," "OK," and "Better" were answers I'd perfected, but it didn't really matter what I said. It was much easier for these folks to lavish sympathies on me than my mother; I didn't have words to express how I felt, and I never fell apart at their feet.

Once we took our seats in the sanctuary and services started, I'd have a whole new set of routines to look forward to. Each time we stood along with the congregation—as the Torahs were taken out of their ark, as we recited the *Sh'ma*—I would believe that everyone behind us was looking at us, and especially at me. They would be trying to get a glimpse of our broken family, wanting to see what tragedy looked like. I wanted to appear traumatized yet strong, like a soap character who had just lost a husband or been convicted of murder. I wanted to appear not so pathetic as to turn people away, but not so together as to make anyone believe for a second that I didn't need attention. Sometimes I would wipe a tear from my eye, whether one existed or not, or place a hand over my face so as to look overcome. I *was* overcome, of course, somewhere in there. I just couldn't feel it.

The highlight was the Mourner's Kaddish, when we would all stand to recite this prayer of grief and of love.

"It is actually a prayer of life, and of the greatness of God," the rabbi had explained to me not long after the accident. "There's not even one word about death in it." She explained this to me before we stood and said it together in my bedroom that day when she came over with the tape of Adam's funeral, when we sat on my twin bed listening to her choked-up sermon. Afterward, when the tape had ended, we had stood together in my room and recited the kaddish together: "Yitgadal, yitkadash sh'mei rabo . . ."

Each time we were in temple I stood and said it the same way, proudly reading the Hebrew version rather than the transliteration, because I'd learned how in Sunday school. And when we were done reciting it and it was time to sit down I'd sing the last line very softly along with Cantor Suzanne, whose voice was passionate and beautiful. "Oseh shalom bimromav, huya se shalom. Aleinu v'al kol Yisrael viumru. Amen. May he who creates peace in heaven create peace for us and for all Israel. And let us say, Amen."

Chapter Thirteen

I HATED my mom for her displays of grief. Not because they often came in public, though that made it worse to be sure, but because, in my mind, every fresh outpouring of emotion for her meant one less for me. It's as if she would steal the feelings from me, a grief thief, expressing woe or horror in reaction to a song or memory or television show in just the way that I would have, if only I had had the chance.

One day that summer I went food shopping with her at Pathmark. It was a month or two after the accident. My mother pushed the cart slowly up and down each aisle, and her face looked jagged and off kilter, her throat emitting a dramatic sigh each time we passed something Adam liked. "Oh, Cheerios," she'd say, voice low and liquid. "Oh, no. Fruit Roll-Ups." Then she just stood and looked at the shelves with her eyes welling up and I seethed, telling her, "Mom, come *on!*"

I seethed because I was no different from her. I could not stand to look at the food either, without being sucked into a memory that was so fresh it was difficult to discern between it and the present moment. Fruit Roll-Ups: Adam would unroll a whole one and peel it off the plastic and then roll it back up, tight, and chomp on it like it was a cigar. Hard pretzels: he ate half a bag of them the night he fell on his face in the living room and had to get stitches. English muffins, Skittles, Life cereal, apple juice, Dannon yogurt, and marshmallows—which we roasted over the hibachi after the sun went down over the cooling sand, and which he insisted on charring while I was careful to stop once mine were a perfect golden brown.

I had to walk ahead of her in the aisle and blink tears back into my throbbing head and breathe in really deeply, with my back to her, taking care to keep it all under control. I could not let her see me cry—partly because it would exacerbate her own tears, partly because I would not give her the satisfaction of empathy.

That got even harder to do at the check-out line.

"I lost my son," she told the woman in front of us. The customer opened her mouth and put her hand to her cheek and shot me a furtive, concerned glance.

"He died in a car accident," my mom continued, eyes glazed like a junkie. "He was just seven. The bastard who hit us was drunk." Her face was all squished up and livid, and when she spoke she sounded like a little child, kind of whining and crying at the same time as speaking. I tried to decipher her state of mind, to decide if she looked crazier than she used to. Would she have worn her terrycloth beach cover-up and yellow espadrilles to the supermarket before? Would she have gone out without washing her hair in the morning?

Suddenly, as if hearing herself from the woman's point of view, my mom covered her face and made a disconcerting, high-pitched choking sound. "I'm sorry!" she told the woman. "Oh, please forgive me!"

The woman looked so full of pity, her hand on my mother's arm and her words of wisdom so useless—"You be strong now, you can do it!"—that I felt lightheaded. I looked away, focusing my gaze on the rack of *Good Housekeeping* and *National Enquirer* magazines, trying to make it seem like I was just there on my own. I could not, would not comfort her.

~

Here's how I saw it: My mom was falling apart. Disappearing. But instead of vanishing instantly, like Adam and Kristin had, she was disintegrating at an excruciatingly slow yet certain pace, as if her skin was sloughing away, the light in her eyes fading into tiny pools of dull darkness.

My reaction to her slow fade-out was twofold: first and foremost, an anger so deep it felt like hatred. Sometimes I couldn't bear to look at her, faltering and whimpering, sighing so deeply that her shoulders collapsed in on her, their grief-heavy weight condensing her whole self, pressing it down, down, down seeming like it should leave an impression deep as an anvil's would into any surface she stood upon. I watched as she did, in my view, nothing to fend off her removal from the world. Somehow the steps that she did take— dragging herself into the rabbi's temple office for ad hoc bereavement sessions, forcing herself to go back to work at her public-school speech-therapist job after the summer ended, reading book after book on grief and loss, like *When Bad Things Happen to Good People* by Harold S. Kushner and *On Death and Dying* by Elisabeth Kübler-Ross—meant nothing to me until decades later, when I could see her through adult eyes. Back then her efforts seemed frustratingly theoretical. She was still slipping away as far as I was concerned, and though expressing and exploring her grief was, in her mind, all that kept her going, to me it felt, stubbornly, like she wouldn't fight back—wouldn't save herself and, in turn, wouldn't save me.

Then there was my guilt-fueled worry, blazing like an eternal flame in my sternum. So I made sure I was around a lot—even if I was holed up in my room, sulking or crying or writing—because if I was on the property, I figured, then at least I could make sure that she was still there too. It was like I lived with an alcoholic, the way I babysat and fretted and thought I could keep everything together if I could only make sure I stayed around to do so. I tried not to make too many plans to go out without my parents, and if I did, I would clear it with them first, ask, "Are you sure you don't mind me going out and leaving you both home alone?" to which they would always respond with what seemed like over-compensating amusement, "Well of *course* we don't mind. We love when you go out with your friends!" And I would ask, "Are you sure? Are you really sure?" and they would say they were, and so off I would go, fear gnawing at my innards at a steady pace the whole time I'd be gone.

It was as if the disintegration process would speed up in my absence, away from my watchful eye, and I would return home to find them both in puddles of tears and snot, flat on their backs, almost gone, like when the Wicked Witch of the West melted into a pucker of black fabric, and then we'd be back at the beginning, like that first night in the hospital, and we'd have to clamber up out of the deepest hole all over again. Fear of that scenario ensured that I never, ever talked about it—never mentioned Adam's name, or even Kristin's, and never made mention of the accident, traversing topics in my mind like a field of landmines, avoiding any single one that could in any way be construed to be connected to it.

We never talked about the accident anyway. They both would try, in their own way, to draw me into a simple conversation about how I felt. "Beth?" I'd hear my mom call through my locked bedroom door, her voice as gentle yet pointed as the hoot of an owl. "May I come in?" And I'd quickly tuck away whatever secret ritual of grief I was immersed in—the book I was writing, the temple newsletter I was reading, the musical jewelry box of Kristin's that Mrs. Sickel had let me keep, into which I had stuffed photos of Kristin and Adam, along with postcards Kristin had sent me over the years from Sanibel Island and a tiny bottle of eye drops, still in its box with the prescription label on it, that my mom had to squeeze into Adam's pupils after a mean kid at the beach lobbed sand into his face. I'd make my way toward my mom's voice and turn the gold knob until the press-in lock popped out and the door would glide open a few inches, revealing her worried self in the hallway, trying not to lean toward me but unable to stop herself, like a magnet near a fridge. "Are you OK?"

"Yes!" I'd answer, never quite letting the meaning of the question sink in. I'd stand there, exasperated, waiting for her to do or say something that would convince me that the interruption was worthwhile. "What?"

"I'm just wondering if you'd like to talk to me about anything," she'd say then, instinctively reaching her hand up to my face, lightly touching a finger to my cheek and starting to smooth my hair across my forehead before I would step back, placing myself just out of reach. Her eyes bored into me so deeply that I'd cringe.

"Nope!" I'd say, flashing her that gruesome smile.

"Are you sure, Beth?" she'd say then, wrapping her arms around herself as she stood there shuddering and alone in the dark hallway. "I'm here for you."

Though I'd want to accept her offer, my insides would instantly seize up, and I'd be unable to allow her in. So I'd close the door and hear her trudge away, sighing.

They'd always launch into the topic without checking first—which felt more like a way for them to make themselves feel better than a way to try and draw me out. Which was oppressive. Worse, the instances came more often than not in the car, when I was trapped.

"Adam was always good at swinging the racket," my father would say more than once as we drove past the elementary school and its brick-red tennis court, where he had taken both of us, on several occasions, to learn the sport. I'd be belted in to the passenger seat of his brown Pinto, fiddling with the radio, when he'd start in, and I'd fantasize about opening the car door and placing my foot out onto the street to slow the car to a halt, burning a hole through the tread of my sandal just like Jaime Sommers would do when she'd stop her runaway blue Datsun 280Z that way in *The Bionic Woman*.

"I think he could've been a great player," my dad would continue. "He had a good eye and a strong arm, and he was so determined. If he missed the ball he'd get so mad! He would stomp his feet and want to try it again and again." And then he'd shake his head and make a sound that was like a strangled breath mixed with a groan, and I'd see his eyes well up when he'd turn to me for affirmation or comfort, I was never sure which, and I would give him nothing, just turn away from him to stare out my window, singing along with whatever pop song blared through the dashboard speakers. And I would think, defensively, Who *knows* what Adam would have been? No one will ever know. But I'd keep my thoughts to myself, and my dad would get a painfully lonely look in his eyes.

Other times my mom would try it. We'd be driving near

the shore and she would say, "I just keep thinking about how much your brother loved the beach, how he would run through the sand to chase the seagulls, or charge right into the ocean to play in the waves." And I would go stiff and silent as a cat who had just spotted an insect near its paw. "I'd like to go back, but I don't know if I can," she'd go on, now crying, wiping the tears with the back of one hand while the other steadied the steering wheel. "It's almost like I'd be a traitor to him, or something. You know? Do you think it would be like that? Do you think he'd be angry with me?"

I had no idea what he'd think, and I resented her for asking me to figure it out, even though I knew, somewhere, that she was just trying to get me to share with her by way of example. The example looked awful, though, so I ignored it, and turned the radio up, and she'd continue crying all alone until a few big breaths would tamp it back down. "He wouldn't be mad," I'd eventually say. But that's all I'd give her.

~

When I didn't respond to their bait, they took a different tack: asking me if I wanted to see a shrink. My mom posed the question a few times, but always in a euphemistic way, because the concept was so foreign to her. And the way she said it—"Do you want us to take you to *talk* to someone, Beth?"—made it seem somehow unsavory. I'd get annoyed each time she asked me, and I would tell her, through clenched teeth, "No! I do *not* want to talk to somebody," when really I wanted to, more than anything.

My parents weren't therapy people. They were a bit too old, born in the '40s, and suburban to the core—born and raised in northern New Jersey, with their most urban residential stints being in Irvington, where my dad grew up, and Elizabeth, where they lived briefly as newlyweds. Plus they were total Conservatives—Jewish Republicans—an oddity that I didn't know was one until after college, when I'd bemoan my parents' Bush allegiance to friends in New York and they'd say to me, "Wait, aren't you Jewish?" Woody Allen's therapy obsession may have been amusing to my mom and dad, but not because it was familiar. /

One time, just a couple of months after the accident, my mother made us all go to a bereavement support-group meeting for families who had lost children. It was held in the dimly lit basement of a church a few towns away, and as we pulled into the lot and parked among the other cars under the glow of a security spotlight, I felt a sickness rise up in my throat. The three of us entered in silence, and I remember the mix of embarrassment and despair that I felt when we entered the room and were told to drag some metal chairs, heavy and cold, into the circle of people who were already seated. It was mostly mothers in the room, about a dozen of them, and a couple of stricken-looking dads. No other siblings. My mom mostly sniffled and wiped at her eyes as the others talked about their own excruciating losses.

"She was so brave right up until the end," said one woman, who repeatedly balled up and smoothed out a haggard pink tissue that she held on her knee. "The nurses all loved her, and when she finally went we all cried together in that dark hospital room. That was nice, to be supported." She forced a smile. My dad looked down at his feet and let out a few weak sighs. I tried to hold my breath in for the entire hour. What did this have to do with anything? is what I wanted to know.

Sometimes I'd lay on my bed in the middle of the afternoon and fantasize about going to a therapist—finding one on my own, so my parents wouldn't have to know, and calling up to make an appointment. It would be in the city, so I'd take a taxi to the train station and a train to Penn Station and find my way to the office, someplace right near Macy's, and it would be a comforting little space with a leather couch and some plants that would look like a living room, just like where Deenie went to get treatment for her scoliosis in the Judy Blume book, or where Marlena Evans, the psychotherapist on *Days of Our Lives*, counseled everyone in Salem.

But in reality, I made do with many of the sympathetic adults within my grasp: my cousin Mindy, on my dad's side of the family, who was kind and beautiful and in her twenties, who lived in Marietta, Georgia, and was the recipient of near weekly letters from me, in which I described to her my sadness and my fears and my wishes. She responded, promptly, to every one, writing to me in lovely, loopy cursive on small white rectangles of stationery that had a clutch of purple irises printed in its lower right-hand corner. My heart would leap with joyous hope each time I saw the matching iris envelope, heavy with her words, mixed in with the pile of condolence cards and bills that arrived in our mailbox. There was also my cousin Susan. I'd write her letters too, probably saying the same things I'd said to Mindy, and I'd call her on the phone and occasionally spend a weekend away with her at her apartment in South Jersey. One time she took me antiquing with her, the first I'd ever heard of such a pastime.

In addition to cousins there were plenty of family friends: Mrs. Fink, the stocky, heavily perfumed mom from the temple, who often rescued me from home with a trip to Häagen-Dazs and a cup of coffee-chip ice cream; Ellen, Mrs. Tuchband's daughter, whom I sometimes called on the phone; Mrs. Zipperson, my former art teacher from grammar school, who had left on maternity leave just before I entered the sixth grade, but who had taken to calling me regularly that summer, one time even having me over for dinner and a sleepover with her husband and baby daughter. And then there was the rabbi, the most therapistlike of them all. On Sundays, either in between or just after classes at Sunday school, I would tentatively approach the door to her office and knock lightly, partly hoping she wouldn't be in there, but mostly hoping, desperately, that she would. She'd almost always be there, and when she saw it was me her studious face would soften. "Come in, Beth," she would say. "Come in and sit down and tell me how you're doing today," and I'd slide gratefully into the sturdy wooden chair in front of her desk, and she'd lean back into the soft blue office chair behind it. Sometimes I'd cry, sometimes I'd ask her questions. "What do Jewish people believe about heaven and hell again?" or "Why don't Jews recite The Lord Is My Shepherd at funerals?" or "So how are we supposed to believe that God exists?" She'd always have a warm and patient answer, and though I rarely believed her, I loved her for trying.

Chapter Fourteen

I SAW him appear out of the corner of my eye about halfway through my Congorilla game, but I had to keep playing or lose my turn. It was only my third or fourth time back to the beach club since the accident, and the kid I noticed was Peter, the older kid who had taken Adam under his wing last summer. He was about fourteen, really tall and tawny-skinned and kind of flabby around his middle, always wearing Hawaiian-print swim trunks, and he'd liked hanging out with my little brother. They'd play catch and go bellyboarding or play Congorilla here in the snack bar. I was trying to get back to the high score I'd gotten last year, but I was out of practice, and when GAME OVER flashed across the screen I felt a jolt of panic because now I would have to deal with Peter.

"Hey, Beth! I haven't seen you all summer," he said when I looked up from the console. He looked sweetly confused, and I knew then for sure that he didn't know. My small clutch of beach pals—acquaintances who had glommed on to me since my crutch-wielding return as if I were a superstar—tightened around me.

"Hi." I was unsure of how to answer.

"I was wondering, where's your brother been? The little redheaded dude . . ." He held his hand out, palm down and about chest high, as if he had to illustrate exactly which little guy he was searching for. I felt like I could faint. How could he not know? I thought. Didn't everybody know? And the only thing I could think to do in my panic was to turn and bolt like the gorilla on the screen.

I hadn't run in a long time because my cast had come off recently so it was more of a limping run and it hurt. But as I flew out of the snack bar and into the early August evening I could feel the warm air on my atrophied calf and the cooling sand under each slap of sore toes and it felt good, inexplicably good, even as fresh tears spilled down my face and I felt a white-hot pain spread wide across my gut. All around me, as I ran, were ghosts—I saw Adam in the ocean to my left, splashing in the pool to my right. There was Kristin, flirting with Scott on her beach blanket, swimming laps, laughing, singing. I couldn't pretend anymore not to see them.

My mom had warned me that it would be too hard. It was back in late July, when we hadn't yet returned to the beach club. That meant only a month had passed, but it was the peak of summer and I was desperate for normalcy. I wanted to put on my swimsuit—a pink-and-white-striped stretchy cotton maillot with a white cinch belt around the waist, purchased at the mall during the last weeks of sixth grade. I wanted to see my friends and sit on the blanket and watch the ocean and wait in line at the snack bar for a bright blue raspberry Slush Puppie and a frozen 3 Musketeers bar. I was willing to overlook the fact that Adam and Kristin would not be there.

I had approached my father cautiously one afternoon, said, "Pop?"

"Yes." He sat forward in his recliner, the room dark and cool. He was staring straight ahead and doing the exercises he'd learned in physical therapy, lifting his injured arm out and in, like the slow-beating wing of a bird.

"Can we *please* go to the beach club? It's hot out, and I'm bored."

"The beach club," he said, and then dropped his arm and looked at me, and smiled gently. "That's a great idea. Let's go." He got up and I hopped quickly on my walking cast to tell my mother, to get her on board. I told her dad had said OK, and that if she came too it would be really fun. But she was incredulous. Accusatory.

"How could you two stand it?" she cried, pacing across the carpet in their bedroom, where the thick shades were pulled down tight. Then she came out into the hallway, glaring at both my father and me. She wore a long nightshirt and glasses, which were thick and out-of-date and which she normally only put on so she could make it to her bed after removing her contact lenses each night. "I'm legally blind," she liked to tell us. But these days she wore them constantly, and I thought they gave her a sinister look.

"How could you possibly bear to sit there on the beach that Adam loved so much? Not me," she spat, tears gathering under her lids before spilling with one aggressive blink. "I will never go back there again!"

"We've got to move on, Deb!" my father yelled through clenched teeth. "If you want to lie in bed all day then you can do that, but I won't do it to Beth!" I was struck both by my

dad's callousness—*how to move on, ever?*—and by his mentioning me. I had a fierce love for our Takanassee Beach Club,
named for nearby Lake Takanassee. We all did. It was not like
the other beach clubs in the area—Surfrider and the Atlantic
and the Spring Lake Bath & Tennis Club, for rich folks, with
cabana boys and full-service restaurants and fifty-meter
pools—but more scruffy and down-to-earth, though still ap-
pealing to that suburban middle-class desire to belong to
something, created out of a former coast guard station and
still painted in the same white and forest green combo. We'd
joined before Adam was born, when I was little and liked to
swim in the pool and chase the ocean waves and collect sea-
shells, especially the pink Playtex applicators that washed up
in batches, which I thought were just another type of deep-
sea treasure until my mother saw me with a handful and bit
her lip. "Put those in the garbage!" she'd command. "Then go
wash your hands and don't ever touch them again!"

When Adam was a baby and my dad started working
summers as a clerk at the racetrack's betting booths to bulk up
his teacher's salary, my mom would take us both to the club
each afternoon—but not before two, when the sun had passed
its peak and was not so harmful to the milky skin of her two
redheads. Until it was time to leave the air-conditioned house
I would eat lunch and watch *The Price Is Right* while snuggled
under the black-and-white afghan that my mom had cro-
cheted.

Adam would sometimes join me, and other times he
would play outside in the shady backyard, while my mother
began her involved routine of packing our huge green Coleman cooler with a fresh salad and homemade coleslaw and
preformed turkey burgers to cook on the beach for dinner,
when my dad would join us after work. I loved sitting there
on the sofa, safe in my cool cave, catching glimpses of the

blinding midday sun through the kitchen window when I'd bring my crumb-filled plate to the sink during a commercial, and wonder for a moment what Kristin was doing at the beach club, and what I might've been missing.

She'd have been there since early morning, when we'd go together for swim-team practice in the pool. But while I'd get whisked home afterward to wait out the sunniest part of the day, she'd stay, slathering her olive skin with Sea & Ski tanning oil and lounging, in sexy Lolita-esque poses, near her mother in one of their low, striped canvas beach chairs.

They sat in a different section of the beach than we did, with almost all of the other families from our neighborhood, right near a row of three cabanas, which were for the richest people at the club—those who wanted something beyond a dark, closet-sized locker that smelled of moist wood and baby powder. The cabana that our neighbors gathered around belonged to Dana and Cara Borneo, whose dad was a department store executive, and their cabana, which was always open, was like a little house, with a table and a microwave and lots of snack foods and even a small TV, which Kristin and I would sometimes stand in front of in our dripping bathing suits to watch the soaps for a few minutes at a time. In front of it was the popular people's part of the sand, where everyone worshiped the sun and sipped cocktails or icy beers and had a boom box going all day long. The mothers—who looked just like their teenage daughters, with deep-brown tans and permed, frosted hair and string bikinis—would all put their low beach chairs in a large circle, so they could call back and forth to each other throughout the day.

"Can ya refill my glass while yer up?"

"Will ya rub some oil on my back?"

They'd have sunbathing paraphernalia that fascinated

me—teeny little white eye guards made of plastic, bottles of oil with no SPF over 4, mirror-like reflectors to be placed on one's lap, and spray bottles filled with water, so that everyone could mist themselves throughout the day.

Kristin's mom didn't have the same sex-kitten quality as the other moms—she wore glasses and one-piece bathing suits with skirts—but she sat with them because they were all her neighbors, and because she wasn't quite friends with my mom.

My mom insisted on sitting way across the beach, closer to the water and the jetty, far away from the neighborhood gang. She liked being peaceful, she'd say, and spoke of the cool mothers dismissively. "They pickle themselves with Manhattans all day long!" she'd say whenever I asked why she wouldn't sit with them. "And they'll have skin cancer by the time they're fifty! No, Beth, I'm sorry, I'm here to relax and read, and to watch you and your brother play in the ocean."

My mom was pale, and regularly saw a dermatologist who warned her of the sun's dangers. So she would set up a massive beach umbrella that she could plant herself beneath in her sand chair, wearing a big floppy hat and sunglasses and a yellow cover-up, absorbing herself in one of her thick library books—Stephen King, Robin Cook, Erma Bombeck—all afternoon.

When we arrived at the beach in the station wagon each day at two fifteen—the pebble-filled parking lot already packed with double- and triple-parked cars that the tanned, shirtless attendants would jockey throughout the morning— we'd usually get a good spot, one recently made available by a family who'd been there since eight that morning and had had enough sun. Then we'd head to our locker, number 116, a small, dark little room that we shared with my friend Melissa's family, and Adam and I would help Mom carry our huge load—my light-green bellyboard, Adam's net bag of sand toys, a balled-up blue beach blanket, huge towels, Mom's little aluminum-framed chair and the beach umbrella, with its heavy wooden pole. We'd leave behind the Zim Zam game and the soot-caked hibachi that we used for grilling turkey burgers; those were for when the crowds thinned out and the sun began to set.

When we got set up on the sand, my mom would hold Adam by the wrist and rub Sundown Sunblock all over him, while I'd do my own. And as soon as I was slathered up I'd give my mother a hasty kiss goodbye and sprint away, toward the cool part of the sand, where Kristin would be waiting for me. "I'm going to find Kristin," I'd tell her, before running from her little shady spot, partially wanting to loll around with her in the quietude, but mostly needing to tear away in shame, before anyone from the other side saw me there with her.

The moms would coo over my red hair—"I'd pay a *fawtune* for that shade!"—and tease me about not having a tan, and they'd offer me barbecue potato chips and Oreos and a Tab. But Kristin would jump up from her sunbathing pose when she saw me. She'd grab my arm and say, "Let's go!" and we'd run off, tittering, to our special spot on the jetty, tucked in between two of the largest boulders, where we could talk about swim-team practice or the cute lifeguards. We'd sometimes sing pop songs, harmonizing into the breezy air and dancing on the slippery black boulders. Other times we'd head straight to the pool, where we'd get on line for the diving board and take turns showing off swan dives or somersaults or jackknives, or we would take our bellyboards into the ocean and ride waves with the boys or head to the snack bar and buy chocolate bars and wait our turn to pump quarters into the Congorilla video game.

But the best of all would be the end of the day, at about five or six o'clock, when hardcore sunbathers who had spent their day in the sand would fold up their blankets and beach chairs and umbrellas and start clearing out. Moms would call their kids out of the ocean or go and fetch them from the pool, and hold towels around them so they could slip off their wet, sandy suits and put on dry underwear and shorts and T-shirts, and then they would all head home for dinner.

Right when everyone else would be leaving, we would start hunkering down for the evening. First my mom would move the car closer, so she could back it right up to the edge of the beach and its knee-high concrete border. Then she'd take out the hibachi, fill it with fuel-treated coals and start it up before getting me to help her carry the big fat Coleman, filled with salads and drinks and dessert, from the locker to whatever wooden picnic table we had claimed with our red-and-white checked oilcloth. Sometimes I'd snag Kristin just as her family was leaving, and get her to stay with us for the long haul. "Mom, can Kristin stay down with us?" I'd ask breathlessly, knowing I had only a few moments before she'd be whisked back home. "Of course," she'd always say. "I made an extra turkey burger just in case."

Melissa's family often stayed for dinner too, and we'd set up our hibachis side by side, guarded from the evening wind by the concrete wall, and cook and wait for my father to arrive from the track. He'd pull up by six thirty and be sweaty and warm in his white short-sleeved button-down shirt and cotton work pants, his posture stiff with hurried stress. But once he stepped out of the car and felt the ocean air and got hugs from us, all damp and sandy, his face would relax into pure, softly-lit joy. He'd go to the locker and change into his swimsuit and do laps in the pool right before it closed, and then we would all sit down to a sunset dinner. It was pure bliss—especially the stretch right after dinner, when the beach would be empty and ours. We would dash through the cool sand and balmy air, still warmed by the last rays of the sun, dizzy with freedom and the vast feeling of possibility. Everything would take on new meaning in that low, ochre light: The lifeguard's overturned rowboat became a balance beam to tiptoe across and their white wooden stand became a clubhouse, perfect for climbing on and lounging in, clad in too-big sweatshirts or red swim-team jackets and sweatpants that dragged through the sand. The ocean became a dark and swirling mystery, its waves looking stronger than they had during the day, its depths endless and a bit frightening, although sometimes when the tide was low and it was a particularly warm night—with a west wind and a clear sky and more than a sliver of moon to light our way—we would enter that delicious inkiness for a night swim. I would scream in delight if my toe brushed a clamshell or a pinching crab, and be at my happiest if I caught a wave to shore in the moonlight. Sometimes my dad would join us to bodysurf, but my mom would always watch us from ashore, proud and happy.

~

In my sprint away from the snack bar, just as my weak foot was about to give out, I spotted the new version of my family. My mother, who had finally relented in her refusal to set foot on the sand, was setting a bowl of salad on the picnic table; my dad was talking to the rabbi and to a family from temple, who had joined us for a barbecue on the beach that night. I could tell as I arrived that everyone was heavy with the effort of happiness.

"Beth, what's the matter? What happened?" My mom noticed me first, saw my shell-shocked expression, chest heaving under my damp one-piece swimsuit.

"Somebody asked me where Adam was!" I cried. "Somebody asked me where he was and I didn't know what to say!" It was as if this boy's question had finally made me realize that Adam really wasn't here, because if he'd noticed, then surely others had. I covered my face and cried and people, warm arms, comforted me from all around.

I needed to hide, though, and my mom helped me to where I was headed—into the car. It was an unfamiliar one, an ugly, witch-green Chevy Citation that our insurance company had hastily provided to replace our totaled silver station wagon, and I hated it. But it was backed up to the edge of the beach for our tailgate party and I climbed into the backseat and just sat there, facing away from the sand and our guests and toward the near-empty parking lot.

"Beth?" I looked up and saw Kristin's father. Mr. Sickel. Gordon. I'd known him since I was little. He was a skinny, funny guy—he had a messy thick mop of brown hair and a big grin and he'd do quirky things like dive into the pool while wearing his big thick glasses, shooting up to find Kristin and me laughing at him. He'd say, "What? They help me see underwater," not a trace of irony in his voice. He was always nice to me, even playful, when I went over to their house. He'd had a "Gordie's Forty" birthday party the year before, and Kristin and I had helped decorate the living room with crepe paper streamers before the adults from the neighborhood started arriving and I walked home, through the shortcut, in the dark, the sound of the swelling party fading in the distance as Kristin waved good-bye through the back sliding door.

I'd only seen Mr. Sickel a few times since the accident— once when he came over to the house to see if I had developed

my pictures from that night, from the ballet recital, to see if
there was one of Kristin that he could have. "I'm just trying to
see if she had anything around her neck, like a scarf, because
they said they found one with her and I don't know what it
was," he'd said, hovering over me in my bedroom, looking
desperate yet resolved to get to the bottom of the scarf matter.
It was very important to me to appear helpful, so I put great
thought into my answer, like a detective.

"She did have on her gold 'K' necklace," I'd told him, "and
I think she had ribbon-wrapped barrettes in her hair. And oh!
I know! There was a red scarf that tied into a big bow around
the collar of her new sailor shirt!" I was pleased with myself,
and showed him the picture to prove it. It was a shot of us
sitting together in the audience before I had to go backstage
and get into my costume. I'm in the background, my hair
pulled back into a smooth, shiny copper bun, and my lips,
theatrically red from stage makeup, in just a vague smile
that covered my braces. Kristin's in the foreground looking
kittenish—eyes wide, smile slight and mature. It was the last
photo of her ever taken. Mr. Sickel had stared at it with a
faraway look in his eyes and then tentatively handed it back.
I snatched it carefully. I didn't want to give it up, so I gave
him the negative and he thanked me and hugged me, and I
averted my eyes from his blank face and shrank from him in
shame because I was still alive.

Now here he was again, looking at me. I didn't want him
to see me, but he was leaning into the car, trying to coax me
out of my panic. "It's OK for you to cry and get upset," he
told me. "You don't have to try to be so brave all the time."
People were always telling me this, always telling me it was
OK, I could cry, I could show my emotion, I could let it all
out. How could I tell them I didn't really feel anything? When
I did, like now, it would come in a wave so intense that it

scared me silent, and I would stomp it back into the farthest reaches of my body until it could not be found, becoming either stony or smiley or, if I was around someone I wanted comfort from, dramatically, over-the-top sad and self-pitying.

"I know I don't have to be brave," I said, still sniffling. I was starting to return to normal, to quiet shock. "It just really surprised me when he asked . . . I mean, I couldn't believe he didn't know, and I didn't know what to say." It did not feel right for me to be having a conversation with this man who had lost his daughter.

"Well, I just spoke to him, to Peter. I saw him after you'd run away. And he's real sorry to have upset you," Mr. Sickel said. "He really didn't know, and now he's pretty shocked I think. Do you feel a little better now that you've cried?"

"I guess so," I said, finally looking into his face. Kristin had had his eyes, I saw for perhaps the first time. Her little sister Tracy had his nose and his mouth and his upturned chin, but his eyes were pure Kristin. I was mesmerized by them for a moment, and then I quickly looked away.

Chapter Fifteen

ONE spring afternoon a couple of years earlier, Kristin and Tracy and I were barefoot on the lawn of their backyard, about to play *Charlie's Angels*. It was a common scenario.

"OK, so let's pick who will be who," Kristin said. Then she added, "Today I want to be Kelly."

It was predictable. Kristin was older, eleven to my ten, and always got to be either Kelly or Jill—the pretty ones—while I was almost always Sabrina, the smart one. I hated that. But while I could have chosen Kelly or Jill—whichever one Kristin discarded—a part of me felt I'd be an imposter trying to portray a character so sultry. So I'd relent and accept my lot in life as Sabrina, even if, like most days, Kristin and I were the only two playing the game. But this afternoon was different.

"I wanna be Jill!" Tracy blurted, puffing out her chubby seven-year-old chest. "I'm Jill."

Anxious resentment flared inside of me. I was no Jill, but neither, by any means, was she.

Tracy had been held back in kindergarten, and was slower in understanding things than other kids her age, preferring to be friends with kids, like Adam, who were younger and smaller than she was. And while she had the same butter-soft skin and honey-brown hair as Kristin, she had more of a round nose rather than her sister's perfect slope, and eyes that didn't have quite the same spark.

Whenever I played at Kristin's house, Tracy followed us everywhere, calling, "Krissin! Krissin!" and begging to be included in our adventures. We'd usually send her away, especially when we played "Boyfriend," during which we would lay side by side on Kristin's bed and act out kissing scenes. We'd rotate the list of *Tiger Beat*–type stars we were in love with—Scott Baio, Donny Osmond, Leif Garrett, Shaun Cassidy—each claiming one for ourselves and then wriggling around on our backs like happy puppies, arms in the air, as we'd caress and hold our invisible men, our lips puckered and kissing the empty space above our faces as we called out, "Oh, Leif! Oh, Donny!" Soon we'd get bored, though, and head outside into the backyard to act out another episode of *Charlie's Angels*. We'd usually send Tracy away from that, too, but on this afternoon we tried letting her join us, just to keep her from whining. Still, I wasn't willing to let her take such a coveted role.

"You can't be Jill," I told her, not concerned with how immature I sounded. Tracy stuck her tongue out at me.

"She's right, Tray," Kristin agreed, gently placing her hand on her sister's head. "You can be Sabrina. But she's a great part. Smart."

I felt a bit in awe of Kristin, as usual. I was still gawky— buck teeth, pale skin with freckles, thick red hair with a mind of its own. But she stood tall and tan, with hands resting neatly on her hips and smooth, freshly Naired and lotioned legs poking out of silky running shorts. And she wore a new T-shirt that her father had gotten her at the mall—a white baseball shirt with blue three-quarter-length sleeves and velvety blue iron-on letters that spelled one simple word across her chest: PERFECT. Nobody's perfect, I'd think to myself each time she had it on.

"If I'm not Jill then I'm not playing!!" Tracy shouted, folding her arms on her round stomach and waiting a beat or two for a response. She got none, though, just Kristin and I glancing at each other, and so she tore away, toward the house, yelling, "Mooooooom!"

We began our game then, sprinting around the yard to catch invisible bad guys, clutching imaginary guns to our hips, creeping slowly around the aboveground pool and using its flimsy, curved walls of aluminum as a shield. Then we darted across the lawn toward Kristin's playhouse.

Her handy father had built the little structure the year before, and it was perfect and sturdy and cute, its pointed roof and front window and bright-yellow coat of paint making it look like a munchkin house from *The Wizard of Oz* stage set, and my heart lurched with envy the first time I saw it. It was so much more adorable than the shacklike plywood clubhouse my father had cobbled together for Adam and me. But I never said anything. I knew how challenging it was for my dad to build anything, and how dogged he was to make our little clubhouse work. Plus Adam and I loved the thing, using it for secret members-only clubhouse meetings, and once crowding into it with Mom and Dad, on the first night of Sukkot, when we ate apples and said a prayer and slid open the square roof hole so we could gaze up at the stars.

After playing out our scene—catching the bad guys in the

playhouse and bursting back out into the yard, victorious—
we sat together, sweaty and giggling, on the back steps of her
house, drinking glasses of Country Time Lemonade that her
mom had mixed for us. Tracy was just inside the sliding glass
doors, sulking and glaring at me. I understood it was because I
had taken her sister away, and I wanted her to know that it was
just temporary, that it was more like I was borrowing her. So I
smiled at her. But her stony face would not soften.

~

A month after the accident I attended a neighborhood barbecue at the Cichettis', our next-door neighbors whose property I'd skirt to cut through to Kristin's house. Laura, the
daughter who was my age, came over and rang our doorbell
to invite us.

My leg was still in a cast, and I stood balanced on my
crutches on the inside of the screen door while Laura shifted
her weight awkwardly on the front porch. Her crooked eye
teeth were not yet reined in by braces, and her glossy strands
of licorice black hair were falling ever so slowly from their
barrettes. She wore running shorts and a boy's T-shirt, and
she had a scabby knee.

Laura forced a smile when she asked, "Do you want to
come over to our barbecue?" She hadn't stood in that spot, so
near our house, in a long time—since fourth grade, most
likely, when we went through a brief period of watching TV
together, bored, while still in our Girl Scout uniforms, after
we'd arrived home from troop meetings on late Thursday afternoons and were at a mutual loss at what else to do with
that no-man's-land hour between *Happy Days* reruns and
dinnertime. She looked out of place now, standing on our
porch, but I'd become accustomed to such discord.

"Who's there, Beth?" my mom called from the depths of

our house. She had been wandering in and out of her bedroom in a tired pair of blue sweatpants and an old, threadbare
nightshirt covered in hot-pink stars for much of the afternoon. Dad was napping in his recliner, his breathing-exercise
tube resting on the lamp table at his side.

"It's Laura," I called. "Cichetti. I'm going over to have a
hamburger at their barbecue." I pushed the screen door open
and she held it for me as I steadied myself out of the door and
onto the porch. "Can I sign your cast?" she asked, eyeing the
colorful scrawl of other friends. I told her sure, as long as she
had a Magic Marker at home.

In the thirty seconds it took to cross out of our property
and into hers, I could hear the festive din rising from her
backyard. I wondered if it would be a mistake, to enter a
happy party knowing that my presence would dampen the
vibe. I was forever branded now as the girl deserving pity. But
part of me liked that—needed it—because it felt like all I had.

I was not quite past the wood-post fence at Laura's backyard when I spotted her: Tracy, slumped on the bench of a
wooden picnic table wearing a blue, pilling one-piece swimsuit. She was alone, poking at a plate of potato salad with a
plastic fork. I froze for a moment, hovering at the edge of the
yard. I saw Kristin's mom, too, next to the big gas grill. She
had her back to me, and rocked nervously from one foot to
the other, holding a paper plate with an open, empty bun. I
headed straight for Tracy, careful not to push my crutches too
heavily into the Cichettis' soft, lush lawn, or to look into the
faces of too many guests. I sat down across from her at the
picnic table, while Laura went to get me some food.

"Hi, Tracy," I said. She stuck a forkful of potato salad into
her mouth, and sat with her shoulders gathered around her. I
noticed she had one of Kristin's barrettes clipped into her

hair—one she'd made in junior high, a simple metal thing braided with silky ribbons that hung about chin-length, dangling a few plastic beads. She had made me a pair in purple and white, but my hair was too thick to fit in them.

"Hi," she said, not looking up from her plate.

"What are you eating?" I was uncomfortable and ashamed, though not entirely sure why. Her sister had been my friend, and my brother had been hers, and I knew we should've sought comfort in each other. But her resentment was palpable. After a terrible silence she spoke.

"Kristin would still be here if it wasn't for you," she said, eyes steely, jaw fixed. "She was going to *your* ballet recital!"

I hadn't even thought of that myself—hadn't yet been able to pinpoint the source of the barbed ball that flared beneath my sternum ever since leaving the ER. And yet there it was.

A fizziness filled my head. I opened my mouth but couldn't speak, and could think only of fleeing, so I pulled myself up onto my crutches. Then Laura appeared with my food, setting a wobbly paper plate with a burger onto the table. Tracy's mom was with her, and could see by my face that something had gone horribly wrong.

"Beth, you OK?" she asked. "Aren't you going to eat something?"

"No thank you," I said, trying to smile. "I have to go."

Tracy sat with her arms crossed on her chest, her nose all wrinkled up. She scared me. Mrs. Sickel looked at her intently and asked, "What happened, Tracy?"

Tracy was unflinching. "I just told her the truth," she said. "That Kristin wouldn't have died if she didn't go to her ballet recital." Her mom clenched her teeth and stiffened for a moment before crumpling—putting her hand over her face and breathing in deeply. "No, Tracy," she said softly. "That's just not true. Beth," she said, looking into my eyes, "it's not your fault. OK? It was not your fault."

I forced a smile again though I felt shattered, and told her, "OK. I know. I just have to go. My mom needs me home." She rested her hand on my shoulder for an instant, and then I steered myself out of there, back into my own yard, not sure where else to go. I wondered, Was it my fault? Could it really be that simple? Did everyone else think it was true?

The sight of our shut-tight house filled me with woe and I pictured my lethargic parents inside, pacing or crying or strewn about, like casualties of war. But in I went, quietly. No one called out from the dark.

Chapter Sixteen

I WASN'T mad at Tracy for what she said. It's almost like I was relieved. Getting blamed helped to alleviate what I only knew much later to be my guilt. I took in what she said, though—buried it deep but held onto it tightly and believed it, if only subconsciously.

I knew her apology had been forced when it came just a couple of days after the barbecue. I had found myself back over at the Sickels' house, desperate for the connection, a glutton for punishment.

"Oh, Beth, good! I'm glad you're here. Come in and sit down. I know Tracy has something she wants to say to you," she said, holding open the front screen door for me and then turning over her shoulder to call, "Tracy! Come out here right now please!"

Tracy emerged from her room pretty quickly, wearing pink shorts and a too-tight Strawberry Shortcake T-shirt and

those same ribbon-wrapped barrettes in her hair. Her face
was expressionless as she gazed in my direction, though not
quite at me, and said, "Sorry for what I said the other day,
that it was your fault. I know it was an accident."

"That's OK," I said without pause, blushing at how forgiv-
ing it sounded.   .

Then Tracy walked past where I still stood in the hallway
with her mom and went into the living room, clicking on the
TV. She sank down into their overstuffed couch and placed
the unwieldy cable box on her lap, flipping through the endless rows of channels until settling on *The Price Is Right,* where
the first contestants had already been called to "Come on
down!" by Johnny Olson, the nasal-voiced announcer, and
were busy placing their opening bids on a color television
with remote control.

Normally, Tracy and her mom would've been at the
beach already by then, and I would have been at home
watching Bob Barker stroll around the candy-colored studio
set all by myself, but it was chilly and cloudy outside, and
the forecast called for thunderstorms, and so there we all
were: Tracy, caught between hating the sight of me and
wanting me around so that I could be a stand-in for her sister; Mrs. Sickel, encouraging my visits, as far as I could tell,
because she also saw me as a sub for Kristin and wanted that
for both herself and for Tracy, and because she was trying so
hard to accommodate me, so it wouldn't seem as if I were
being blamed.

And then there was me, trying to please not just Tracy
and Mrs. Sickel, whom I really thought I could comfort in
some way just by hanging around, but myself. Being at their
house made Kristin seem not only close by but containable—
like a precious ether that I could have enter my body and soul
by some improbable sort of osmosis. I thought, on some level,

that I could actually become her, which was an ideal scenario:
It meant that she wouldn't have to be gone, and that I, in
turn, could cease to exist.

"Beth, come watch with me already!" I looked over at
Tracy to see her patting the empty space near her on the
couch, flicking her eyes off of the television screen and onto
me for just a moment. She wasn't smiling, exactly, but I sensed
something like a peace offering in the gentle way she touched
the couch. I headed toward her and eased my way down onto
the soft cushion, just in time to see a heavyset woman with a
poodle perm shriek with joy and squeeze Bob Barker after
winning a trip to Tahiti. Tracy laughed. It was my favorite
kind of TV moment.

~

I went back again a few days later, on another non-beach day,
when it was hot and muggy and thickly overcast. I'd had my
cast removed the day before, and had my swimsuit on underneath my T-shirt, so Mrs. Sickel suggested we take a dip in
their pool.

"Wait till I explain my plan for the sand-castle contest to
you girls," she blurted out to us as we hopped around in the
tepid water, not talking to each other, trying to cool down
and pretend that Kristin was still around. I had a pit in my
stomach because I knew it was just Tracy and me, and because I could feel the faint, arm-hair pricking motion of the
far-off thunderstorm moving toward us in the heavy, languid
air. I wanted to do gymnastics—underwater handstands and
backflips and cartwheels—but Tracy couldn't do it like Kristin could, as she had to hold her nose and do all the moves
sloppily and one-handed, so instead I alternately bopped
around and floated on my back.

"What sand-castle contest?" Tracy asked. She was

dunking the crown of her head backward into the water, smoothing it back like Kristin used to do, but instead of having the desired mermaid effect it just made pieces of her bowl cut stick up.

"At Takanassee! I think you girls can win first prize." She looked pleased with herself, as if the sand castle talk was really making her happy as she stood there in the scorching backyard, lawn yellowed in spots by the sun, hands on her hips. She wore a white beach cover-up, not so different from the ones my mom always wore, like shorts and an elasticized halter top, but all in one piece, pulled up over a bathing suit. She looked sweaty and really tan, and was tall and big-boned, her brown hair in a short, round cut like Tracy's.

Mrs. Sickel was one of those moms who did all the creative school assignments for her kids. I'd seen her make shoebox dioramas and report covers and pie charts for Kristin over the years—hunkering down with tubes of glitter and a big bottle of Elmer's glue and thick pieces of construction paper spilling across the top of their kitchen table while Kristin and I watched television—and the sight always caused me a bit of shocked jealousy.

"Mrs. Sickel made Kristin's diorama, and it had this neat, real-looking pond made of light-blue cellophane!" I'd report to my mother.

"Mrs. Sickel was doing Kristin's homework for her?" she'd ask, her voice heavy with judgment. I'd clam up then, afraid I'd said too much, and she would shake her head and state, "In this house, you do your own homework. Got it?"

I did. But that summer, as a stand-in for Kristin, I got to try it Mrs. Sickel's way.

The sand-castle contest was one of the beach club "events" that I would have never done on my own, because it was too early in the day, when the sun was too strong, when I was usually at home watching TV and eating lunch, waiting with Adam for our two o'clock beach departure time. Also because the events were too cliquish and competitive—once I had entered the annual "Crazy Hat Contest," and thought for sure I would win. My mom had made me a sort of kitchen-themed helmet. She turned her aluminum colander upside down and tied a bunch of big spatulas and spoons and whisks from the little holes, so that they hung all around my head like a head of heavy weird hair. But there were kids with much more elaborate creations—a beehive wig adorned with birds and wasps and flowers, space-age headgear made of special tinfoil, bonnets made of spun sugar or entire dollhouses filled with furniture that stayed atop a head with one thick ribbon that tied neatly under the chin. I didn't win in any category, and I felt so sad for my mom, whose cleverness seemed too homemade for the cutthroat crowd.

The sand-castle contest was the last thing I wanted to do, but I told myself that Mrs. Sickel's happiness depended on it. I began picturing elaborate wet-sand mansions, with moats and turrets and little hollowed-out rooms, built just far enough from the tide line to remain intact for several hours, and looked at Tracy—paddling lazily on a blow-up raft, her stroke clumsy and young—and I wondered how the pair of us would accomplish such a feat.

But Tracy seemed reeled in by the notion of competing. She half-smiled and her mother grinned, and then Mrs. Sickel made us guess what her idea was. "It's very trendy," she said. "Very *now* in pop culture," she said. She was like this, really up on fads, which was why, the day after I'd first see a specific pair of Jordache jeans or Candies shoes advertised on TV, Kristin would be wearing them. They seemed no more wealthy than we were—same model ranch house, same American-made cars, similar food—and yet I always seemed to be lagging behind with knockoffs, because my mom just couldn't comprehend the importance of labels.

I thought for a moment about Mrs. Sickel's clue and then ventured a guess. *"Star Wars?"*

"Nope. But not bad," she said. "Keep guessing."

Tracy tried. *"General Hospital?"* I pictured us sculpting Luke and Laura's wedding in the wet sand. Impossible.

"No."

"MTV?" I offered. It was the trendiest thing I knew of.

"No," she said, unable to contain herself any longer. "Pac-Man!" she yelled, clapping for herself. "We're going to make a Pac-Man screen in the sand." This seemed very high-concept to me—too one-dimensional, not enough building—but I didn't have a more clever idea and figured she had some tricks up her sleeve, so I forced a smile and said, "Cool." Tracy did the same.

We didn't look at each other while Mrs. Sickel told us the plan—that they would pick me up the next morning at ten, supplies in hand, and head down to the beach to begin our creation. I climbed out of the pool into the windy, gray air and wrapped a thin Pepsi-Cola beach towel around my shoulders. Then I walked quickly home through the neighbor's yard and reached the laundry-room entrance just as a fierce summer storm broke out. I told my mom about our plan as soon as I saw her. She was standing in the kitchen, leaning on the counter and staring out into the backyard. It was almost dinnertime, but she wasn't cooking. Just staring. I hoped we still had a neighbor's casserole in the freezer.

My mom wasn't impressed with the sand-castle plan. "Why doesn't she let you girls come up with your own idea?" she said. I shrugged, not caring either way.

I felt protective of Mrs. Sickel suddenly, and defended her by telling my mom that I loved the Pac-Man idea.

She made me put sunblock fifteen on before even leaving the house the next morning, as it was way too early for me to be heading to the beach. But today was supposedly a special occasion. She thought I was excited about it.

Mrs. Sickel rapped lightly on our front screen door at ten on the dot. Tracy waited in the car.

"Hi, Debbie," she called in to my mom. She stood on the porch in the same beach cover-up as the day before, and she spoke with a sort of forced merriment. "I'm here to pick up the sand-castle champ!"

"Oh hello, Judy," my mom said, voice low and sad, pushing open the door and inviting her in for a minute. "Where's Tracy?"

"She wanted to wait in the car. The brat!" She laughed, kind of nervously, and my mom scrunched up her eyes and put her fingers to her temples and started to cry.

"Oh, Judy, how are you?" She said it to the floor, into her hands, and she kept crying little moany sobs, like she was trying to keep them inside but couldn't quite contain herself. I marveled at how fast it always came on, and I wanted to go back into my room and close the door and stay there, but instead I just froze in place and looked at Mrs. Sickel with sympathy. She came over to my mother's side, though, and let her eyes well up, and put her long arms around my mom.

"I'm OK," she said, her mouth forming a what-do-you-expect-me-to-do sort of smile. "And so are you, right?" My mom hated this game, I could tell, but they were just different, and there was nothing to talk about, so she forced herself to stop crying and said, "Yep." And then, to me: "Try to stay out of the sun, Beth. And good luck in the contest."

She kissed me goodbye, and I felt her wet face on my

cheek and I wiped off her tears on my way out to the Sickels' car, a yellow Chevy Citation with soft tan seats. It was pulled into the driveway just behind our own ugly green loaner. It was jarring to have matching cars with Kristin's family—wrong, somehow—but there it was, real and hideous.

Tracy was in their front seat, eating Chips Ahoy! cookies out of their blue bag. She said a barely audible "Hi," her mouth filled with crumbs, and bent forward so I could slip into the backseat behind her. I thought I could still smell Kristin in their car—her suntan lotion, her flowery shampoo—and I felt sick about it for a moment. It was compounded with the guilt I felt for leaving my mother and for wanting to act like everything was still OK. I leaned my head back and sighed, giving myself over to the day.

On the way there I tried to see into their ordinary movements—Mrs. Sickel's steering, Tracy's playing with the radio dial—to discover their secrets to survival. I tried to see what was different now in their car, on its dashboard, in the strands of their hair and their smooth stretches of skin. But it all looked unchanged, normal. So I peeked into the bulging bag of sand-sculpting supplies that sat next to me—tubes of food coloring, yellow butter-flavored popcorn salt, bright pink cake-decorating sugar crystals, clear blue sprinkles—and Mrs. Sickel heard the rustling, and began excitedly explaining what everything was for.

"We'll first try to color batches of sand with the food coloring, but if it doesn't work, we'll just create the playing screen and then shake the color on top, using the salts and sugars I got at the Pathmark," she said. It was amazing, how she could pour all of her grief into a child's contest, and never crack in front of us. Tracy asked question after question, but I zoned out, watching the strip malls and familiar landmarks—

railroad tracks, Scoops Ice Cream, the karate school, the old red church—and thought about how Kristin would've never in a million years agreed to do something as silly as a sand-castle contest.

When we pulled into the beach club, the lot was almost full. Mrs. Sickel had to park at the farthest edge of it, near the jetty that divided Takanassee from the private beach in the next lot over. They didn't have a locker like we did, so I helped them unload low canvas-and-aluminum beach chairs and a couple of towels—no sun umbrella here—from the trunk. Tracy grabbed our bag of supplies and ran ahead.

All the usual sun-worshiping mommies were already there sitting in their huge circle when we arrived. It was clear that they were curious about my arriving with Kristin's family, but as they peered over the tops of their sunglasses to take in the situation they quickly shifted into their bubbly, joyous selves, waving exaggeratedly to us, helping Mrs. Sickel with her chair, and offering us snacks from a big mound of potato chips and low-fat cookies.

"Nice to see you here so early, Beth," said one mom, Mrs. Borneo, who was so nice and rich and pretty that I wanted to curl up in her lap and have her pet me just about every time I saw her.

"I'm here for the sand-castle contest," I told her, anxiously pressing my finger into my forearm to see if I'd gotten sun-burned yet. "I'm doing it with Tracy." Tracy looked up from a bag of potato chips when she heard me say her name.

Mrs. Borneo smiled sweetly. "That's just lovely," she said. "Good luck."

"Girls!" It was Mrs. Sickel, finished with setting up her beach area and ready for action. "Let's get this show on the road!" Tracy sucked the salt off each fingertip, rolled up the bag of potato chips she'd been devouring, and hoisted herself out of the warm sand. A thin coat of it stuck to the back of her thighs, as well as the elbow she'd been leaning on. She wore her blue one-piece suit, and her thick hair held one of Kristin's barrettes above her right ear, giving her an extraneous, flapping wing. I got out of Mrs. Sickel's extra beach chair and yanked up my pink terrycloth halter top, which was attached to shorts and elasticized around my waist, just like Mrs. Sickel's. I had worn it over my red one-piece suit, because, though I was five feet and four inches tall and 104 pounds, I had recently started feeling self-consciously fat.

"OK, let's go win," I said to no one in particular.

We trudged like ducklings behind Mrs. Sickel, who was making a beeline for a specific spot in the sand. It was far down the beach, away from where the women sat in their circle and even farther from where my mom liked to stake her claim with the beach umbrella, and when we got there I stood with my back to the ocean for a moment, taking in this new perspective. It was such a break from the beach-club routine, this spot, that it jangled my nerves. I wanted to get it over with already. When I looked at Mrs. Sickel, she was on her hands and knees.

"Help me clear a nice big smooth square area," she was saying, using her forearm to sweep the moist sand into a flat, slightly swirled surface, like an iced sheet cake. Tracy got down in the sand with me and we did what we were told. Then our leader pulled out a picture, torn from a magazine, of the Pac-Man characters, and instructed us in how to form the zig-zag–bottomed ghosts at various spots around our "screen." The sand felt good between my fingers, pliable and slightly cool, and I thought of how Adam could dig at the water's edge for hours, making moats and drip castles and elaborate tracks for his Matchbox cars as I went belly-boarding in the ocean behind him, sometimes watching his small, wiry figure as I bobbed on the water, waiting for a wave. I could usually spot my mom, too, from that vantage point. She'd be in her beach chair, under the umbrella, reading. But her eyes would be on one of us, almost always, and sometimes she'd wave if our eyes met. She always looked content to me.

Finally our sculpting was done, and, after quickly figuring out that dyeing the sand was too elaborate a process, we got out the colored salts and sugars and put the finishing touches on our creation. We used the butter-flavored popcorn salt to make Pac-Man himself nice and yellow. And then Mrs. Sickel said, "Don't forget this, guys," and pulled the pièce de résistance out of her beach bag: a small sign that she'd had me pen earlier in big, rounded block letters on construction paper that said, cleverly, PAC AT-TAK! She taped it to a flat wooden paint mixer, stabbed it into the sand, and smiled. We smiled too, as it didn't look half-bad.

Although with one glimpse up the beach, toward the towering castles and mini skyscrapers made with exacting molds and spade-like little tools, it was clear that ours would be too homespun. I watched as Chris Peterson, the owner of the beach club, began threading his way through the entries, nodding and smiling and patting kids on the back. He had a couple of other adults with him, and they all took their time inspecting everything. We were the last in the row, and when he got to ours he let out a big chuckle and clasped his big, fleshy hands together excitedly. "It's great!" he said, still laughing to himself. "Really clever!" I blushed when he said that, since I had had nothing to do with the idea.

Chris was an extremely tan, short, and muscular guy who always wore khaki shorts with deep pockets and Top-Siders so worn out it was as if he'd spent weeks lost at sea. Sometimes he had a thick white smudge of zinc oxide on his nose, like the lifeguards, and he always wore dark, Ray-Ban sunglasses. When he talked his mouth gathered in one corner, like he was chewing on something, and sometimes he'd get so excited that a spray of spittle would come flying out from between his lips. On that day he spoke calmly, taking his sunglasses off and smiling, and then looked piercingly at Tracy and me.

"Congratulations," he said, pulling two blue ribbons out of his pocket. "You two are the winners." He shook our hands and gave Mrs. Sickel a hug, and then hung the ribbons on the PAC AT-TAK! sign. Tracy started jumping up and down, and her mom pumped her fist into the air a couple of times, saying "All right! Way to go girls! Way to go." She looked happy for a few minutes, but then deflated, until Tracy asked, "Can we get hamburgers at the snack bar to celebrate?" That cheered her quickly, and she motioned for us to follow her. And as the three of us headed up the rise of the beach together, hurrying to avoid the pinch of heat that had settled into the sand from the midday sun, I had a realization: We shouldn't have won. We didn't deserve it. But as soon as I had seen the look in Chris's eyes I knew what was going to happen. I knew that we would have to win. We were bereft of our siblings, trying to carry on, doing it in a way that was so public, so desperate, it would have been impossible to not be rewarded with a pity prize. I don't know if Tracy or Mrs. Sickel realized this, or if they even cared. But to me it was shameful. Still, I thanked Mrs. Sickel and I ate my cheeseburger and I smiled at Tracy for the rest of the afternoon. But when I got home I went to my room and pulled my blue ribbon out of my beach bag. I shook the sand that clung to it into my wastebasket, stared at it for a moment, and then put it into a drawer.

Chapter Seventeen

"WHO do you like better, Rick Springfield or Air Supply?" It was the August after the accident, and Dana Borneo was holding up two record albums, one of each. I was desperate to give the right answer. "I love both!" I said, although, while I found Rick Springfield beautiful enough to squeal over and had memorized the words of every single song on his albums, I had never been quite as moony over Air Supply, whom I found to be strange looking and skinny and too girlish with their long and fluffy hair. I was crazy over their new *Now and Forever* record, though, and it just happened to be the one that Dana brandished in the air on that stormy summer afternoon, when I had miraculously found myself in her finished basement, sprawled on the plush wall-to-wall carpet with my head leaning on the ottoman of their low and cushy couch.

"Rick Springfield is more of a hunk, though. Look at those

eyes!" Dana's older sister Cara spoke with a mellow resolve, and I felt relieved to have agreed. "Put *Working Class Dog* on first," she commanded, sprawling onto the couch and then propping herself up on her elbow, fixing her gaze onto me. "Beth, can I French braid your hair?"

A bolt of warmth shot through me.

"OK."

I quickly ran a hand through my heavy locks to make sure there weren't knots.

"Cool. I'll be right back with a brush and stuff." I watched as she hopped up and toward the stairs. She was a full-fledged teenager, fifteen years old, and she had a taut, curvaceous body and cap of dark brown hair that bounced with her every move. She was a cheerleader at the high school, and she moved like one—as did Dana, who, though she was a year younger than me, still impressed me with her dark eyes and long, light brown hair and body that was as muscled as a gymnast's.

"Do you have this album?" she asked.

"Yeah. I love it," I told her.

"Cool."

She dropped the needle on a bit clumsily, but soon the basement was filled with the rock 'n' roll beat of the first track, which poured through the high-end hi-fi system with a beautiful force I'd never heard the likes of at home.

"Let's dance!" Dana yelled over the music, holding her arms outstretched toward me. I jumped up, incredulous, and did a silly sort of Hustle-inspired, rock 'n' roll partner dance with her.

There was something happening that summer: I had become more popular overnight. I knew it wasn't such a great thing, really, since it was simply because I'd survived a tragedy, which had made me a curiosity, but I savored my new standing—especially with people like the Borneos, whose father was the vice president of Bamberger's department store, and who had always been nice to me but never particularly interested. Kristin and her mom sat near them at Takanassee, though, and they, like everyone, had thought Kristin was cool. They had started paying attention to me earlier that summer, and we'd already spent several afternoons lounging near the snack bar, sharing frozen Marathon bars and orders of thick French fries. And now, I guess, since I had been with Kristin in her last moments of life, I had attained a sort of cool status too.

Mrs. Borneo had called my mother the day before with an offer to take me to the beach with them—word was out among the other beach club mothers that mine didn't want to go so often anymore—and when the August day turned out to be a stormy one, Dana called and asked if I wanted to come over and hang out with them anyway, and I made my way there—a two-minute walk around the block opposite ours—delighting in the unfamiliar route that I'd walked only while trick-or-treating or on my Girl Scout Cookie routes. I felt like maybe I'd found some new friends, and that maybe I wouldn't feel my losses so acutely because of them. I rang the bell at the Borneos' and it played that long ding-dong pattern and before it had ended Mrs. Borneo was at the door.

"Beth! Come in," she said. "The girls are in the basement, so go ahead down. Too bad about the beach, but we'll take you down another time."

"OK, thanks," I said, scanning the living room for signs of wealth. There were modern-art paintings on the walls and a carpet shaggier than ours, and a low glass coffee table, but nothing too out of the ordinary. Downstairs, Cara and Dana were lounging around wearing their bikinis under deliciously thick hooded sweatshirts and looking bored as they listened to records—which led to the dancing, and to Cara's return with hair-braiding products along with a bag of Ruffles that she tossed onto the end of the couch.

"Dana, let Beth sit down," she said, patting the spot of carpet in front of her and waving a comb in the air. Dana led us through a final spin and let go of my hand, then grabbed the potato chips and pulled the sides of the bag until it opened, inhaling the salty puff of air it released and then reaching in for a handful before holding it in my direction.

As I danced I thought of how our babysitter Robin had taught us the Hustle. She would be watching us on a rainy Saturday night and she'd put on a Captain & Tennille or Bee Gees album and take my hand and lead me onto the dance floor—the center of the moss-green carpet of the living room—and talk me through the out-in, in-out rhythm of bringing our chests together and apart, and the slightly country way of grasping hands and moving them up and down, making our elbows pointy and our wrists bent. Adam would take spins with her too, never quite learning the steps but delighting in letting Robin flip him around before dissolving in a fit of giggles and rolling to the side so I could continue my lesson. "This is what 'cut the rug' must mean!" I told her once as we danced, noticing how we ruffled the nap of the carpet and recalling one of the old-fashioned phrases my father liked, which he would use when inviting my mother or me to dance at a Bat Mitzvah or wedding or even just around the house.

I twirled away from Dana and plopped myself down on the floor, back up against the couch so that Cara could easily reach my head.

"Your hair is so pretty," she told me, combing out any tiny tangles that had materialized since morning. Kristin had taught me how to work them out with little pain, starting at the bottom of a knot and combing through it little by little, until it was smooth.

"Thanks." People were always complimenting me on my hair, on its color and thickness and the way it shone in the sun like a penny. I loved hearing it but never knew quite what to say.

"Sometimes I would French braid Kristin's hair at the beach," Cara said. "Her hair was really pretty too."

"Yeah," I said, feeling the air inside my lungs diminish ever so slightly and the skin of my face begin to tingle. "She always used to complain that it was too thin." I both wanted to talk about her all the time and never wanted to talk about her again. I wondered if I'd betrayed her by mentioning her hair, then closed my eyes for a moment and imagined it, the fine, pin-straight strands in tones of flaxen and cherrywood wrapped tight around those pink, spongy curlers she liked to use when we had sleepovers, which my hair was too thick for but which gave her perfect ringlets when she'd unwind them in the morning, sitting up but still in bed because she couldn't wait another second to see if it had worked.

"How's your book going?" Cara asked the question, but Dana sat on the rug next to me, ready to hear the answer. My "book" was the story of the accident, which I'd begun writing by July, in cursive with a blue pen on wide-ruled, loose-leaf binder paper that I'd asked my mother to buy me on a quick errand at the mall, in McCrory's. I was on page 100, and had taken to showing it to anyone who expressed an interest. I would sit there, wide-eyed, watching whomever read it and waiting eagerly for any sort of feedback, from a blink to a full-on "Oh my God." Cara was one of its biggest fans, devouring my new pages every few days as if it were a soap opera she just couldn't wait to catch up with.

"It's OK," I told her. "I'm about halfway through, I think."

Cara tugged at my hair as I strained to keep my head upright. Dana jumped up to flip Rick Springfield's album over, and I thought of how I would listen to Casey Kasem's American Top 40 with Kristin on rainy Saturday afternoons, and how Air Supply would always have at least two songs in the lineup. This could be just as good as being friends with Kristin, I tried to tell myself. Cara and Dana could be my new friends.

I thought about the question they had asked me a week before, which I couldn't answer at the time. "Is it true that Adam and Kristin were both decapitated?" Dana had asked. Cara shot her a look but then turned her gaze on me, curiously. "Um, I don't know," I told them, confused. "Where did you hear that?" Dana said it was in the newspaper. That night I asked my mom what "decapitated" meant.

"Decapitated? Why?" she asked, knitting her brow.

"I'm just wondering."

"It means your head gets chopped off of your body. Why are you asking about such a terrible thing?"

I pictured that reality for just a split second, but then felt dizzy and shoved it away. Plus I could tell by the way she answered me that this had not happened to Adam or Kristin—and if it had, she didn't know anything about it. And I didn't want to know about it either. I decided that that afternoon in the Borneos' basement was as good a time as any to set the record straight.

"Oh, so remember you had asked me the other day about whether it was true that Adam and Kristin had been, um, decapitated?" I tried to sound casual, but the word felt foreign and disturbing in my mouth.

"Yeah?" Cara said, securing the braid on the right side of my head with a tiny blue coated rubber band.

"They weren't. I checked with my mom. So no, it's not

true." I laughed uncomfortably, then continued, emboldened by the fact that I now knew the meaning of the word. "I guess I would've remembered it, anyway," I said. "Right?"

"Wow," Dana said. "Right." She had joined me on the carpet to watch Cara do my hair and to listen, with full attention, to the decapitation answer.

"What *do* you remember from that night?" Cara asked. She was halfway through the other braid, pulling tighter with each strand, making my left eye water and my scalp ache.

"I remember everything," I said, quietly. We had been over this before, but it seemed they could not get enough of the story. They took turns with rapid-fire questions, hungry for more details.

"Did you see the other car coming?"

"No. Nobody did."

"What were Kristin's last words?"

"I'm not really sure." A girl at the temple had asked me the same question. I found it an odd one—she wasn't on a death bed, hadn't known her words would be her last, so whatever they were would've been insignificant, most likely. Still, it seemed so important to them, so I racked my memory, trying to think how our late-night chat about the onset of summer, the end of the school year, the mod furniture in the window of the storefront we passed, had sounded. I had no idea. "'I can't wait till summer'?" It sounded plausible.

"Oh God, how sad," Cara said, fastening the finished braid down at my shoulder blade. I turned so I could see her, leaning sideways into the plush couch.

"Yeah," Dana added, tying her long, uncombed hair back into a stretchy pink headband she had kept wound around her wrist.

"Was it very bloody?" Cara asked. "I mean, if you don't mind me asking that."

"I don't mind," I said. The question brought a familiar throb and burst of lightheadedness to the spot behind my left eye socket. But really, I didn't mind. I kind of liked it, actually—talking normally about the accident to people with whom I had no baggage. Talking to my parents about any of these details was out of the question. I knew that implicitly, even if I didn't understand why. "It *was* really bloody. I was soaked with blood, actually, right through my shirt and pants and everything. But it wasn't even mine. It was Kristin's."

"Oh my God, are you serious?" Dana looked freaked out.

"Yeah," I said. "It was kind of weird."

"What about Adam?"

"I didn't see any blood on him at all." I thought about that for a moment, thought about what it implied. Internal bleeding? A banged head? Or maybe blood that I just never saw.

"So you weren't knocked unconscious, then?" Dana asked. "I mean, if you remember everything."

"Um, no. I don't think so." I wished I could've said that I had been; it would've been even more dramatic.

"Well maybe you were and you don't remember," Cara offered.

"I guess," I said. "I mean, it's possible. I'll have to ask my mom. She wasn't unconscious. Neither was my poppy."

Cara snorted. "Poppy? Wait, is that what you call your dad? *Poppy?*"

I felt my face flush so deeply my eyes watered. I had blown it after all. "Um yeah," I told her. "Well, I mean, just sometimes."

Dana sniggered. "Poppy? Really?"

"Look how red you are!" Cara said. It made me even redder.

"Why, what do you say?" I asked.

"Dad!" Cara and Dana answered together.

"Dad." Another foreign word in my mouth. It had always sounded so cold and formal to me. And typical—not individual enough for my very own father.

"Anyway, it doesn't matter," Cara said, shrugging. "Dana— put on Air Supply!"

Rick Springfield had stopped at some point during the talk of blood and unconsciousness, and now the orchestral strains of Air Supply filled the room, and the two sisters lay back on the carpet, side by side, arms straight up above them in a pantomime of a serious conductor. Then they released peals of laughter and let their arms flop down and were still, like satisfied girls in their just-made snow angels. My face was still tingling and my heart still pounding because they had laughed at what I called my father.

"I'm going to look at my hair," I called over the music. "Even the Nights Are Better" had just started, making the muscles in my throat constrict. It had been one of my and Kristin's favorite songs.

I padded up the carpet-covered stairs and leaned too heavily into the light plywood door, flinging myself into the main level of the house. The late-day light was a golden syrup, filtering through the last bit of heavy clouds that were slowly breaking up. The air was fragrant with sautéed onion and garlic, and filled with classical music that seemed to pour out of speakers in every corner. I peered into the kitchen and saw the back of Mrs. Borneo, who moved between the stove and the fridge and the sink with happy bounces, grabbing spoon and then towel and then knife and then salt, humming along with the increasingly frantic piano piece.

I thought of my mom, of how she would have been moving happily around the kitchen not all that long ago. She'd make dinner every night—meat loaf or chicken or London broil or hamburgers—and I would set the table, and then she would clean up, load the dishwasher, and, if we weren't watching a TV show that night and if I didn't have to do my homework quite yet, I would join her for our ritual: listening to music together in the living room.

She and my father had recently replaced the big old dial-knob radio with a new stereo system, which had a digital-face radio, a double tape deck and a record player that could take five LPs at once, dropping them down one by one onto the turntable, where the needle would magically settle into the first, scratchy groove. Though I still listened to records in my room on my own little record player, I had started joining my mother here to listen to her own collection when I was about ten, most often to hear records by Jane Olivor. She was a schmaltzy, passionate belter like Barbra Streisand.

"But with a much better range," my mom would say, "and so much emotion! I never cared for 'Some Enchanted Evening' before I heard her do it."

Her voice moved me, too. But mostly it moved my mom, and being so close to her while she was overcome with emotion—the joyous, passionate kind rather than the weepy, sad kind that came from watching *Little House on the Prairie* or the nightly TV news together—was wonderful for me. It made us close, and it made her stay in one spot, alone with just me, for at least one whole Jane Olivor album, and sometimes even two.

There was a chair in the corner, next to the stereo, that we would take turns sitting in or sometimes squish into together. It was shaped like a throne, with a high, sturdy back and manly arm rests. Its upholstery was crushed velvet in the most soothing shade of icy gray blue, and I liked to rub its nap back and forth as I would to a cat, watching its color go from pale blue to deep blue between my thighs. Usually, though, I would wind up on the floor, stretched long and lean on the thick car-

peting. Jane Olivor would start singing and we would enter a
trancelike state together, and often during "Vincent" I would
sing: "Like the strangers that you met, ragged men in ragged
clothes. A silver thorn, a bloody nose . . ."

"Beth, it's *rose!*" my mother laughed once, hearing my mistake. She laughed long and hard, and I was discomfited, but I
loved that she'd heard me and that I could make her laugh in
the middle of a song that usually made her cry. I loved lying
there with her almost more than anything else. It was our
time, and it was special, and I never wanted it to end.

After the accident, I knew intuitively that it would
end—that our shared hours of basking in music were to go
the way of the beach and playgrounds and certain driving
routes that went past Adam's friends' houses, and certain
songs that would have to be quickly shut off when they
came on the radio—but I tried to pretend, at first, that nothing had changed.

"Mom, will you listen to Jane Olivor with me?" I held my
favorite of the singer's five albums to my chest. "I miss it.
Maybe it'll make you feel better." It was only July, a month
after, and she was still wandering around in a constant daze,
on the verge of tears, her hair needing a cut and her clothes
needing a change.

"I can't," she said, putting the last of our dishes from dinner into the dishwasher and shaking her head sharply. "It's too
soon."

"Please," I said.

"No, Beth!" she snapped. "I don't think I'll ever be able to
listen to that again. I can't, oh I can't . . ." and she held her
damp, dirty dishrag to her face and cried. I cried too.

"It's not like Adam liked her!" I pretended that she wasn't
making sense. But really, I understood why she couldn't do it,
why she couldn't hunker down with me in our favorite nook

in the living room, wedged between the piano and the stereo, and listen to the music we loved. It was a joy, like so many others, that now lay on the other side of a massive abyss. It was from before. Done, finished, dead.

~

I slipped into the tiny half bath at the top of the Borneos' basement stairs, flicked on the light, and quietly shut the door behind me, staring at myself in the mirror. The French braids were neater than any I'd had before, except for maybe when Kristin did them for me right after I'd taken a shower one time, when my hair was slick and heavy and easy to manage. I looked into my eyes and thought their blue looked a little faded, thought my face looked a little pale—less freckled and sun-kissed than usual at this time of year. Then I grimaced to get a look at my braces and thought of when they'd had glass in them, which I remembered as if it had been a dream. I looked, I thought, just as I felt at that moment: like my heart ached. I knew that Cara and Dana—and anyone else in the world, for that matter—couldn't really replace Kristin well enough. These were not my people; it was time to go home.

When I started back down the basement stairs I could hear the last strains of "Two Less Lonely People in the World," and the familiarly harsh melody of a sibling argument.

"I don't care! Mom said!" Dana whined to Cara, who was standing on the couch, bouncing softly up and down. When Dana saw me she smiled, and Cara turned to me.

"So, do you think it looks good?" she asked.

"I love it! It's really neat," I told her. "But, I should be getting back home. I have to help my mom with dinner." It was a lie—I never helped, just set the table and did some of the clearing afterward. Plus I had a feeling it would be a take-out night—subs or fried chicken or pizza. I just wanted to get back home, back to something known.

On the short walk back I decided I would no longer call my father Poppy. I was too old for it, and it sounded funny. "Dad," I said out loud, practicing. "Hi, Dad. Hey, Dad, what's on TV?" It kind of made me sound grown-up, I thought. And, though it sounded like I was talking to a stranger when I said it, I kind of was. We all were strangers now.

Chapter Eighteen

I WAS not going to cry. But it was my first day at Memorial Junior High School, my first day in seventh grade, and I wanted to look perfect. I wanted to make Kristin proud. And my hair was already failing me.

"Mom! Where's my mousse?" I stared into the bathroom mirror, my eyes welling up fast, and tried to will my drying cowlick to behave. My new haircut had seemed like a good idea last week, when I sat in the chair of the salon in the mall and decided I needed to add some layers to my one-length long hair. I should've known, though, that the angles probing the sides of my face would not feather properly.

"In the cabinet, right where you left it," my mom said, rushing by the bathroom toward the kitchen. "You look beautiful! Now stop playing around in the mirror or you're going to miss your bus!" I gave the sides of my hair one more tug each with my new vent brush and then flicked off the light. I just couldn't look anymore.

The first day of junior high was something I had planned to experience with Kristin. She was going to help me make a fashionable start—braid my hair for me the night before, tell me what jeans to wear with what blousy top, how to do just enough makeup for the boys to notice me. I knew I had to do it without her, though.

When it was time to go I kissed my mother good-bye and pretended not to see the tears in her eyes, and then left the house with uneven feathers and no braid and made my way to the bus stop. It was just about two blocks from the house, on the corner of Sandspring Drive and Weston Place, at the foot of the steep hill that I would walk up to get to grammar school, but going there—standing on a corner at a specific time, in the sleepy, blurry early morning, was a completely new experience.

Up until that point I had been a walker—I think my only time on a school bus had been for class trips and maybe once or twice when I went home after school with Beth and Brenda, the twins I was friends with who lived just far enough from Woodmere School to have to ride the bus. So as I walked to the bus stop that morning in the late summer air, I took in the new experience, thinking about how I would've been meeting Kristin there, and how I would've left Adam at home to walk to Woodmere on his own, and how now I would instead have to board the bus with people like Heather Dietz and David Holub—neighbors who were Kristin's age and none of whom I had really been friends with since we were about seven or eight years old. And then there would be the ones who were my age, also just starting seventh grade—Joanne and Laura and Anthony—more sort-of friends who were a huge part of .

my childhood, but not so much in my world anymore until they all made their way over to our house that summer, dragged by their moms, to pay us an awkward condolence call and leave a tin of cookies or pan of lasagna.

I knew I would be early that first morning, so I walked slowly along our quiet street, avoiding cracks in the sidewalk and inhaling the just emerging scent of summer fading into autumn—the smell of school. I passed the Cichettis' and the Naomolis' and the Fishers' and the Kitchens', trying not to peer into their front doors and hoping no one would come out at the same time that I passed so that I could have the walk to myself that morning. I was nervous about going to a new school, and I needed time to ease my way in.

At least I looked pretty good, I thought. I wore a plaid, short-sleeved blouse with two front ruffles, one rippling down each side of my torso, which I loved because its dark tones were slenderizing. They were tucked into new Bon Jour jeans that had white stitching and that new-denim smell, like slightly sour milk, and though they were way too loose in my opinion (my mother refused to pay for the skin-tight size), my mom had hemmed them on her sewing machine just a couple of nights ago so that they draped perfectly over the insteps of my feet, on which I wore brown sandals with a low heel, just as Kristin would have done. Wearing heels bothered my just-healed foot, which was already a bit achy with the morning dampness, but I kept it to myself—even when my mother cocked her head and asked, "Beth, are you sure it's not going to hurt your foot to wear these things?"—so that I could have the right look for my first day of school. I wore a new maroon backpack, empty save for some new Paper Mate erasable pens and a Trapper Keeper; I knew it would be filled with new books by the end of the day.

As I rounded the corner of my street and approached the next one, where the bus was supposed to pick us up, I saw Heather, wearing tight Levi's and a tank top and smoking a cigarette. Joanne was already there too, planted firmly in brand-new navy Pumas, and David was standing off to the side, hands shoved in his pockets, looking geeky and uneasy around the girls.

"Hey, everyone," I said, joining them there.

"Beth. Hey. So, how are you?" It was Heather, someone out of my social circle for a few years already, but someone I secretly yearned to still be friends with. She was badass and pretty, with hair as blond and shiny as corn silks that stood in perfectly sculpted mug handles along each side of her head. The way she looked at me now was half pitiful, half starstruck. I realized right then I should probably get used to it.

"I'm good! How about you? How was your summer?"

She looked thrown, but I held fast to my happiness. "Great," she said, exhaling a long stream of smoke over her shoulder and squinting as she did it, her thickly masacara'd lashes at half-mast. "It was great."

"Hey, Bethie!" said Joanne, my best friend in kindergarten and first grade, now more of a friendly neighbor. She was kind of a chubby tomboy with piercing blue eyes and dark blond hair that she wore either in pigtails or unevenly clipped barrettes, like today. I could tell in an instant that, unlike Heather, who would've liked to talk about the accident with me, Joanne was perfectly happy to go along with me and ignore it. So we made small talk, after David nodded his head in acknowledgment, reaching a quiet point just as Alyssa came along. Alyssa lived next door to Kristin. I'd never been drawn to her, and when Kristin and I had playdates we'd leave her out unless she spied us in Kristin's backyard and came ambling over on her own, standing at the edge of the yard until we said, "Hey, um, come on over." On my first morning of junior high school she looked smaller than usual—almost meek.

"Hey, Alyssa," I said.

"Hi, Beth."

A silent understanding passed between us—*it's just you and me now . . . we don't like each other much, sure, but we both really loved Kristin, and we've just got each other now*—and we looked at each other, really looked at each other, and knew we'd become some sort of friends.

"Don't be nervous," she said. "Junior high is really not so different than Woodmere. The teachers are nice." She smiled. "Are you going to try out for choir?"

"Yes, definitely," I said. "I think try-outs are like next week or something. Kristin said they're . . ." I stopped, because when I mentioned her name Alyssa's eyes widened with alarm. "Sorry, I just . . ."

"Do you miss her? Like, a lot?" Alyssa asked, her voice low and conspiratorial. "Because I miss her a lot." Her eyes welled up.

"I do," I said. "I really do." The bus came along then and we got on. We sat together and craned our necks to see Kristin's house as the bus rolled past it. Her shade was pulled down.

We were quiet for most of the ride, and I thought about some of the things Kristin had told me about Memorial School.

"So you get, like, your own locker for your books and your lunch or whatever," she explained.

"Can you decorate it if you want?"

"I guess. Some people do but I haven't yet," she said, sounding jaded. "You also change classrooms for each subject.

Like, we have science in this smelly lab room—I hate science!
We're doing dissections and it's gross . . ."

"What's dissections?"

"Cutting up worms and looking at their guts!"

"Disgusting!"

"I know. We're doing frogs next. But anyway, so we
also have stuff like home ec, where you sew—I'm making a
pillow—and shop class, where the teacher is a total perv.
You can't wear a skirt in his class because he'll try to look
up it!"

"Really?"

"I've never seen him do it but I think it's true. I'd never
wear a skirt in there. Oh and then there's homeroom, in the
morning. And I love that best of all because I'm in choir
homeroom, with Mr. Collins."

Choir was the be-all and end-all for girls like us—
dramatic girly girls who craved attention and who could sing
on key. While just about anyone who wanted to could make
it into the school chorus, choir was selective—you had to
know how to carry harmony, have stage presence, be good
enough to do a solo. Kristin was one of the dozen chosen
choir girls. She sang alto and got dressed up for seasonal con-
certs and sometimes did duets or solos, she told me. Making
it in was my number-one goal of the year.

When we got to the school—a low brick building not so
different from that of the elementary school—Alyssa pointed
me in the direction of my homeroom, which smelled like
formaldehyde. I didn't know what that was yet, but would
find out in a couple of months, when we would dissect impossibly long, rubbery worms with Miss Samson, who was
rotund and had metallic breath. She was a substitute for Mrs.
Boyd, who was on maternity leave.

But today it was Mrs. Boyd who stood at the front of the room, a soulless science lab, with rows of high black counter-like stations that each had a tiny sink and two stools. The cinder-block walls were empty, and one wall had windows that looked out to a grassy interior courtyard where, it seemed, no one had or would ever go. Potted plants edged the shelves along the windows. And up front, written in large script on the blackboard, was MRS. BOYD. HOMEROOM 7-A.

She had blond hair cut short, like a boy's, and kept her hands folded and resting on the shelf of her round belly, which was beneath a buttoned blue and white checkered smock shirt. She was taking attendance in a flat but friendly voice, summoning us up to her desk/science lab sink to pick up a packet of papers with our daily class schedule, hall locker number and combination and some other handouts about school policies.

"Michael Collins?"

"Hiya," he said, pretending to trip on his way up. A red-headed class clown.

"Robert Davies?"

"Here." He was tall, and sounded bored, and slinked up to the front and back.

"David Fisher?"

"Here." I watched him with some comfort; though we were hardly friends, he lived across the street from me and I had known him since we were toddlers. He was one of the few in my class who had come from my grammar school and not one of the other two schools in town.

"Nancy Fox?"

"Here!" The voice was so perky, I had to turn around to see who it belonged to. It was a tiny girl with a beautiful face—a button nose and dark brown hair that was parted in the middle and swooped back into symmetrical, rolling waves just like Jaclyn Smith's. As I turned to look at her she was swatting the arm of the boy next to her, stage whispering "Shut up!" through an impish, flirty smile.

"Beth Greenfield?" She paused then, as if startled, and as I approached her she looked me in the eye with an expression that I'd become well-acquainted with over the summer. "Oh, I know who you are," she said softly, sadly. "Welcome." I smiled at her, faintly, and felt my cheeks burn as I made my way back to my seat. Would everyone here know who I was? I hadn't thought about that, but the answer was probably yes. Kristin had been a star student here last year, and this year she'd be glaringly absent.

I sank into my seat and instinctively fingered the leather bracelet that had belonged to her. It was from the mall—just a strip of brown leather with a snap closure that had "Kris," with two butterflies imprinted in it by a machine. I had gotten it a week or so after getting home from the hospital, when I went over to her house and sat in her room and her mother asked me what I'd like to take to keep and remember her by. I had wanted to say, "Everything—her bed and her flowered curtains and her Jordache jeans and the Farrah Fawcett poster on her wall and that pile of barrettes and just the air in here; can I bottle the air?" But instead I chose a small jewelry box that played music when you opened it, and the stuffed brown monkey she had brought to our sleepover that never happened, and the bracelet. I'd grabbed the bracelet at the last minute, remembering when we'd gone to the mall and gotten two of them together, both with our names and two butterflies each, but hers brown and mine blue. From that day on I wore hers instead of mine every single day for a year, kissing it anytime I removed it to take a shower or go swimming, and once again when I put it back on.

After attendance was finished we were led out into the

hallway to try out our lockers. On the bottom of two rows was mine, a narrow metal compartment about the size of a small television turned sideways, and I privately thrilled over having such a grown-up space of my own—a locker like those I had only ever seen in movies about high school students.

"Excuse me, would you mind switching with me?" I looked up from my squatting position to see Nancy Fox, the one with the well-feathered hair, smiling at me with her perfectly straight white teeth. "Mine's on the top row, and I'm really short and, well, I can hardly even reach! You're lucky. You're tall." She demonstrated the problem by showing me how she had to stand on her tiptoes to reach inside. "See?"

"OK," I said. "No problem. I don't like having to squat down anyway."

"Thank you!" she seemed genuinely excited. When we switched places and exchanged combinations, she leaned into a large brown paper shopping bag and began unloading a stack of shiny new textbooks into the space that had briefly been mine.

"Why do you have all those books?" I asked. "I haven't gotten any yet."

"I get a second set to keep here in school and I'll take another set home. I can't carry them back and forth every day. I have rheumatoid arthritis and it hurts my arms."

I must have widened my eyes as I studied her delicate, bony wrists and exceptionally spindly arms.

"Don't worry—it's not like it's catching or anything!"

"Oh I know! I just . . . I never heard of anyone having arthritis so young."

"Well I'm just a special case!" she was self-deprecating and cute and flashed me a big smile. "So, how *are* you?"

I had heard that overly concerned tone before, and it made me feel found out. "What do you mean?"

"Oh, I'm sorry, I just . . . the funeral. My neighbor went to Kristin's funeral and . . ."

"Did you know her?"

"No. But my neighbor, Traci, did. She's in eighth grade, and they were in choir together," she said. We stood there floundering for a moment. "I'm trying out for choir as soon as they have auditions. Are you?"

"Definitely. I can't wait." I couldn't, it was true. But right then all I could focus on was the fact that Nancy too knew who I was, and all I could hear, over and over again in my head, was the phrase "Kristin's funeral." "So, like, does everyone know who I am or something?" I asked. "Mrs. Boyd said she knew. It's weird."

"I don't know. Probably," Nancy said. "It was like, all over the papers and everything. Don't worry about it, though. I'm the girl with arthritis and two sets of books! Now *that's* weird."

I chuckled, shaking my head at her.

"I'm psyched you're going to be in choir too," she said.

"Well I'm just trying out!"

"I hope we both make it. I think we should be friends."

"Me too."

Nancy, it turned out, reminded me of Kristin. She was pretty and popular and knew how to flirt with the boys, who responded with gobs of attention that she pretended to dislike. She was a bit compulsive about shopping and fashion, and her mom bought her all the real brands—Izod Lacoste polo shirts and preppy Bermuda bags with wooden handles and white Candies sneakers and Calvin Klein jeans. She knew just exactly how to apply mascara and hairspray and how to turn up her collar and roll up her pants legs. And she had a beautiful voice, too.

∽

I woke up even before my six a.m. alarm clock went off on the day of choir auditions, and all day I practiced my song in my head—"Open Arms," by Journey, whose sheet music was in too high a key for me. So after the last bell of the day rang, when my turn finally came to stand by Mr. Collins's piano while he played along, I told him, "I'm going to sing something a capella for you," and hoped I had impressed him with my music terminology.

"OK," he said. "Let's hear it." Mr. Collins half smiled at me in a way that let me know he knew I wanted to impress him, but not that he necessarily was. He was the school music teacher and director of both the choir and the chorus.

I noticed how his bony knees formed little points under his out-of-date plaid trousers, and how, in the morning, during homeroom choir practice, his hands shook as they hovered above the piano keys and his breath smelled of bracing mouthwash. None of it mattered to me because he'd known Kristin, and he'd loved her, and he was always so nice to me. Besides all those loving quotes in the *Asbury Park Press* article, he had given the eulogy at her funeral. Mrs. Sickel had told me about it, and from that moment on I knew I would get to know him well, and that I would join the choir and show him how alike we were, Kristin and I, and that I would kind of fill in for her. I thought about this as I sang.

I made the choir, and after that, my homeroom switched from Mrs. Boyd's science lab to Mr. Collins's music room, where the choir girls—plus one boy, Michael, who was Mr. Collins's son and who had a still-unchanged soprano voice—would gather first thing every morning for an eleven-minute practice session that began with "do-re-mi-fa-so-la-ti-do" scales and then segued into one of our signature, three-part-harmony songs, like "Morning Has Broken" or "Babe." I was an alto, and so never got to sing melody, but I loved the challenge of it—always having my voice dip way below that of the sopranos and second sopranos, growling out notes that seemed off-kilter by themselves but which blended perfectly with the main tunes that the high-voiced girls were belting out. Kristin had been an alto, too.

Mr. Collins was always particularly gentle with me. It was as if he was both protecting and lauding me for having been with Kristin when she died—just like all the other girls in the choir who had been there the year before, in her presence. These were her other friends whom I hardly knew—the popular, flirty, pretty ones, with names like Tricia and Nancy and Jodi and Kelly—and they took right to me. I had status then. I was in, vicariously. Sometimes we'd talk about her. They would ask me the questions that had by now become standards, like that old "What was the last thing she said to you?" and "How did it happen, exactly?" They'd reminisce about seventh grade and sometimes even cry, like when we sang a song that would remind them of her, or when it was her birthday, or just because. Sometimes I'd sing as if I were her, or both of us, and it would make me feel like she was with me.

But I had Nancy—she made the choir, too—and that made Kristin's absence easier to bear. Nancy was a second soprano, which was perfect for us to be able to harmonize and practice together when we weren't at school. It was good to have a new best friend.

~

The night after choir tryouts I had a dream that would recur, in some form or another, over the next twenty years. In it, I am walking along my street to the bus stop in the crisp, early light of morning. I think I see Kristin up ahead, standing on the corner and talking to some people I don't know, but I realize I must be seeing things and make a concerted effort to keep my eyes on the pavement of the sidewalk. But when I get to the corner, I see that it is indeed Kristin, and I panic, because I know that if I let her know that I thought she was dead, she will be angry, and then she'll really disappear, for good this time. When I get up close to her I see that she has a blurry, ethereal quality, but her face is glowing and happy. Though I try not to look her in the eyes, I cannot contain my joy at seeing her, and I exclaim, "Kristin! Where have you been!" and she says, "I've been here." She is not nearly as excited about seeing me. I try to hang back and wait my turn to speak to her, like waiting in a reception line at a wedding, and I steal glances at her whenever she is looking away. She looks older, but no less beautiful. I try to shoot some of the other people knowing looks, so I can gauge whether anyone else is shocked to see her alive, but no one responds. Then I silently scold myself for all of the time that I'd wasted grieving, rather than simply being with her.

Chapter Nineteen

Early in the school year I stumbled upon the closest thing yet to a real therapist: Miss Boyd (no relation to my homeroom teacher), Memorial's new school social worker who one day came around to all the health classes to explain that she was available to talk with anyone who was having "emotional problems." I'd already felt drawn to her—to her piercing eyes and warm, solid presence—before she said that part, but with that statement I felt lightheaded and panicky, because I knew this was for me, and that this was finally my chance. After she left the classroom, I asked for a bathroom pass and then followed her down the empty, carpeted hallway, my heart pounding fast in my chest.

I spoke only when I'd gotten right up behind her. "Miss Boyd?" She turned slowly, like she'd kind of been expecting someone to follow her, and she smiled when she saw that it was me. "Um, I was wondering if I could come and talk to you sometime," I said, my voice quavering. "It's just that, well, my brother and my best friend died in a car accident in June, and I sort of just really miss them."

She already knew all about it, of course. But I still felt that I had to explain it to her. When I told her what had happened, and that I missed my brother and friend, she said, "I bet you do. That sounds like a very difficult thing to deal with, but I think that it's wonderful that you want to talk about it, because it will help." I breathed in deeply to stop from crying right then and there. "Do you have any study periods this week? Because that would be the perfect time to come. And if you like it, we can make it a regular thing."

I started two days later, amazed at how easily I was let out of my study hall just by handing in my pass from Miss Boyd. But the study-hall teacher, of course, knew all about me too. "No problem, Beth," she told me. "See you next week."

One week turned into every week and sometimes more— half-hour sessions during gym or home ec or even Spanish, which I savored, that I looked forward to with a yearning that bordered on obsession because they felt like the only time reserved for me to truly be myself before reverting to the contented, overachieving pre-teen that I presented myself as to the world.

At first I spent time going over the details of that night— replaying them out loud chronologically, without having to be drawn out with questions. Sometimes I'd be cold and emotionless, recounting the evening like a reporter, still in shock even six months later. But every once in a while it would hit me that what I was saying was true, and that it had happened to me—that I had seen Kristin's blood and that it had soaked through her hair and onto the seat and through my clothes, and that I could still hear the sound that the cars made when they collided, metal on metal and then glass on asphalt, as if it was the actual end of the world—and then my voice would catch and I would look into Miss Boyd's eyes and they would be teary, and then I would cry in a burst that felt so good but that I would never allow to last very long.

Soon I tried talking about my feelings. I told her that I missed both Adam and Kristin desperately and that I sometimes was lonely. And I admitted to her that I despised my mom when she cried, and didn't know what to do when she tried to get me to talk to her. Talking to Miss Boyd was easy. She seemed to hear every word, every inference, and I liked looking into her face: calm and dusted with a soothing constellation of freckles, warm brown eyes that shone often with empathetic tears, thin upper lip that drew easily into a smile and then a deep-throated laugh that I adored, all fringed by thick, brown, curly hair that fell to her shoulders.

She'd ask me questions: "Why is it so hard for you to share your feelings with your mom?," which I could never, ever answer, or "Do you ever feel like the accident was your fault?," to which I'd sometimes answer with an instant, defensive "No!" and other times with, "Well, it was my ballet recital we were driving home from," because I thought it was what I was supposed to say. It was way too soon for me to admit that guilt, though—or to even know it was there.

I soon began to obsess over Miss Boyd and our sessions, and look forward to them in a way that had me spaced-out in class, living for that time together as though it was the only thing getting me through. I'd also feel a stab of slightly shameful jealousy whenever I'd notice another student slink into her office—usually it was a bad kid who would be going in to talk about divorced or abusive parents, or using drugs or getting drunk in school or cutting too many classes. It was never an English-geek like me, who wrote poetry and played clarinet in the band and sang in the choir and had hair with a cowlick that prevented it from feathering properly, but a burnout, a stoner, a slutty girl who smoked and had sex with boys and cut classes.

Usually it was someone like Sandy Manning.

Sandy was in the seventh grade too, but I knew her only from afar because she was in a different crowd. She was a tough girl who hung around all the kids I was most afraid of. But early in the school year her older brother had died in a car accident, and that gave Miss Boyd an idea.

"So, Beth," she began one afternoon. "You know Sandy Manning, right?"

"I know who she is," I said, flaring my nostrils. But then I remembered something about her that made me soften. "Didn't her brother die too?" I asked.

"Mmm-hmmm," she said, a vague smile forming. "What would you think of having your sessions together for a while? Kind of like a support group?"

I didn't like the idea at all.

"I don't know," I said. "I think I'd rather keep having my time alone with you. I don't even know her. And what would we talk about?"

She said we could still have one-on-one sessions, but just add in one with Sandy. "I know you're very different, but I bet a lot of what you're feeling is the same," she added. "And I think you could help each other, actually."

I agreed—but mostly because I was so fascinated with Sandy, and what had happened to her since her brother died early in the school year. I didn't know her before junior high because we went to different grammar schools, but I'd heard that she'd been a serious figure skater. Her father owned the local ice rink, and I remembered sometimes seeing her there when I went to skate in wobbly circles with my dad on Sunday afternoons. Sandy would be one of those girls who wore short little skirts and tiny sweaters and beautiful white skates, and who always stayed in the center of the rink. She never seemed cold or shy, and practiced jumps with such a focused grace that it was nearly impossible to circle around her without becoming mesmerized and losing balance.

But she had recently abandoned it all, from what I had heard. Now she was a bit heavy and unathletic-looking, with shoulders that sloped forward when she moved her compact, five-foot-tall frame through the halls. She looked like she was about twenty years old, with lots of purple eye shadow and distant eyes that seemed lost behind a permanent haze, and had huge breasts that she liked to reveal with a standard burnout uniform: long flannel shirts opened low to show cleavage, tight acid-washed jeans and ankle boots with skinny heels. At lunchtime she smoked cigarettes outside of the cafeteria door and called out things like, "Yo, Tommy! Eat me!" to her boyfriend, who had perpetually red, watery eyes and a gravelly voice. Sometimes they made out by her locker until a passing teacher said, "Break it up, you two."

The more I thought about it, the more I realized that I couldn't wait to start my sessions with her. I couldn't wait to see her up close, to have her speak to me, to find out if the unfathomable grief of losing a brother was enough to close the chasm between us.

Our first meeting was awkward—Sandy stomping in late, eyes never quite meeting mine, me right on time and waiting, in my usual chair, chatting nervously with Miss Boyd. When we were all there, it was quiet for a minute, except for Sandy cracking her gum, and then Miss Boyd started. "So I thought it might be a good idea to have you girls here together," she said, seeming a tiny bit nervous. "You don't know each other well, I realize, but you've both lost brothers. You've both been through a very difficult time." I looked down at the floor then, my face throbbing, stomach in knots, and I think Sandy did the same. "This is your space, and it's a safe one, and in it you can talk about your experiences and your feelings. Who would like to tell their story first?"

I was quiet. But Sandy shrugged and said, "I will. Why not?" So she told us that her brother, Johnny, was older, eighteen, and that she adored him. "He always made me feel really special," she told us. But one night he was out really late with his girlfriend—partying, drinking, driving around in his muscle car, which he loved working on—and never came home. "The phone rang in the middle of the night. I was sound asleep," she said. "And then I just heard my mom screaming and crying." Finally, her nonchalance faded and her voice cracked, and her eyes welled up when she told the next part: He had hit a telephone pole and died instantly, but his girlfriend survived. No one was exactly sure how it happened, she said, but when I heard her say that they had been out drinking and partying, I had a pretty good idea—and couldn't help but think about how he could've killed someone else—though I didn't say a word. I just felt a new and gnawing nervousness about telling my own tale.

When it was my turn to talk I was surprised by the sound of my own voice, which sounded tinny and faraway and not at all like my own. I had not quite developed a standardized way of telling the tale yet—though I would perfect one in years to come, having short versions ("No, I'm an only child." or "I had a brother but he died when we were young . . ."), medium versions ("A car accident. A drunk driver hit us, and my brother and friend were killed."), and various long versions, which could include details from the ballet recital and the actual intersection to Kristin's blood and the rundown of everyone's injuries. For Sandy, I didn't get quite so detailed.

"It was in June, and we were driving home from my ballet recital," I began, entering a flat, emotionless zone that had by then become second nature. "It was me, my mom, my dad, my best friend, and my brother, who was seven. Another car hit us—a drunk driver—and my brother and my friend died. I broke my foot and my dad was really hurt. We were all in the hospital for a week."

When I'd finished I saw stars, and was surprised to realize that it made me feel a bit sick, reliving it all in front of an audience. I looked at Miss Boyd for grounding and she smiled at me with her eyes. Sandy was quiet for a minute, and then: "I can't believe you were in the car. I can't believe your friend died too." I had managed to inspire awe in this girl, who seemed like she'd seen way more in life than I already had. But I, too, had apparently seen my share. This could work after all, I thought.

We continued meeting on a weekly basis, warming to each other more and more every time, and also expanding the scope of what we shared, revealing more and more about our lives at home, our friends, the way we saw the world.

One time during our session with Miss Boyd, Sandy told us that she'd had sex with Tommy in the woods, during a party. She didn't actually say it, but she looked at me and said, in a tone both accusatory and ashamed, "We did what you would probably not even *consider* doing. But I did it. You'd probably think I was a slut if I told you about it."

"No I wouldn't," I said. But I was too frightened to ask any questions, and Miss Boyd said, "We'll talk about it later, Sandy."

We became unlikely pals. My other friends would say, "Ew! Sandy's such a druggie!" and I can guess what her stoner friends said about me. But we didn't mind, because we needed each other too much. We went religiously to our sessions and took turns talking about our mothers and our brothers and our guilt, articulating our ideas in completely different ways, but understanding each other nonetheless. We only hung out socially a few times. Once we went to the mall, where we spent most of our time avoiding her rowdy friends, who hung out in front of Sam Goody in "the pit"—a place where the floor went down a couple of steps into a sunken lounge area that was edged by benches and protected by the cement planters that formed a wall around the area. But one time we ventured in there together—she noticed her brother's friend, and just had to go in and say hi—and so I followed her as if I had been in there a million times. But really I was fascinated and nervous as I made my way down those three little steps, into the smoky air, where every laugh, it seemed, was directed at me. Her friends—skinny guys with long, ratty hair and Judas Priest and Metallica baseball jerseys, and a couple of girls with wide hips shoved into skin-tight black corduroys, all puffing away on Parliaments—eyed me like the interloper that I was, but they were vaguely nice, or indifferent at least, and when we left I felt cooler by association, though I knew I'd never venture in there again.

Sessions with Miss Boyd were where our differences truly fell away. And though Sandy was usually stalwart, one time she came in crying.

"I'm, like, a total ugly mess today," she announced, plopping heavily into the chair that had quickly become hers. It was one of those old-school, molded-plastic Eames chairs that came in dusky shades like seafoam and fleshy pink. I was in one just like it, and both were in front of Miss Boyd's desk, so we could face her and also the windows behind her head, which looked onto a skinny little grass courtyard and the red brick facade of the biology wing. Before Sandy had burst in—late, as always—I had been talking to Miss Boyd about my upcoming Bat Mitzvah, and what I was going to wear, and about how much I would miss Kristin. And then in she flew, the smell of cigarette smoke trailing her.

"It was like, really fucking cold in my house when I woke up this morning," Sandy said, sniffling and shaking and rummaging through her big sack of a corduroy purse till she found her CoverGirl pressed powder. She opened it, and it was broken into several pieces, and she used her thumb to rub a tan film off of the little scratched-up mirror before she peered into it, wiping at her runny black mascara while she went on. "I couldn't find anything clean in my drawers, so I looked in this really old pile in my closet and that's when I found this," she said, stopping for a second to click the powder closed and thrust her chest out at us. She was wearing an unremarkable black hooded sweatshirt that was about three sizes too big. "It's Johnny's!" she said. "I remember I stole it from his room last winter and I never gave it back. And it fucking smells like him, you guys. It fucking smells *just like him!*" Sandy started crying again. Miss Boyd pulled the perforated top off of a fresh box of tissues and handed it to her. I edged my chair closer to Sandy and put my hand on her warm shoulder, and she surprised me by leaning her still-damp, grape-Bubble-Yum-shampoo–scented head into me and putting her arm up around my neck, pulling me into a clumsy hug. I froze there, and took a whiff of her sweatshirt, and smelled what must have been her brother: faded laundry detergent and musky cologne and stale smoke.

"Smells can be very powerful," Miss Boyd said, looking at us so intently with those keen eyes that I, too, began to cry. Sandy fell away when I took a deep, weepy breath and looked at me. "So what did Adam smell like?" she asked, suddenly composed.

"I-I don't know," I stammered, kind of offended.

"Come on, yes you do."

"I can't remember." I was suddenly shy, and I wanted to keep the memory of Adam's scent—new jeans and fallen oak leaves and pretzels, when he was much younger, Ammens baby powder—all to myself. I blew my nose and looked at Miss Boyd pleadingly.

"Beth was just talking about her Bat Mitzvah, about how she's nervous about having to put on an act and seem happy for a full day," she told Sandy. "And she was telling me about the Jessica McClintock blouse she tried on last night at the mall." I was humiliated. Sandy was still sniffling a little, but she managed one of her throaty laughs.

"God, we are so different," she said, eyeing me like a stranger. "Isn't it weird?"

"Yes," I said. "Totally."

We'd take turns being the more depressed one, which was good, because then we'd get to take turns being the strong one too. On some days we'd talk about how we couldn't see the point in school, or even in getting out of bed. Sometimes Sandy would seem surprised when I agreed with her. She'd say, "But you're so together, so good," and I'd say, "But you're so cool," and then we'd look at each other and get silent and our eyes would well up with some kind of love, because everything would be stripped away except for us and our thirteen-year-old–girl pain. In those moments in Miss Boyd's little office, with its beige wall plastered with a poster of a kitten that said HANG IN THERE, Sandy and I would totally get each other. Our overwhelming grief, we'd be amazed to find out again and again, was the same. And for the moment, at least, it was all that mattered.

Chapter Twenty

"THEY say all the firsts are difficult." My mom was on the phone with someone, probably the rabbi or another temple friend, talking about New Year's Eve, which was just two weeks away and filling all of us with anxiety because we didn't want it to be tragic. Nobody talked about this, of course, but the fear of midnight and watching the ball drop and trying to bring any feeling of festivity into our house, still so heavy with sadness, was something I know we all wanted to avoid.

We had already made it through Thanksgiving, the first one ever when we ate at a restaurant, because Mom thought we should try something different. We chose a nearby fancy place, the Cypress Inn, which was a low, white building on Route 35—just a couple of lights south of where the accident had happened and across the street from one of our two local malls, Seaview Square, where the anchor stores of Stern's and

Steinbach's were like the poor stepsisters of Bamberger's and A&S of the Monmouth Mall. When we showed up for our reservation, there was a valet parking attendant, so Dad pulled right up to the entrance and we filed in, all making expectant, excited faces at each other while we waited to be seated. It was a sad scene, though—the dining room filled with other small families, tucked around turkey platters and glasses of wine, with no real festive air to be felt at all. I had a lump in my throat throughout the entire meal, and felt at times that I would choke on the effort of merely swallowing cranberry sauce or mashed potatoes, and I knew my parents felt the same. But we finished our dinners and got out of there, back onto that haunted highway, relieved that Thanksgiving was officially over.

We had also made it through Hanukkah—eight nights of me lighting the candles and singing the blessings with my parents by my side, singing along but stumbling over the new melodies I'd learned in Hebrew school, coming in strong with me for the "Amen" part. I'd acted like nothing was wrong each night, like no one was missing, like the three of us in front of a menorah was how it had always been. My mom got a new one that year, replacing the low, flat, blue-engraved silver plated one with a more classic, candelabra-style gold-metal piece. I didn't really like it, because it didn't have as much character as the old one—which had Hebrew writing on it along with tiny images of lions, as well as many years' worth of old candle drippings that had become a permanent part of the design—but I didn't say anything as, each night, I put those cheap, quick-burning pastel-colored candles from the supermarket into the clean, unclogged holders. I understood that she wanted to start fresh, and I didn't want to discuss it, so I just carried on, singing "Baruch atah adonai, elohanu melech ha'olam . . ." and then hugging and kissing both of them and saying "Happy Hanukkah," as always, and acting extra-pleased with whatever gift they went and retrieved from their bedroom each night. I could see the welled-up tears in my parents' eyes, and the barely dulled pain in their faces, which flickered behind their skin like a fly caught behind a window. It moved erratically and was barely contained, but I was a pro at ignoring it—at smiling into the pain and refusing to ac-knowledge it, and sometimes even at making it settle down a bit, melting into the spaces behind their eyes and making it-self at home, in a permanent, somehow peaceful, sort of way.

New Year's Eve would be harder, though, because it wasn't like the night would be over with the lighting of some candles or the unwrapping of a gift. It had a universal weight to it that threatened to highlight any speck of sadness or loss that lived silently among us—and to remind us, unflinchingly, of the New Year's Eves we had shared before, with special dinners and noisemakers, each of us struggling to stay awake until midnight so we could all hug and kiss and welcome in the new year together. I always got particularly excited about it—I liked that universality, the lack of Christmas-like barri-ers and the glamour that seemed to come with champagne toasts and noisemakers and dressing up and midnight, al-though the closest I had ever gotten to such an adult bash was in Miami Beach one year, when Mom and Dad had gone off to a hotel for a couple of nights and left Adam and me with Grandma and Grandpa. Grandma Lil had awakened me, as promised, at eleven forty-five, so that I could come and groggily join her at the party she had made. I was only half awake but I remember being excited over the handful of blue-haired snowbird couples who filled her living room with warmth and happiness, sipping scotch out of tumblers and eating handfuls of pistachios and Andes mints out of small blown-glass bowls. Now, with Adam gone, I simply feared the approaching December thirty-first, imagining a scene in which we'd all sit and watch the ball drop glumly, my mom crying as I turned up the volume, pretending none of it was happening. But that night my mother got off the phone and announced her big idea.

"Beth, how would you like to do something really special for New Year's Eve this year?" she asked me, standing in the doorway between the kitchen and the family room, raising her voice to be heard over the commercials that blared before my show, *The Facts of Life*, returned to the screen. She held a dish towel in her hands, and I heard the dishwasher kick on behind her as she finished up the nightly post-dinner routine that my dad and I generally avoided. My dad was in his chair, across the room, his head buried in that day's newspaper, but he put it down on his lap at her question and grinned. Clearly, they had already discussed the plan—the thought of which filled me with sweet relief, whatever it was.

"Yes! Please!" I told her. "What would we do?"

She got a gentle smile on her face and said, "I thought we'd go to upstate New York, to a resort in the Catskills. They have a New Year's Eve special that I found in the paper."

I had no idea what the Catskills were all about, just vague memories of my mom's stories about going up there for parts of the summer when she was a girl, staying in a big, crowded old house with her mom and aunts and swimming in a lake. She said we'd go for the weekend to a place called Kutsher's Country Club, the name of which—"country club"—filled me with visions of fancy meals, lavish quarters, golf carts, and an all-out black-tie affair on the big night.

"So we'd go away overnight?" I asked, surprised that they would spring on such an expense, when the only time we usually went for overnights was at Christmastime, when we went to Miami, and sometimes during Easter break, when we visited my dad's cousins, the Bernankes, in their big Southern house in Dillon, South Carolina, and had a family Passover seder that often overlapped with my birthday, bringing a thickly iced cake with candles into the joyous mix.

"*Two* nights!" my mom said, pleased with herself, adding that there would be plenty to do during the day—sledding and ice-skating and maybe some skiing lessons, or if it's too cold outside, there were indoor activities like swimming in the heated pool or makeup classes for the women—and that nighttime would be a slew of performers and delicious banquets and holiday parties.

"Makeup class!" I exclaimed, imagining myself made over, with long, dark eyelashes and a sweep of lipstick. "I want to go to the makeup class!"

They laughed, and my dad rolled his eyes playfully. "So it sounds like a good idea, right?" he said.

"Yes!" I said, filled with hope.

~

The drive up was like entering another land—one without interstates or fast-food chains, and with a seemingly endless supply of Orthodox Jews, whose dark, formal dress belied the casual farms and fields and old, weather-worn houses. I asked my father to stop the car so I could snap a photo of a place that advertised KOSHER PIZZA, because I'd never seen those two words together and it seemed like an oxymoron, or at least an amusing curiosity, and when I got out of the car at the edge of the empty two-lane road I could smell a faint hint of cow manure under the icy-clean country air, which was much more bracing than it had ever felt at home. Then I was back in the warm, cozy confines of our Citation, surrounded by magazines and crossword puzzles and school books that I hadn't cracked and a pillow from my bed, all piled in for the three-hour drive north. It was our first road trip, albeit a short one, with just the three of us, and it was both relieving and terrible to have the entire backseat to myself.

We reached Monticello and pulled into the resort's parking lot just as the late afternoon's bright sun was starting to slip behind the mass of bare trees that surrounded the property, and while my dad checked us in at the front desk I watched the swirl of people move through the lobby from all sides, some wearing swimsuits and toting towels, others in parkas and bulky boots. I tried but couldn't quite picture myself in the mix. I had a nagging feeling of being an outsider here—of being at a camp where everyone already knows each other from years before and of being the new kid, with my parents just as uninitiated as me—and I decided I wouldn't try to blend in until after we'd gone to our room and then gotten the lay of the land.

"Beth, you are in for a treat tonight!" my mom said, coming toward me from the front desk, a slip of paper in her hand. "Rita Moreno is performing in the main concert hall. She's such a talent! You'll love her."

"Who's she?"

"She's been in lots of movies, but to you she's the woman from *The Electric Company*," she said. "She's the one who screams, 'Hey you guys!' at the beginning."

"Cool," I said, buoyed by the fact that she was, at least, a famous TV star whom I would recognize.

Our room was big but pretty standard, with two double beds covered with striped bedspreads, dark-wood furniture, a TV, and some big windows that looked out onto a frozen, snow-free courtyard. I picked a bed and flopped down on it and started reading the special holiday schedule that they'd given us at check-in. It was sort of camp-like—or how I'd imagined camp to be, since I'd always refused to attend, partly out of homesickness but also because I was perfectly content with going to the beach club every day—with scheduled group meals in the dining room, lots of unstructured time with various activity options and nighttime parties and performances galore, culminating with the big New Year's Eve ball tomorrow night. I was most looking forward to that, because it seemed like it would be glamorous, and I had brought the perfect new outfit: black trousers and black flats with a white tuxedo-top blouse that had a black bib sewn right into its front. I got up and pulled it out of my suitcase and hung it up on one of the heavy wooden hangers in the closet, but as I did it I felt an uneasiness creep into me. It was the thick sadness I'd hoped to keep at bay for the three days we'd be gone, but there it was, stubbornly settling over my chest, as usual.

"Hey, Beth, let's go exploring," my dad said, with manufactured excitement in his eyes. "I want to see what the grounds are like."

I put on an extra layer for the penetrating cold that awaited us with the sinking sun and then bundled up. We left my mom behind to settle in and went roaming about, first poking our heads into the heated pool area, which was too steamy to let us stay for more than a minute. My dad seemed happy. "Wow, Olympic-size," he noted. "I'll have to do my laps in the morning."

Next we peeked into the main dining room, where hushed staffers were moving about in preparation for the start of dinner hour, moving chairs and setting tables and putting huge metal steam trays into place over blue glowing sternos. "Should be good food here," my dad said, raising his eyebrows up and down a few times like he does when he is impressed with either food or beauty, "since it's Jewish." He was way too obsessed with what was Jewish and what was goy in this world. If anything exciting ever happened—in sports, politics, entertainment, you name it—my dad would get absurdly thrilled if the person in question was Jewish. He'd tell the story of the person's accomplishment and then he'd wait a beat for dramatic effect and say, "And you know what? *Jewish.* How about that?" I would roll my eyes, abashed by his pride, and say, "So what?" and leave the room in exasperation.

We headed outside where the chilly air was refreshing and clean, but not quite freezing enough, I realized, for what was supposed to be a place to ski and ice skate and go sledding. We followed the map to the practice ski trails, but found abandoned hills of brown, matted grass. "Well, we don't ski anyway," my dad said with a shrug. I suggested we go and check out the ice-skating pond, which I was looking forward to trying out in the morning. But when we arrived we saw that it was not even partially frozen—just a small, pitiful circle of slate gray water, rippling slightly in the chilly, late-day breeze. I posed so my dad could take a photo of the moment, and put a sort of "What can you do?" expression on my face, mashing my hands into my pockets.

The three of us got dressed for dinner, heading to the group dining room and settling in at a long, rectangular table with a couple of other families. I suppose we chitchatted with them over our plates of salad and brisket and green beans and potatoes, but I can't remember much of anything about that evening—not even about Rita Moreno's show, which followed our meal and thrilled my mom. The only part I'm certain of is what happened after her performance, outside of the stage door, where we all waited with a small clutch of fans to meet her and photograph her and get her autograph, and where my mom broke down in front of her.

When she swept out of the stage door and into the harsh fluorescent glare of the hallway where we waited, Rita Moreno looked gorgeous, with matte skin that was rosy with a post-performance glow. Her stage makeup had been removed, except for the thick black mascara that coated her lashes and a mild slash of brownish lipstick that gave her mouth a fresh sheen. Her hair was pulled back into a clip, though springy curls escaped all around her face, and she wore a chic black sweater and slacks, and looked absolutely pleased to find a handful of fans awaiting her.

We waited until a family in front of us posed next to her for photos, had her autograph a big black-and-white photo, and told her how much they adored her show. Then it was our turn. My mother stepped right up and took her hand, and leaned into her in a needy way that I'd seen many times before. It made my stomach drop.

"I have been a fan for a long time, and I was so touched by your performance," she told her, eyes getting dangerously misty. "I lost my son just a few months ago—he was only seven—and this is our first New Year's Eve without him, and I wanted to have a special time for my daughter here, my dear Beth." She pulled me toward her and I was mortified. I looked to my father for help but he only stared at the floor. "I want to thank you for giving us a special night." Rita Moreno looked a bit confused but was ultimately very kind, giving my mom a hug and looking genuinely sympathetic. Then she took my hand and squeezed it and looked at me deeply.

"I loved you on *The Electric Company*," I told her. Then my mom gently placed me next to her and stood back, and snapped our photo. I have it still, and when I look at it now it's like I was superimposed into the frame, smiling so that my braces showed, my awkwardly angled hair frizzing at its edges. I barely remember the moment, but have this solid evidence tucked away in a photo album with other surreal images from the weekend: my mom and dad posing at the New Year's Eve ball, all dressed up but looking so stiff in their party clothes, red cardboard "1983" hats plastered with scarlet feathers and perched atop their heads; a grown man dressed as Baby New Year, diapered and weird, sitting in a crib, with another guy his same age but in a robe and fake white beard as Old Man New Year standing beside him; me, in my cherished tuxedo outfit, a thin belt cinched around my skinny middle and a paper noisemaker stuck between my lips. Armed with all the props of a party, we look like we should be having a blast.

I no longer remember how we passed our afternoons there, only the nights. And at the New Year's Eve party we arrived at the crowded, festooned dining room to learn that there was a separate seating area for kids and teens, and that's where I was supposed to be. It was presented like a special treat, like, Wow kids! Don't worry about having your parents cramp your style at this place, we've got a seriously happening soiree planned for you all! The thought made me homesick.

"Can't I just sit at your table?" I pleaded. My parents realized that if I sat there it would displace someone else. Plus, I would be the only kid in that part of the room, and I understood that it just wouldn't be appropriate. "It's OK," I said. "I'll go with the strangers."

I wandered into the area reserved for me and the other kids and found my table. I was not interested in these people, in making new friends, in trying to think of something to say, in leaving my parents all alone in the other room on the most important night of the year. I settled into my seat and began to pick at the salad that was waiting for me. There was a boy across the table from me and no one else yet, until a dark-eyed girl in a red sweater and black skirt came along.

"Hello," she said, slipping into the seat beside me. "Happy New Year." She had an accent and I thought it was Russian.

"Happy New Year," I replied. She told me her name was Anna, and that she'd come with her parents from Brooklyn—a mystery to me, and the place where my cousins lived, but where we had never visited—and that only a year before, they had emigrated from the Soviet Union. I told her about the other Soviet Jewish families I knew, who had recently joined our temple, and that we lived in New Jersey. Though our conversation quickly became stilted, I decided I'd latch on to her for the evening. We bumbled through dinner together, trying to find reasons to bond but never quite hitting on any; we didn't watch the same TV shows, didn't like the same music, barely spoke the same language. But she, I could sense, was desperate too. The gaggle of teenage boys at our table asked our names and where we were from, and then told us theirs, and that they had all come in a group, with their families, from Long Island, which was another place of mystery to me. Just after dessert was served—a slice of multi-colored spumoni topped with a swirl of whipped cream—they all hopped up from the table and made a beeline toward the dance floor, which sat, practically empty, at the far end of our dining room.

"Come on!" one of them called back to us. "It's the Clash!"

I wanted my ice cream and so hastily polished off half of it, then ran with Anna to join what had become a mob of all the kids in the room. "Rock the Casbah" was blaring, followed by "Stray Cat Strut," and we joined the fray, a bit timidly, and then let ourselves get tossed into the center of the undulating crowd. I kept thinking: This should be fun. This should be awesome. Why doesn't it feel that way? Why doesn't it feel like anything at all?

It had gotten late, and I saw my parents hovering with some other adults several paces away from the dance floor. They waved when I caught sight of them, and my mom pointed to her watch and I realized it was just before midnight. I ran to them, first turning to wave a quick goodbye to whatever random teens danced around me, just to show them that I had made friends.

"Well you look like you're having fun!" my mom beamed. I wish I could've left right then, gone back to the room with them, been asleep before the big moment.

"Yeah, everyone's really cool," I said. My dad pulled me into him for a hug, and then I heard everyone in the place doing the count down—"Five! Four! Three! Two! One!"—and then a huge and hearty "Happy New Year!" and "Auld Lang Syne," filling the speakers. They both hugged me, and I felt my mom's shoulders bounce up and down twice, fast, and I knew it meant that she was crying. I peeked toward her face just to make sure, and saw that she was—proof that nothing had been changed by this trip after all.

"Happy 1983," I told them, then took the paper noisemaker out of her tight grip and blew it. "1983! Can you believe it?" They smiled sadly, and I thought of the year before, when we went out for Chinese food and then came home and watched the ball drop and Adam fell asleep by eleven. I remembered how good it had felt to be in the house, cozy, and I began looking forward to leaving the next morning, even though it would only be the three of us heading home.

Chapter Twenty-One

I DON'T know what I must have been thinking that late afternoon, the skies still gilded and the top layer of warm air peeling back to reveal a surprising crispness on that luscious late-spring day, as I made my way over to the Sickels' house. I was thirteen—an adult, according to Jewish beliefs. I had just gotten home from my Bat Mitzvah, the big event finally come and gone, and before even changing out of my beloved frilly outfit—the navy skirt swarmed with pink roses and edged with white satin piping, the high-collared blouse a pure-white confection of lace and puffy sleeves—I announced that I was going to see Mrs. Sickel, and left the house, clomping across the driveway towards the neighbor's side lawn in my still-stiff ballet flats, moving like a homing pigeon towards Kristin's house, the place I felt drawn to again and again in the months after the accident. Though I went less frequently

than I did that first summer, occasional visits there still comforted me.

"Beth," my mother called out after me, standing in the
front doorway and still glowing and impossibly happy from
the long afternoon party, "are you sure that's a good idea?"

"Of course!" I said, looking back at her but still scuttling
down the driveway. "I want to tell her about the day."

"OK," I barely heard her say. "But be back soon! All your
relatives will be here for the evening." Grandma Ruth was already at the house, and I heard her hiss to my mom, "Where
is she *going?*" just before I was out of earshot.

I somehow believed that Mrs. Sickel really wanted to see
me. In my head she was the new Kristin—she was cooler and
funnier than Tracy and she seemed to genuinely like to see
me when I appeared—and Kristin would have wanted to
know all about my Bat Mitzvah and so therefore, I figured,
her mother would too. She hadn't shown up, though, sending
Mr. Sickel and Tracy alone. Tracy had been seated with all
the kids, wearing a starchy blue sailor dress and white knee
socks with Mary Janes and a ribbon in her hair, which was in
a fresh, neatly brushed bowl cut. She had played all the
games—musical chairs, Coke-and-Pepsi, limbo—right along
with everyone else, even though she didn't know many of my
friends. Mr. Sickel had sat at a table with some other neighbors and beach-club couples, although every time I caught
sight of him he was sitting rigidly in his blue-gray suit and tie,
looking poker faced and lonesome, and I wished that Mrs.
Sickel had been there with him, even though Mr. Sickel had
apologized to me softly near the entrance of the social hall,
explaining to me that it was "just too hard" for her to come. It
was the first I'd ever heard of her having a difficult time with
her grief—she'd always put on such a show for me—and part
of me didn't quite believe it.

For me, the day had meant everything—not only because I'd get to be the star, but because I knew it meant that my parents would be happy, or at least have to appear to be happy, for the afternoon and evening, and maybe throughout the entire weekend.

My Bat Mitzvah was just ten months after the accident. My parents had discussed putting it off for a while, but then had a change of heart, because they wanted life to become normal for me as quickly as possible. And I was extremely ready for that. I proceeded toward the big day as if there were no missing brother or friend, as if nobody would have mixed feelings about a celebration, as if the near one-hundred-percent response rate among invited guests would have happened anyway. To me this was not a day to get through—it was a day of genuine happiness to be savored.

I threw myself into the preparation like I never had with anything before—never missing a Torah lesson with the rabbi, practicing at home in my room and deciding early on that I wanted to chant both my Torah and haftara portions, even though such tradition had never been followed in our Reform temple before. I turned the whole thing into a sort of show, and I wanted to be dazzlingly talented and at ease in front of everyone I knew and loved.

I had practiced my chanting with Cantor Suzanne—a pretty, strong, black-haired woman with a surprisingly bohemian vibe, who sang with such passion at Sabbath services that she'd close her eyes and look somewhere between tears and ecstasy and rock herself gently, the silky fabric of her long black robe making a swishing sound as it brushed back and forth over the tops of her sandals. To supplement our lessons she ordered me a set of cassette tapes, which had a deep man's voice chanting my parts, and I played them over and over again on the tape recorder. I learned to read the chanting markers over the Hebrew—the little squiggles and dashes that indicated a trill or a dip or long-held note—and I looked toward them as guides as I held my little pink rectangular practice books in my hands each night in my bedroom.

It was also the look of the event, though—the design of the social hall, the color scheme, the style of my dress—that held my attention. My mom threw herself into it too. It must have been a great distraction. We picked out the invitations together, hunched over albums and albums of samples in the cramped basement office of a stationery company in Long Branch, near the florist, Van Brunt, that would take care of our rose-and-daisy bouquets attached to huge clusters of helium-filled pink and purple balloons that were to float directly above each table. The invitations were cream sheets of parchment paper engraved with pink cursive and flowers and a tangle of vines in each corner, and when the custom-printed stack arrived we picked up the thick and satisfying brick of paper, brought it home, and sat and sent them all out together, complete with the pre-stamped response cards and that thin sheet of vellum slipped into each envelope, which I painstakingly hand addressed in hot pink calligraphy.

I loved finding those response cards in the mail—even more so than the flood of sympathy cards that had come throughout the previous summer and fall. The response cards were brighter, more hopeful, evidence of the reality that we were moving on. With each one we received I tore into it to see who had signed it and what they had written, and then imagined whomever it was out in the congregation, watching me as I chanted, and then dancing the hora with me in the social hall. I couldn't wait to have a day that was all for me—with no mourning or sobbing or invoking of losses. I couldn't wait to be the center of attention.

Our core family members from my dad's side all flew into town two nights early (my mother's family was scattered all around New Jersey still), and trickled by for visits before checking in to their hotel. I was in heaven, with Grandma Lil and Grandpa Norman and Essie and Sol all flying up from Miami, and the Bernankes from South Carolina—Aunt Rita and Uncle Mort and Mindy and Marc, all of whom I could not get enough of, with their sugary Southern accents and the way they made me feel as if I were the most special person in the room. Also arriving that night was my great aunt Doris, the eighty-year-old grande dame of my dad's side of the family, with snow-white hair and thick glasses and a cropped fur jacket that I coveted whenever she'd wear it on cool Miami nights, exiting the lobby of her grand waterfront condo and slipping into our rental car for a dinner excursion and smelling of rose petals, letting me hold her soft, papery hands, which felt like velvet in my own.

"Such a darling girl," she would say, looking deep into my eyes. "Such a darling."

When everyone left our house that first night, though, I began to feel guilty. Adam was missing it all, and Kristin wouldn't be among my friends at the Bat Mitzvah, and yet here I was basking in the attention—thrilled by it—and not feeling properly sad. I picked up a book that I'd been saving—*Tiger Eyes* by Judy Blume, her latest, and the only one I hadn't read yet—settled onto my bed and began reading it. I knew it was about death, the death of a girl's father, whose name was Adam, and I thought it could make me cry. Luckily, there was also a little brother in the story, a seven-year-old, and so it hit even closer to home than I'd imagined it would. It made me sad and weepy, and thus satisfied, and I read it deep into the evening, even after my parents poked their heads in to say goodnight and I switched from sad to over-joyed for them, and they closed my door behind them and went into their room and turned out the lights. I finally put it down and fell asleep, but went right back to the pages in the early morning, finishing it just in time to head to the mall with my mother for our manicures, filled with perfect levels of both grief and joy.

At night we hosted a dinner for all the relatives who were in town. My mom put out platters of carved turkey and sliced cheeses and little dishes of black olives and sweet, sliced pickles. For decoration she had bouquets of bright yellow for-sythia stems, picked from the newly in-bloom bushes along the side of the house, and one particular item that made my temples throb: a white baby's bowl-and-dish set, imprinted with whimsical Peter Rabbit images.

"It was a gift from a neighbor when you were born," my mom told me, smiling as she set up the dish set on the kitchen counter, near the coffeemaker, just before guests started to arrive. She looked pleased with herself that she had thought of this detail—something from my babyhood to juxtapose with my burgeoning womanhood.

"Are you sure that was mine?" I asked her, thrown. I knew for certain that it had been given to Adam not long after his arrival. I remembered helping to open the box, waving the bowl in front of his elfin face, handing each piece to my mom so that she could put them away in the cabinet, since "good" dishes and silverware and goblets were not to be used in our house, but stored away and protected.

"Of course I'm sure," she said. "They were given to you by a neighbor, though I can't remember who it was."

It was the Reeds, I thought of saying. It was when the Reeds still lived next door, after they had adopted their own baby, and named him Jeffrey, and had gotten that yapping little beagle that made Adam cry. But I just said, "OK. It's cute," and left it at that, and went into my room to press the tears back into my head.

Months earlier I had gone to set the table for dinner, grabbing a stack of three plates from the cupboard over the toaster oven. I had to make a conscious effort to not grab four—though I did by accident one time that first summer, which flooded my mom's face with such horror and pity that I made sure to never do it again. So I grabbed three and set them down, and was filled with nostalgia when I saw that one of them, made of white plastic, was made by me at age eight or so. I'd done it through a craft kit that my mom had ordered—draw pictures with markers on special round slips of paper, mail them in to the company, and receive plates magically bearing those images just a few weeks later in the mail—and the stick-figure image I'd drawn was of myself, wearing a purple poncho, standing in the rain.

"Oh I remember those!" my dad said, taking his seat at the table with one eye on the six o'clock news.

"Cute," said my mom, placing a halved grapefruit in a pastel-colored Tupperware bowl at each of our places.

The third plate, though, shocked me. It was one made by Adam, bright and alive, the shakily drawn faces of the four of us, stick legs poking out from where our necks should have been, pulsing with his life force. We all fell silent for a second, and then my mom put her hand over her mouth. My father whispered, "Oh, jeez. Oh, yeah." And I put the plate back in the cabinet, grabbing a blank olive-green one instead. The next day I went to look for the plate, to study it, to hoard it in my room. But someone had beaten me to it. It was gone.

My Bat Mitzvah day began as a blur. I barely remember the service—just nailing my chants and seeing the faces of everyone I loved beaming up at me, and the rabbi and cantor giving me special, proud, encouraging looks. I knew the air was heavy with emotion. I realized that the tears in people's eyes would not have been of quite the same quality—and may not have been there at all, for some—if the accident had never happened. But this was only a pinprick of thought in the farthest reaches of my mind, and one that I wouldn't give any direct attention to, because to do so would ruin my moment, and confirm that, once the day ended, things surely would go back to the muted gray, the dreaded loneliness of before. So I slipped back into that comfortable state of denial, and decided to take all the adulation as something pure, something unaffected by grief. I stuck to it even in my speech, which had a heady theme of change, and chose to not add a part about "people who could not be with us today," because I just didn't want to. I wondered, later, if people found it odd, but I didn't dwell on it for long.

The reception was held in the temple's social hall, a grim, character-starved box of a room with cinder-block walls and faux parquet floors, separated from the sanctuary by a wall that collapsed like an accordion to make one massive space on the High Holidays, when every temple member showed up for at least a few hours, and a sea of gold bridge chairs was necessary to accommodate all the suddenly religious among us. Using the social hall was much cheaper than renting a banquet hall, and, we reasoned, it made sense to walk from the staid sanctuary into the lobby and then right around to the other side of the collapsible wall into a room that had housed plenty of Bat Mitzvahs and weddings in its day.

We transformed it with flower arrangements for each table—explosions of pink roses and fat daisies and tall reeds of purple statice and, tied to the center of each, the burst of balloons. We hung pink crepe paper streamers and a wide sheet of pink oak tag that had seemed massive in the store but which became dwarfed after we'd taped it to the wall; I had fashioned it into an autograph and graffiti board by drawing a facade of bricks with purple marker and writing GRAFFITI WALL in big bubble letters across the top, and then attaching string to the purple marker and tying it to the corner.

The long buffet table was a cornucopia of beef-tenderloin medallions and salad and steaming trays of whipped potatoes, the servers dressed in crisp white shirts with black vests and slacks, as in a fancy restaurant. My friends were seated all around me at one long table, and we spent much of the time playing musical chairs and limbo, and dancing to the music of Tuvia Zimber, a thin, bushy-bearded guy with a definite hint of body odor who picked and banged at his electric keyboard like a one-man klezmer band. We had found him on a recent foray into the city, when we'd gone to eat at Sammy's Roumanian Steakhouse on the Lower East Side, a favorite with suburban Jews, where small pitchers of thick yellow *schmaltz* sat on tables next to plates of garlicky skirt steak and broiled chicken and egg creams, while across the street in Sara Roosevelt Park, junkies wandered like emaciated shadows, glaring at us and our full bellies as we hailed a cab to head back to Penn Station at the end of the night.

The whole time we ate at Sammy's, Tuvia Zimber had stabbed at his electric piano, playing songs like "Hava Nagila" and "Siman Tov" along with rollicking klezmer pieces. My mother just loved him, delighting in his deadpan expression and fancy finger work and, after a few phone calls to track him down, he agreed to come to Jersey to play my party, where he bolstered his musical repertoire with '80s Bat Mitzvah standards like "Celebration" and "Eye of the Tiger," as well as verbal cues for games and candle lightings.

In between all the dancing and game playing, I was greeted by a near constant stream of relatives and friends of my parents, who gave me long, hard hugs and fat checks. They all helped hold up the illusion of the happy day for me—just as Dad did when he got a bit tipsy and red-faced, and laughed and waved when he let a group of men lift him up on a metal bridge chair and carry him around the dance floor high above their heads, exposing the slightest bit of hairy leg above each falling-down dress sock, and throwing his diagonally striped tie just a bit off-kilter. He looked so happy, so truly glowing and satisfied and proud that I had believed right then, in the moment, that the simple fact of me looking gawkily pretty and reading Hebrew, had lifted my father out of his sadness and grief and made our family whole and happy and safe for just one day.

I believed it when I saw my mother, too, who was beaming and sweet in her cornflower-blue dress. And my grandparents, posing for photos and squeezing me with what felt clearly like joy to my naive and lanky self, and various cousins lighting baton-length candles on my cake and posing stiffly for the photographer as they pressed their lips into my cheek and wrapped their hands around my small arms. My friends played along too. Scott danced with me, and even managed a tolerant, brace-face grin as the photographer took several shots of us, just as I had instructed him to do.

~

It was only as I hurried across the front lawn and onto the porch and rapped lightly on the Sickels' screen door that it occurred to me I might not be the most welcome person on this day—that maybe Mrs. Sickel *was* having a difficult time, and that if staying away from my Bat Mitzvah and all those other still-living thirteen-year-olds was what she needed to do, then seeing me in my Gunne Sax blouse, practically out of breath with excitement, was possibly not what she wanted. But I realized it all too late, when I had already heard the light footsteps on the way to answer my knock at the door.

"Oh, Beth, hello," she said, sweetly but wearily, pushing the door open to welcome me in. I stepped comfortably into the foyer as usual, taking in the heavy, ever-present scent of laundry and the drawn curtains in the living room. The house felt different that day, and I realized, with disquiet, what it was just as her tears started: Mrs. Sickel was not hiding her grief.

"I just couldn't come, Beth," she told me, removing her glasses to wipe at her eyes. "I'm so sorry. I just couldn't do it." I put my hand on her arm to let her know that it was OK, and was surprised when she pulled me to her, embracing me and crying freely. I started crying then too, and we stood there, as the last drops of daylight filtered in on us through the screen door, sobbing with each other like never before over our shared loss. I loved her so much right then and missed Kristin intensely, finally feeling her absence from the day. We eventually pulled away from each other. Sniffling and wiping at her eyes, Mrs. Sickel excused herself to get us some tissues, which we blew into and balled up before looking into each other's eyes. And then she said, "So please, tell me about the day already, will you?" and led me into the living room, where we sat together on the bench of their organ—one of those complex, many-layered keyboards with various pedals and buttons that produced samba, polka, or waltz beats on demand. Kristin had been thrilled when they purchased it not long before she died, and we'd sat together on this very bench, banging out polka versions of "Heart and Soul" or "Chopsticks" with each other, or as I played my latest piece from piano lessons—"Für Elise" or "Solfegietto"—as she sat and watched in appreciation.

"I love your outfit, by the way," Mrs. Sickel said to me. "Stand up and twirl around for me." I did, somewhat awkwardly, and then sat back down with her, telling her about the food and the dancing and my chanting during the service. "Oh, and I danced with Scott!" I blurted out, immediately sorry that I had; he was more Kristin's than he ever was mine, and it was probably just too close of a reminder in that moment. But she played it right and humored me, just like her usual self.

"Really?" she said. "Did you kiss him too?"

"No," I told her, relieved that Kristin still had one up on me. "No, we definitely didn't kiss. And I think he just danced with me out of pity or something."

"Yeah, probably!" she said, teasingly, though it stung. I blinked back a fresh round of tears and swallowed the lump in my throat, and wondered where Tracy and her dad were. The house was silent.

"Well, I should probably get back," I told her. "My relatives are all coming over soon."

"Yes, get outta here already!" she said, standing up with me and walking me to the door. "But thanks for coming to visit. And I'm sorry again for not being there."

I hugged her again. "I understand," I told her. "It's really OK."

Then I stepped out into the indigo twilight and headed down their front path, my new shoes clack-clacking again on the cement. As I made my way home to my own family, across their side lawn, past Kristin's old playhouse and through the neighbor's oak-shrouded yard, my heart felt heavy with a realization: I would not be going over there anymore. I knew it for sure with a mix of both pain and relief. It was time for me to move on.

Chapter Twenty-Two

Fʀᴏᴍ the football field I could barely make out my parents—small, still silhouettes up in the bleachers, behind the blaring white lights of the game. It was halftime, and I was dancing with the five other baton twirlers and the whole cheerleading squad to "The Horse" as the high school marching band played it, raising my arms and lifting my knees, one at a time, as I hopped up and then spun around, catching a glimpse of the much-more-crowded, festive bleachers on the other side of the field each time I turned. Though our games were usually on Saturday afternoons, this one was an away game, at Shore Regional, and they held theirs on Friday nights, which added an air of excitement to the weekly ritual.

I don't quite know why I became a baton twirler my freshman year—probably the same reason I'd soon become a spiky-haired glam-rock groupie, an alternative-rock drama-club freak, and, eventually, a Deadhead: all desperate, fickle attempts to find where I belonged, to figure out who I was. I seemed to always be trying on and casting off personas during those years—way more than any of my peers seemed to be doing.

Twirling was cool, though—more tough-girl than being a cheerleader. Plus it required a bit of rhythm and grace, skills I had worked on in ballet all those years, and the outfits were sexy—black sleeveless bodysuits with high necks and three V-shaped rows of silky white fringe pouring down the front. We wore them with nude hose and fat white well-polished boots that we topped with homemade fluffy pom-poms of black and gold yarn. Our captain was Stacy, a skinny, apple-cheeked girl with braces and huge breasts and brown hair brushed back into fat wings who dated a beautiful blond football player named George. Alyssa, Kristin's next-door neighbor, was on the team too, which drew us even closer together.

My parents supported my random venture, coming to as many games as they could, standing in the bleachers and taking photos of me from too far away, creating roll after roll of shots that had me and my teammates as little, scantily-clad figures, barely discernable from one another, peppering the massive field like a flock of gulls on a wide and empty beach.

"Did you see Dan when he ran off the field before?" Alyssa leaned toward me as the song ended, flashing me her metal-mouth grin. "Such a hunk!" Dan McGuinness was a walking cliché—captain of the football team, tall and blond and built, and dating the most popular cheerleader on the squad. We couldn't help but fawn.

I raised my eyebrows and nodded in agreement before Stacy blew her whistle and picked up her baton, holding it in the crook of her right arm as she stuck her hands on her hips and began marching in place. We all followed suit, and the band—a gangly, motley crew of mostly older kids whose names I didn't know—started bleating out the intro to "Sea of Love," my favorite song in the repertoire. The brass section blared and we did our steps and our twirls, and I exaggerated every movement, feeling alive and free and in the spotlight. Out in the bleachers I saw a camera flash and thought that it was probably my father, taking more photos that wouldn't really look like anything. Still, I smiled big for him, and made sure to point my toes each time I lifted my feet to march.

Things had started feeling both better and worse that year. Better because the accident was farther away than ever, and because Mom didn't burst into unexpected tears as frequently. Also because I was finally out of the junior high school—where everyone knew who I was and what I had lost, and where Kristin's spirit had never stopped inhabiting the halls—and into the big regional high school, where I could find new friends and begin to reinvent myself. Worse, though, because it wasn't far away enough: Mom still cried and often seemed lost in sad thoughts, which annoyed me and made me constantly dread the moment that she might totally fall apart again. It felt so stupid to me, still grieving after two whole years—especially since I had made the conscious decision to put it all behind me back in June, right after my eighth-grade graduation.

Until then, though, I had dramatized every milestone. Like Adam's eighth birthday, in the November after he died, which my mom had quietly acknowledged that morning. "It's your brother's birthday today, you know," she said. Of course I had known it; I had awakened that morning thinking about it, and that night I sang to him quietly, while sitting in my room and clutching a flimsy postcard from Mr. Steak, which had come a week before, addressed to Adam, inviting him to come in for his free birthday meal. I had snagged it in my daily mail-grabbing ritual and squirreled it away for the macabre occasion.

Later came eighth-grade graduation for the class that Kristin would have been in. I don't remember how I convinced my mom that I had to be there, but there I was, sitting near the back of the room. The ceremony was held at the Post Theater on our town's army base, Fort Monmouth, because it was classier than the stuffy cafeteria filled with folding chairs would have been. My eyes welled up when the class sang the theme from *Ice Castles*, and my cheeks flushed when the principal, Mr. Danielson, announced that there would be a new award instituted that year, presented to two outstanding, well-rounded students: the Kristin Sickel Memorial Award. I don't remember who won it (though I did, predictably, the following year), just that its existence floored me. But besides that the ceremony was anticlimactic and depressing, proving once and for all that Kristin was gone, and that all of her classmates were growing up and moving on without her.

A year later, at my own eighth-grade graduation, I gave the farewell address before the two hundred kids in my graduating class.

"As we each leave here tonight to enter high school, we will strive to become more independent—facing new challenges, taking advantage of all life has to offer, and thinking more about our futures, each contributing something to the world in our own way," I said in my speech. I had been chosen to speak due to a combination of my straight As and, most likely, pity—just like when I had won the sand-castle contest with Tracy, and the talent show earlier that year, singing "Think of Laura," a cheesy, light-rock Christopher Cross

song popularized on *General Hospital* when Laura Spencer was
presumed to be dead after being kidnapped by the evil Cas-
sadines. I'd sung it with tears in my eyes, for Kristin, and
every teacher in that school knew it. Nancy, who belted the
perennial favorite "Maybe" from *Annie,* in near-perfect pitch,
was jealous. But how could I not have won?

I stood at the podium wearing a high-necked, powder-
blue Gunne Sax dress exactly like Nancy's white one. We
both wore ivory hose and pastel ballet flats. My hair was short
and permed into a thicket of curls, and I wore brown mascara
and pink lip gloss. After my speech I stood onstage with the
choir and sang "We've Only Just Begun" and every time we
returned to that chorus—"We've only just begun . . . to live"—
tears leaked down my face because I thought about how Kristin had only just begun to live too. I sobbed in Nancy's arms
after we got our diplomas.

"I'm moving on without her now," I told her, wiping black
mascara juice off my cheeks, barely able to explain why I was
such a wreck. "It's like I'm leaving her behind."

I was still wiping my eyes and trying to get a hold of myself when Mom and Dad and Grandma approached me in the
crowd, but they thought I was just being overly dramatic
about graduating. If they knew the real reason for my melt-
down, they never let on. And neither did I.

It had been almost five months since that day, and there I
was in high school, twirling out on the football field as if I
hadn't a care in the world. We all went to sit in the bleachers
when the halftime show ended, twirlers huddling together
a row or two behind the band members in the raw, early-
November air. My parents were right behind us, and as soon
as I finished clambering my way up the aluminum benches,
feeling a stab of vertigo each time I dared to glance down
between those flimsy strips, my mom handed me my latest

favorite possession: my varsity jacket, black with gold trim, with a hood that unzipped down its middle to lay flat across my shoulders, revealing MRHS in big woolly block letters. My name was sewn in cursive on the left breast.

"Put this on before you get a chill!" my mother said to me, wrinkling her brow at my bare arms. Instead of rolling my eyes at her I took it, happily, and could not jam my chilly self inside the cool, quilted lining fast enough. "All that moving must have kept you warm, though," she added. "You looked great out there. All you girls did! I wish I could move like that!" Everyone said thanks and Stacy went with Alyssa to get hot chocolates for us all. Then the lights blared and the band stood up to play and the football players came running back onto the field and I squinted until I saw Bobby, a JV player whom I'd kissed at a party recently. I was wondering whether we were dating or not, and what would constitute such a thing, when I caught an alarming tone and posture coming from my parents over my shoulder.

"Well then you can go without me!" I heard my mother hiss. She was hurling her wounded-accusatory-martyr voice— an angry sort of whisper/yell that sent shivers down my spine—toward my father.

"Oh would you come *on* already?" he pleaded. I stole a quick glance at them, saw my mom's slumped, impenetrable posture and her wet, steely eyes and felt my stomach tighten.

I zipped my jacket and forced my knees up into it, blowing on them and pressing my lips to the thick nylons that encased them. Don't cry, I thought to myself. Do. Not. Cry.

"Beth, come on," my mom called behind me. "The game's almost over. Let's get going."

"The game is *not* almost over!" I snarled, with a bit more anger than I would've liked. "I'm not leaving yet!" The other twirlers were on their feet, engrossed in the action on the field, stomping their boots to the beat of some blaring marching-band rally, probably not hearing a word we were saying. I felt so far away from everyone, so left out, amazed and so disappointed that after two years I could still feel that so much turmoil separated me from everyone else, who would have probably pegged me as happy. The more I had tried to avoid the truth, the more pronounced it had become, like a pebble in my shoe that felt bigger and harder the more I continued to walk on it. Stacy and Alyssa returned then, holding out rectangular cardboard trays stocked with Styrofoam cups of cocoa, and I took one, settling in, showing my mom with my posture that I wasn't going anywhere.

We left as soon as I finished my cocoa, that much I know. What I don't remember anymore is what set her off in the first place—what caused my mom to break down and cry in the car, and my dad to breathe out through his nostrils, exasperated. I know it was something about Adam—probably about her seeing something or someone that reminded her of him, which would've caused her to fall apart, which then would've caused my dad to tell her to stop dwelling on it all, leading to a fight about how it hadn't been long enough to move on and what was wrong with him anyhow?

Whatever it was, it was the breaking of the dam, and the powerful gush it released left me drowning in the backseat, fingering the silky fringe of my uniform and holding sobs in my chest until I felt as if my heart would stop.

When we pulled into the driveway I felt almost as nauseated as I did that first day home from the hospital, when I noticed a new sadness in the gray-brown shingles and saffron shutters. Only tonight it was worse, because I was noticing it all over again, years later, when I had tried so hard to convince myself that the sadness had receded. But at that moment, in the weak ochre glow of the front porch light, I realized it had only grown more massive, more all-encompassing. My mother's cries grew angry and jagged, and she hopped out of the car and slammed the door behind her, getting inside the front door before my father or I could even set foot out of the car.

"Come on, Bethie," my dad said to me, all low and quiet like he was issuing a warning about doomsday. I wrapped a sweaty hand around my thin, icy baton, and stepped out of the car onto the tarred driveway, the weight of my boots suddenly feeling too much for me to lift, so I dragged my feet along as my father pulled open the heavy garage door and held his hand under it while I walked in. It was a running complaint among us that the garage was a horrible mess, but I secretly liked the disarray, found comfort in seeing the lawnmower shoved up against my sand-flecked bellyboard, an ancient wooden croquet set stacked against the rusting blue Zim Zam game and a waist-high stack of newspapers waiting to be brought to the recycling plant. I breathed in the familiar scent of cold must and faint gasoline, hoping it would fortify me for whatever lay inside.

I stepped tentatively into the laundry room—another less-than-organized space, painted in a garish mint green and home to not only the washer and dryer but closets jammed with coats and hats and boots for every conceivable climate. I noticed my mom had dropped her purse, a tightly packed brick of stiff leather, onto the floor. ("What do you *have* in there?" I always asked her, astonished by its heft anytime I'd picked it up to hand it to her, causing her to cluck her tongue and roll her eyes and declare, "My *life!*" which told me nothing.) The house was country quiet and dark, save for the faint emerald glow from the VCR's digital clock in the living room, until my dad flicked on the overhead light in the kitchen. My mom appeared out of the dark recesses of the bedroom hallway, clutching her car keys.

"I'm leaving," she said, barely looking at either of us. Her face was splotchy and her eyes were hard, and she wore jeans and her white Reeboks and a zipped-up sweatshirt. She looked like she was serious.

"Oh would you come on, Deb?" my dad asked, this time with a hint of fear in his voice.

"No, *you* come on!" she said. "I'll see you later." And then she turned away from us and walked toward the front door.

"Where are you *going*!?" I shouted after her with a ferocity so intense my throat burned. The desperation in my voice startled me, and made my mother stop, but only for a second.

"I'm going out," she said flatly. And then she said, "Don't worry about me, Beth. I'll be fine." But the way she said it— like someone who was saying one thing but clearly meaning another—made me worry even more. And it made me furious, too. I stood in the front door, alternately fuming and fretting, and watched as she walked with purpose across the edge of the front yard, got into her car and slammed the door, and then backed swiftly down the driveway, peeling out—the tires made an actual screeching sound—like a pissed-off character in a movie.

I turned away from the door and saw my dad standing there, a wounded look on his face. "Don't worry, Bethie," he said, using the same low voice he had used out in the driveway. "She's just upset."

My throat was so constricted I could barely eke out a sound, but I managed to tell him, "Well she doesn't have to leave!" before rushing to my bedroom to dissolve into a mess of sobs.

She'd felt missing to me in so many ways before that

night, but never so aggressively gone. Usually we just ignored her pain, our pain, the empty chair at the dinner table, the absurdity of calling Adam's room "The office." Usually the truth of our situation didn't explode in our faces this way, because none of us ever let it. I pressed my nose against the window in my room, half expecting to see my mom's car already returning to its spot in our driveway, next to my dad's brown Pinto and the dormant rhododendron bush. But it was silent and dark out there; not even my neighbors across the street, whose geeky son was a year older than me and friends with some guys in the marching band, had returned home from the football game yet.

I cried hot tears as I sat on the edge of my bed and yanked off my boots, dropping each with a thud onto my newly exposed wood floor. My mom had helped me tear up the hot-pink carpet earlier that year, after I'd learned somewhere about the concept of bare-wood floors covered with throw rugs, and how it was a much more chic, grown-up look. We bought a large rag rug in shades of peach and sage and put it down alongside my twin bed, and though it was colder at night than the shag had been, I thought it looked much better.

I stood in front of my full-length mirror and watched myself as I cried. I had watched myself sob in this place so many times, but not so much lately, and I was taken with the way my forehead flooded with redness as I drew my breath in and out. My twirling uniform looked suddenly tacky in my bedroom's light, but I left it on, too exhausted to even wriggle out of it. I sat down on the floor then, alternating between weeping so strongly I was lost in it to short periods of complete calm because I felt a certain kind of peace, just knowing that my frenetic mother was out of the house.

But where could she have gone? And why? I imagined her

racing along Route 35, past The Spot: the traffic light at
the intersection where Route 35 crosses Deal Road, where
the low cement highway divider will forever remain cracked
and crumbled from where our station wagon slammed into it.
Whenever we passed it, which was often, I would be in awe over
the craggy, dirty crevice that our car made in the cement, and
that it never got repaired, and also at how unremarkable an
intersection it was—jughandle, gas station, Foodtown strip
mall. I pictured my mom racing past this, eyes already slits,
sobbing all over again when she sees it and then maniacally
running red lights until she comes to the edge of a cliff and
drives right off of it without slowing, into a rocky, watery abyss.
Of course there was no such landscape anywhere in the entire state of New Jersey. Still, I visualized this scenario over
and over again, working myself into a frenzied panic until,
though it was out of character, I turned to my dad.

When I opened my bedroom door I was struck by the silence in the house. Usually by then my father would have
turned on the television and settled into the couch in front of
the late-night news, keeping one eye on the screen and one
on the *Asbury Park Press*, the unfinished sections from the
morning spread messily across his lap. Instead it was so quiet
I thought he had fallen asleep as I crept along the short, carpeted hallway toward the living room, glancing at the wall of
photos on my way. For as long as I could remember, Adam
and I had figured in equally on that wall, one half for each of
us, the centerpiece on each side being one of those big framed
collages—a black mat cut out with preset spots for about a
dozen photos—filled in with images of us both through the
years. But at the end of that first summer my parents took
down all of Adam's individual pictures and removed the photos from his collage, inexplicably filling the ovals and rectangles back in with old photos of themselves: a sepia-toned

shot of my smiling dad at two, wearing brown overalls and sitting on the sidewalk in front of his father's North Jersey soda shop; a black-and-white head shot of my mom, doe-eyed and long-haired, in high school; a too-far-away photo of my parents on their first trip to Europe, earnestly posing together in front of Buckingham Palace. Only one image of Adam remained. It was in a family photo—me at five, Adam at one, standing with our parents at the edge of the water on Key Biscayne—that they had, for some reason, decided to leave in the collage. We had been visiting my dad's parents on our yearly pilgrimage to Miami and decided to have a day away from them, just the four of us. I remember being thrilled at how empty the beach was, and amazed by the warm shallow stillness of the water, which glowed pale cerulean like something out of a Caribbean fantasy. I gazed into that photo, noting the brightness of Adam's red hair and the light in my mother's eyes, and the way my father had kneeled down next to me, wrapping a strong arm around my small waist. Then I moved along so I could find him.

"Dad?" My voice pierced the gloomy quiet of the house.

He was reading the paper after all, and looked up from it with weariness. "Hi, Bethie," he said glumly.

"What if Mom doesn't come back?" I hadn't expected to blurt out such a thing, planning instead on saying something nasty and blaming. But this is what came out of me, along with a torrent of tears, which horrified me.

"She's going to come back," he said, smiling the tiniest bit as if to prove to me that anything else would be ridiculous. But as he spoke he put his paper aside and got up out of his chair and put his arms around me, pulling me into him as he started to cry—really cry, with noise and deep breaths and wet tears that I felt in my hair and where my bare shoulders poked out of my twirler uniform. "We just miss him so much!" he sobbed.

"We try to go on and be strong, but it's hard sometimes! And your mom, I think, just needed to get away." I continued to hold onto him and to cry, thinking, I am actually crying with my father and not running away. How truly, alarmingly desperate. His crying was so deep, so guttural, almost as intense as his painful moans had been that night in the car. I cringed from the intimacy of the moment, and only let myself languish there for a few moments before pulling away.

"OK, well I'm going to change," I told him, swiping at my eyes and suddenly yearning to end our scene.

"OK," he said. He stood there unmoving, bereft, letting me know with his arms, and the way they hung, still suspended in the air, that I'd torn myself away from him too soon. I briefly considered flinging myself back into his warm chest but didn't do it, and instead returned to my room.

I heard my mom come in about an hour later, when her voice, commingled with my dad's, woke me slowly from a deep and syrupy sleep. I had changed into sweats and dozed off on top of my made bed, with my light on and my R.E.M. tape playing softly, and I hadn't even stirred when the cassette clicked off. My clock radio's face said 11:58. She'd been gone for less than two hours; it had felt like a week. Part of me was so jealous that she got to tear off like that, and I suddenly yearned for my driver's license.

Another part of me began to awaken for the very first time: my rebellious side, my run-for-your-life side. My mom's half-assed yet terrifyingly real flee had stirred something in me, and made me realize that, while getting older may not make the grief hurt any less, it gave one access to the tools that could help facilitate escape a little better—car keys, new friends, even alcohol. I switched off my light and got under the covers, and made a mental note to throw myself into all of it, headlong.

Chapter Twenty-Three

I KNEW I was asking for trouble when I showed up for Sunday school in the same over-the-top outfit that I'd worn to Samantha's party the night before. But I was fifteen and disaffected, and I did it anyway. I had decided on my own to continue Sunday school past my Bat Mitzvah so I could have my Reform-Jew confirmation. But somewhere between thirteen and that day I'd turned hard and resentful.

"Beth, can I please speak to you out in the lobby?" It was the cantor, Suzanne, her black curly hair shorn into a mullet and topped with a somehow-hip, embroidered yarmulke. She didn't wear her robe for teaching choir, like she did during Sabbath services, but she always looked like an eclectic mix of together and artsy—like that day's outfit of a prairie skirt paired with a blazer, and odd, furry little ankle boots. I followed her out of the sanctuary, shaky on my spiked heels because of the hangover that I just couldn't get past. When we were out in the empty, gold-carpeted lobby, she looked me up and down and frowned.

"Beth," she said, looking me searchingly in the eyes, "This is not an appropriate outfit to wear in the sanctuary. I think you know that." Suzanne gestured to my bare belly, which was revealed in a three-inch space between my cropped, sleeveless black sweater and my skin-tight white cotton pants that were covered with a dizzying black pattern that looked like a blurry version of Chinese script. My hair was gelled into pointy peaks that crunched to the touch, and the rims under my eyes were penciled with extra-thick strokes of kohl. I pursed my lips, caked with deep purple, in an attempt to not look rattled. But I was mortified.

"I'm sorry," I said, humbled. "I slept at my friend's house last night, and she lives a five-minute walk from here, and I forgot to pack another outfit." I could have easily borrowed a decent pair of jeans and a clean T-shirt from Sam, but I just didn't want to because it wouldn't have felt like me. At that moment, though, I would have given a lot to not feel like me. I shot Suzanne a pleading look and asked, "What should I do?"

She was gentle with me. She knew my parents, and my whole situation. "I think you can wear my jacket to cover you," she said. "Here." Suzanne slid the blazer, an awful, maroon, cheap-polyester thing with shoulder pads, off of her stocky frame and handed it to me. I was ridiculously happy to have it and I put it on, loving the warmth that the slippery fabric held.

"What's going on with you, Beth?" she asked. "Is everything OK?"

What could I possibly tell her? I got so trashed last night that I blacked out and threw myself at three guys, fooling around with one after the other, and then I passed out. It made me happy at first, all the attention, because one of them, Rob Lewis, a JV football player, had put his face between my legs and for a moment I felt loved, but then when I wouldn't give him a blowjob—wouldn't even touch him down there—he pushed me back on the bed and left the bedroom in disgust. I passed out before the sun came up and then I puked in the woods on my walk over here this morning. Now I feel wracked with guilt because I told my mother that Sam's parents would be home, but really they were in the Bahamas and my older friend from drama club, a senior, posed as Sam's mom when mine called to make sure I wasn't lying. And actually, right here, in temple, is one of the only places where I feel safe, where I still feel like the good girl that I used to be and am not ashamed by it, so I can't believe that I'm blowing it right now. And usually, when I'm not here, which is most of the time, I think about killing myself. So nothing, nothing at all, has been OK since the accident, actually, even though that was so long ago—three whole years almost—that it's embarrassing.

"Everything's fine," is what I told her instead. "I just forgot a change of clothes. I won't do it again." With that she nodded, and we went back into choir class. I sank down low in my pew, singing quietly but with passion to the new arrangement of "Eliyahu Ha Navi" that we were learning for Passover. The melody was sweet and sad and I had to seriously focus to not let the grief in my core well up enough to spill out. My eyes leaked just a bit as I sang, Holly and Lauren from class singing next to me while giving me curious sideways glances. Lauren's father had been our lawyer after the accident, and I could not look at her without thinking of it, without wondering how much he had told her about the man who had hit us. Did she know more than I did? Did she have some sort of magical clue of information that would allow me to move on? Instead of asking her, I sang, staring straight ahead, letting the music wash over me. "Eliyahu ha na vee. Eliyahu ha tish bee."

~

I continued drinking through most of high school. I'd look forward to it all week sometimes—look forward to just sitting around with friends from drama club and sipping from bottles of peppermint schnapps or vodka, right in their quiet bedrooms, or going to parties and filling my plastic cup again and again from the ever-present keg. Then I'd get a ride home and I'd slink into the house and fall into another round of bed spins and vomiting into the white plastic tulip-shaped waste bin that I kept under my desk. I would slide it right up next to the side of my bed and empty my guts into it a few times before falling into a dead sleep, awakening early to the stench, and creeping into the bathroom to take the crusty bin into the shower with me, where I would rinse it out while throwing up and gagging over the drain and trying to wash my hair, and then I'd pat the thing dry, wracked with tremors, and place it right back under my desk where it belonged.

Those were the lucky nights. Usually, my parents would sit up and wait for me to get home, and then, when I'd come stumbling in at midnight trying to look composed and genial, my dad would come up to me under the pretense of wanting to kiss me good night. But what he'd really be doing was getting a good sniff at my breath, which, though I would have just sucked on anything from peanut butter to raw onions to mask the liquor, was undeniably that of a very inebriated girl. I would roll my eyes dramatically when I saw my dad, groggy with sleep but sitting up in his recliner, his thin cotton bathrobe wrapped around him and the handful of strands in his comb-over puffed out to one side in a soft tangle. A patch of old-man skin, pale and hirsute and practically obscene, would appear at his chest or thigh and I would grit my teeth, embarrassed in front of no one. And then in would walk my mom—her face twisted with worry and subtly distorted by her thick, nighttime-only glasses. She'd look disgusted, as if I'd spat in her face or failed out of school or just fooled around with some guy at a party.

The night would start out nicely enough. It would be a Friday or Saturday, I would have just had dinner with my parents, and then I would put on a revealing outfit, add a final layer of Aqua Net to my teased hair, wait to hear the honk from Lisa or Rebekah or Cassie or Liz and then grab my bag, bought at the army-navy store, festooned with colorful buttons from New York City stores like Canal Jean Co. and Antique Boutique and stuffed with dark purple lipsticks and translucent face powder and mints and gum, and snap off the light in my bedroom.

"Beth, please be careful," my mom would say, appearing near the front door, wiping her hands on a dish towel she'd still be carrying around from post-dinner cleanup.

"And no drinking," my dad would add, stepping into the foyer from the living room, where he had assumed his nightly position of laying on the couch to simultaneously read the *New York Times* and watch the *MacNeil/Lehrer Report*. He would have a suppressed grin on his face, as he often did when he was trying to be a disciplinarian; I think he never felt comfortable in the role—still too close to a misbehaving youth in his mind to believe he was a strict parent who was in control. It made it hard, at times, to take him seriously.

"OK!" I told them. "I have to go! Lisa's waiting!"

Of course I was going to drink, I thought. What else were we supposed to do at a party? Still, as I headed out the door I felt a fresh stab of guilt because I was leaving my parents at home alone. The grief that hung throughout our house had, in my opinion, dissipated only slightly in the three years since the accident. And still, every time I headed out of that muckiness and into the cool, dark, unrestricted night, I felt that I was leaving them to drown in sadness. I'd keep asking them if they minded me going out.

One weekend—indistinguishable from so many others—I clomped in my high-heeled ankle boots across the perfectly trimmed and fertilized lawn to the driveway, where Lisa sat in the driver's seat of her forest-green Triumph TR7, bopping her head to Squeeze's *45's and Under*. The end of "Tempted" poured out of the car windows, and I felt precariously unfettered and giddy in the mild spring breeze as I anticipated another night of oblivion.

"Hey, nerd," Lisa said, using our favorite endearment of the moment. "You look cute."

"Thanks, nerd! So do you," I said, breathing in the scent of her: Design by Paul Sebastian perfume, Clinique's loose face powder, and the requisite Aqua Net. Her hair was poofier than usual and she had a thick layer of foundation on her face, with extra globs smeared over a pimple on the side of her nose. I had my own outbreak covered—a crop of tiny whiteheads at the left corner of my mouth—and silently hoped they wouldn't be visible in the dark of the outdoor party.

We drove with the music at full blast and the windows opened just a crack, so the wind wouldn't destroy our sculpted hair, and yelled above the music occasionally to talk about who we thought would be there.

"Probably Kelly and Amy and that whole crowd," Lisa said, snarling her lip.

"Ew, I know!"

After a fifteen-minute trip we turned off the highway onto the short, dark dead end where Mark lived, and had to park almost immediately because of all the other cars that already lined the street. We checked our lipstick in the rearview mirror and climbed out of her low two-seater and started toward the action. My stomach flipped like it always did when I approached a party; would I look sexy enough? Would I drink too much? Would I be able to mask my beer breath from my parents when I got home?

"Keg's that way," said a boy in a football jersey who I didn't recognize, pointing toward the back of the small house that we had entered from the front. We grinned and went out the back door of the house, where we found the keg, as promised, under the harsh glare of the porch light. Clutches of teens filled the yard, which was sprawling and on a slight slope that went up to the edge of a patch of woods that bordered the highway. Bryan Adams blared out of a boom box that was set on a picnic table, and we spotted Mark, laughing it up with a crew of fellow football players from our school. When he saw us he came over.

"Hey, ladies," he said. "Thanks for coming." He filled two red, jumbo plastic cups to the brim with watery beer and gave one to each of us; Lisa sipped and I gulped, going for a second round in no time. I loved the numb, tingly feeling that washed over the tip of my lips and my nose and my fingers, and the way that all the thoughts in my head swirled into a happy puddle. I just never knew when to stop.

She drove me home by midnight, right after we'd both exchanged spit with different guys and then begun worrying about the time. I stumbled up the path to our front porch, trying to steady myself before going inside. But it was useless.

"You've been drinking again," my father announced, his

voice heavy with disappointment. It was not quite a question, but not a statement either. I think he was holding out hope that maybe I wasn't actually drunk after all.

"I just had a beer. Big deal." I was slurry, and my voice was thick with disgust right back at them.

"You're not old enough to have a beer," he said, the tension rising between us. "Plus, I think you've maybe had more than that."

"So I had a few beers!" I offered. "I was at a party. I'm a teenager. I had a few beers, just like everyone else. That's what we do. We gather together with a keg and we drink beers. Can I please go to bed? I'm exhausted." I brushed by him then, trying to steady myself, annoyed by the sight of them, at the graveness of their concern. I could tell my mom had gone to bed, not able to fall asleep, while my dad had chosen to wait in the den, with the TV on low, and that he'd probably fallen asleep hours ago in this vigil position. My mother, as usual, was the first to yell at the back of my head as I loped into my room and threw myself onto my bed.

"Don't you walk away from us, missy!" she called after me, screeching. Then her voice changed from angry to desperately pleading. "Why do you feel you need to drink like this, Beth? Why?"

"Because it's *fun*," I sneered. "You've never been drunk in your life so you wouldn't know! I think you should try it sometime!" I was obnoxious but truthful—my mother is practically a teetotaler. She gets silly and red-faced from just one glass of wine at a restaurant, and she's never taken drugs— except once before I was born, she told me, when she was so distressed after her miscarriages that her obstetrician prescribed her Valium. But she said it made her all speedy instead of calm, and she ran up and down our quiet suburban street in some sort of a teary, manic panic.

My father likes wine with dinner sometimes, and can keep the same bottle of Johnnie Walker in the kitchen cabinet for years, savoring the occasional pour, usually at Thanksgiving or some other special gathering. His only brush with inebriation, he says, came when he was a teenage lifeguard in the town of Bradley Beach, and had polished off a bottle of bourbon with a couple of buddies on the quiet beach one night after work. It had made him "wild," he told me, prompting him to dive into the ocean and swim and swim and swim, not stopping until he was so far out that one of the guys had to paddle out to help drag him back to shore.

"Jews don't drink," was a common refrain of his, always uttered in a defiantly proud tone that struck me as naive. I would scoff at his proclamation—just as I would at all of his Jewish-obsessed comments—and sometimes I would take his comment as a challenge. *I* was a Jew, after all.

My mother quickly moved to the inevitable, lowest slam of all. "A drunk driver killed your brother," she said, as if I had forgotten. "How could you drink? How can you stand it?! I smelled the liquor stink coming out of that guy at the scene of the accident, and I won't be able to go near the stuff ever again!" I hated how she went on, with such drama, how she somehow found a way to point the finger of blame at me. I screamed at her that it was not related, that she was crazy, that everyone I knew drank and their brothers didn't die in drunk driving accidents. But I took it all in— her words, her tears, the guilt. I buried myself under my blankets as they stood above me, still hurling worried questions and punishments that I knew would never stick. The room, so pink and silly and foreign, would always spin around my head at this point—so far, far away from my friends who had snuck into their houses and made it safely to bed without stirring a parent, so far away from the joint

I'd just smoked and the jumbo plastic cups of warm beer I'd just slugged and the mouths of older boys I'd just devoured because I so desperately wanted . . . what? Approval? Attention? Forgiveness? And then eventually my parents would exit, slamming my door and leaving me alone with my thick-tongued misery.

~

I did have a couple of friends who did not drink. They were my bookish friends—the ones who hadn't even made out with anyone yet—and they were also the ones who had banded together to found our high school's first chapter of SADD, or Students Against Driving Drunk. I was horrified when I'd first heard they were doing it—self-conscious and self-abased and guilty that I wasn't involved, but I just couldn't do it. I couldn't risk sitting in a classroom after the final bell of the day had rung, hanging out with this handful of well-meaning peers and trying to look like anyone else, like a normal student who just happened to choose SADD as an extra-curricular activity, the same way I might've chosen debate club or field hockey or chess. They'd ask me to join periodically, but I'd always say no.

"We're planning this great presentation," they'd say, always with obvious caution. "We're screening a new film that we might get Miss Fox to let us show in gym class."

"We're trying to get permission to get a smashed-up car, from an actual drunk driving accident," they'd say, "To display in front of the school before the prom."

They got the car, and for a full two weeks before the prom I saw it there, on the front lawn, a twisted hunk of a sports car in the distance as my school bus approached each morning. I would quiver each time, the sick feeling spreading out from my gut, the students' din around me fading into a buzz, just like the night of the accident when my mind had become a snowy TV set. "Whoa, that's intense," someone near me would say. "Yeah, whoa," I'd say back, trying to sound normal. I'd inspect the wreckage up close some mornings, looking for blood or bone or other signs of life. I wondered what had become of our car, if there were any traces left of Adam or Kristin—any bits of their teeth or hair or skin pressed into the red vinyl seats or dusty carpeted floors or crushed gray metal. If I knew in which graveyard our car lay, I wondered, would I actually go and see it?

I wanted so badly to be big enough to go to those SADD meetings, to maybe even use my experience to help others— to tell my story and dissuade others from ever causing such trauma to anyone. But how would I even begin to unravel my tightly wound, stable facade to let all those people in? I knew I couldn't do it. So I just stayed far away, and hoped they could forgive me.

Chapter Twenty-Four

THERAPY resumed again at some point during my sopho-more year in high school, when I tried weekly sessions with the official school psychiatrist, Dr. Whitehead. But this time it was because my English teacher had set up a manda-tory appointment for me. She'd been growing concerned with my tendencies to wear all black, appear stoned in class (I wasn't—just glassy-eyed and distracted), and write morbid suicide poetry, like

> *I am a figure*
> *In a mob-shot of the world*
> *Printed on a sheet*
> *Of black construction paper*
> *Cut me out*
> *And make room*
> *For another futile sketch.*

I scoffed at her worrying, but secretly I was pleased to start the attention sessions again.

Dr. Whitehead was a very tall African American man with a shiny-bald pate and a pencil-thin mustache. He wore a suit and tie and polished shoes every day and was the most dapper thing going in that whole school. And though he looked uptight, he was laid-back and warm. "So how's it going today, Beth? Tell me about your morning so far," he'd say each time we met, leaning back into his chair and just smiling, looking like he would've happily waited hours for me to respond. During our first appointment he cut right to the chase and asked me if I was high. I smirked, telling him, "I wish! I've only smoked pot a few times," which was true. I basically stuck to drinking—keg beer, peppermint schnapps, cheap red wine or grain-alcohol punch. I added, "I'm just not really very happy." I went to see him each week during study hall and we had talks that went like this:

"This school is such a stupid waste of time," I'd say.

"In what way?"

"Everyone's phony."

"What makes you say that?"

"Their lives are perfect."

"You don't know that," he'd say, gently.

"I do know that," I'd insist. "I can just tell."

"Do you have problems?" Dr. Whitehead would ask. "Are you depressed?"

I liked that it was a direct question, with no predetermined answer built in like when my mother spoke—when she asked me things like, "You'd never do anything to hurt yourself, would you?" or "You know better than to start smoking cigarettes, don't you, Beth?" Pretty quickly, Dr. Whitehead and I were talking about the accident week after week, which made me cry, which surprised me, as I thought my badass escapades would've stomped out any lingering bereavement.

"I just miss them *so much!*" I'd wail. "It's *not fair!* I just want to die."

Dr. Whitehead didn't seem particularly shocked by my outbursts, always remaining supremely calm. Nothing I did got a rise out of the man. He told me logical things—that my emotions had been shut down for years, and that now, as a sixteen-year-old, I was beginning to feel my grief profoundly. But I didn't know how to express it, so I was "acting out" and depressed. It made me roll my eyes. One day I left his office and scrawled a poem into my biology notebook:

> *Thanks so much*
> *For that helpful quote.*
> *Now I think*
> *I'll cut my throat.*

It made me feel better than any session had—as did drama class, my life raft, thanks to the really depressed new kid, Tim Simpson. Tim was pale and sad looking, and about twice a week he wore a black T-shirt with a Shakespeare quote scrawled across its front: WHY HE THAT CUTS OFF TWENTY YEARS OF LIFE CUTS OFF SO MANY YEARS OF FEARING DEATH.

"Cool shirt," I told him during class. We had broken up into small groups or pairs to rehearse scenes that we would do in front of each other. I was with my friend Jo, who would attempt (but fail at) suicide by eating a bottle of Tylenol in another month or so, and we were about to practice our depressing scene from *The Children's Hour.* But first I told her "be right back" and sauntered over to him—he was alone, sitting on the radiator alongside the windows, thumbing through the book of scenes. He brightened at my compliment.

"Thanks," he said. "I made it. Want me to make you one?"

I imagined wearing such a cry for help around the house, in front of my mother, around all of my friends in school. "No, thanks," I told him. "It wouldn't look right on me." He shrugged, but then he smiled, and I knew I had myself a new pal.

One afternoon, not nearly long enough into our fast friendship, he told me the secret to a successful suicide. "The most effective way to kill yourself," he told me, "is to slit your jugular." His eyes sparkled when he said it, and then he grinned and shot his eyebrows up and down, and rapped on the side of his neck for effect.

"What's a jugular?" I asked, sucking down the last slurp of chocolate milk from the waxy half-pint I'd bought for lunch. We were sitting in the cafeteria, the last two left in the room besides the janitor whose job it was to fold up all the long metal tables and their connecting benches and wheel them against the walls, turning the lunch room back into the all-purpose-room/theater. Drama was next, and instead of heading upstairs with the rest of the class we'd decided to wait it out there, balanced at the edge of the stage, where we knew every-one would be trooping in any minute. We'd been working on monologues, and today we were going to take turns doing them alone, at center stage. Tim and I had both chosen, predictably, the "Out, out brief candle!" one from *Macbeth*, and we could do it in our sleep. So we waited, calmly chatting about death.

"The jugular vein is the most important vein in your body, big and thick and pulsing with life, and it's right on the side of your neck," Tim told me. "It would be scary, and really bloody, but you'd go fast. Check it out." He put a clammy hand up to my neck and held three fingers hard up against it. Within seconds I felt lightheaded—and thrilled and scared—and I batted his arm away. "Isn't that cool?"

He looked positively radiant. It was funny about Tim.
He was the first boy ever whom I felt like I was friends with
whom I didn't get all weird and flirty and nervous around.
There was no sexual tension, just a shared fascination with
depression and suicide and death. He was skinny, gangly, and
pasty as bread dough, and his longish brown hair was perpetually stringy. But he was smart, brilliant even, and his eyes
were piercing.

"Tell me again how you did it last time," I said, hoping
we'd have enough time for the drawn-out version of the story
before our class arrived. My request got him so excited that
he stood up and shook off his black leather motorcycle jacket,
letting it fall into a heap on the stage. I yanked it up and put
it around my shoulders, and his musky heat enveloped my
chilly arms and my thin black Echo & the Bunnymen T-shirt.
I pulled my knees up to my chin and kissed the silky black
and blue paisley print of my vintage pajama pants, leaving
behind a deep-plum stain. My hair, crimped with a hot iron
and then teased into a hair-sprayed nest, fell in front of one of
my eyes, thick with black eyeliner. But I could see him well
enough.

"It was a Saturday night," Tim said, pacing a bit now on
the shiny beams of stage left. The second bell of the period
rang out and echoed in the now-cleared cafeteria, and the
janitor trudged out, his massive ring of keys jangling at his
hip. "I had my stepdad's switchblade hidden under my bed,
and I crawled halfway underneath and pulled it out." He
paused for dramatic effect. "As soon as I had my hand on the
blade I felt safe, and ready, and—I don't know—*happy*? What
is happy, Beth? Do you have any fucking clue?" Just then Mr.
Liebenberg and our class of a dozen other misfits banged into
the room, ruining our moment. Good thing, really, because

Tim was about to go off on one of his tangents, and I always felt slightly left in the dark by them. He had really *done* it, he'd really cut his wrists and been sent to doctors, and I just thought about it a lot. And this depressed me even more, because it made me feel like a fake.

I made only one sorry attempt at cutting my own wrists, if one could even call it that. It was one day after school, during my freshman year, when I arrived to find my mother deep in one of her afternoon naps, burrowed in her bed with the shades drawn, once again, and the door partially closed. She never shut it all the way—I think it was difficult because of how the thick wool carpeting slowed the door down from underneath—and as I got older I realized that it was a bit strange that the door was never shut tight (when did they ever have sex?), but I got used to it. Seeing her door partially closed was enough to tell me to steer clear, which I would have done anyway, and I went directly to my own room, right next door, to put on U2's *The Unforgettable Fire* cassette and flop onto my bed and sulk. I had been obsessed with the idea of killing myself for weeks, and wanted, on that day, to really sit with the thought for a while. I know I was never really serious about it, just dramatically desperate for something I couldn't quite pinpoint then—something like punishment or pardon. Or both. What I would sit and think about is how I didn't want to be left on the earth without them, without Adam and Kristin—forever a pair now, and such an unlikely one— although that desire to flee always felt hollow. It could have been the guilt of surviving that drove me, that made me want to run and hide and make myself disappear, although I could not recognize it then, and hardly can do it now.

Whatever it was that made me want to remove myself led me to pick up a very sharp pin that day and dig it into my

wrist. The pin was one of those long ones attached to the
back of a button—either the Smiths or the Cure or the
Unique shop in the Village—and it was the sharpest thing in
my room. I remember bending it back from the button and
then lighting a match and sterilizing it, as if I were about to
pierce my ear, and then I stuck it slowly and methodically
into my right wrist. Of course I went just to the left of a nice
blue vein—it was the trial run, I told myself, to see how much
pain I could bear—and though I remember sticking it in
pretty far, there was not much blood at all. I kept digging
around in there, made a nice narrow hole, and then was too
scared to go on. I pictured what it would look like to really
make a slash, with a razor, and to let myself bleed. I knew I
was supposed to be in a bathtub, something about clotting,
and that even if I did have a razor that I was willing to use it
would probably not have done too much in my bed. I imagined my parents coming to knock on my door to tell me it
was time for dinner, getting no answer and then pushing their
way in to find me sprawled in some unnatural way, bloodied
and pathetic, and it just didn't seem at all fair. I couldn't take
away myself, their only child left, and put them through another tragedy. And when I had this realization I wept, because it wasn't fair that I couldn't kill myself just because
of them.

So I left my room and walked down the short hall to the
bathroom to grab a Band-Aid. I hated the house at that time
of day—when it was freshly dark outside, and I had missed
the sunset because I was so distracted, and there were no
lights on in the house because no one had been aware that
daylight had come to an end. The air felt so close in that new
cloak of darkness, so stuffy and sleepy and sad, like all the life
had been sucked out, and though we were all in the house
and breathing, we were soulless, hollow, grief-stricken pods,

all in the same pain but spread too far apart to realize we were in it together, all moaning and crying and crouched in our own corners because of the distance I had insisted be there. And now no one knew how to fix it.

"Beth? What are you doing?" I was in the bathroom, hunched over my wrist at the sink and patting down the Band-Aid, when my mom appeared, groggy and squishy-faced, in the doorway.

"Oh, nothing," I said, startled and afraid to explain how I cut my wrist, of all places. "I just have a little cut. It's nothing."

"OK. Are you sure?"

"Yes!"

"Your dad and I thought we'd go get some Chinese," she said. This brightened me a bit. Anything but sitting around that sad kitchen table with an empty chair. Anything but being in surroundings so intimate that something emotional could happen. Plus, I was always up for hot and sour soup and some chicken in garlic sauce.

"Oh good," I told her. "I just have to change." My mom flicked on lights in the house, she and my dad got dressed, I had a Band-Aid on my wrist, and we went out to dinner.

She noticed it the next afternoon, when we went shopping for new ballet leotards at the local dance shop. I had returned to ballet at Mrs. Carroll's studio a couple years before, in eighth grade, after taking some time off to let my foot heal. I remember when I entered the studio that afternoon it looked smaller than I'd remembered and a bit distorted, like I was gazing at it through a fish-eye lens, and that the girls in class treated me gingerly, as if I might have a breakdown at any moment.

"How *are* you?" they asked, eyeing me up and down to see how I was different.

I was surprised at how much being there didn't bother

me. I simply took my place at the bar and worked my way through the plié and *tendu* and *rond de jambe* combinations, shaking out the pain in my foot every now and then, but really losing myself in the music and the movements just like I always had. The only time I really got spooked was just before the ballet recital, which, though it was to be held back at the old small church we'd used for years before Our Lady Star of the Sea, felt a bit like returning to the scene of a crime.

That afternoon in the small dressing room I pulled on a plum-colored Lycra leotard with spaghetti straps and a puckered strip between my small breasts, and when I stepped out through the heavy white curtain and into the shop to show my mom, she caught sight of my wrist.

"What happened there?" she asked, grabbing for my arm. I wrenched it away.

"Nothing!" I told her.

"What do you mean, 'nothing'? Right on your wrist like that? Beth, you would never try to hurt yourself, would you?" She looked suddenly daunted, her forehead creased in a way I knew was meant to convey anger, but which actually looked like thinly disguised fear.

"Of course not! God!" I said, as if it were the most insane thought possible. "What do you think of the leotard?"

She looked through me with distracted eyes. She knew something, but wasn't sure what, and she didn't really want to know. "It's fine," she said. "Do you want it?"

I nodded, self-consciously holding my wrist behind my back.

"Then let's get it and get out of here," she said curtly. I wriggled out of the stretchy film of polyester, my mom bought it, and we marched to the car in silence. I got in, she started up the car, and I clicked on the radio, already tuned to the local alternative station, WHTG, which I'd listened to on our way over. A Smiths song was playing. Perfect. I turned it up and stared out the window and heard my mother sigh.

Chapter Twenty-Five

THERE *were* a handful of times, years later, when I allowed us to talk about it. One of the first would have to wait until I was in college, home for winter break during a beautifully crushing snowstorm.

It hadn't started to come down yet, though the sky was heavy with silver clouds as I made the familiar drive home from Connecticut in my little car—a Ford Escort the color of Cookie Monster that my father had bought for me when I turned twenty. The first thing I did with it was to anoint its rear window with a Grateful Dead sticker, which made my dad wince; the second thing was to take it on a cross-country drive, my friends Julia and Liz joining me for a stoned, month-long roundtrip of meandering and camping, of ogling sights from Old Faithful to the surreal, drip-castle landscape of the Badlands.

As I entered New Jersey and neared home to a cranked

soundtrack of Paul Simon and Traffic and Jerry Garcia, I passed parkway exits for towns I'd driven by my whole life: Elizabeth, South Amboy, Middletown, Hazlet. I felt free, comfortably suspended between my past life and the present.

At home, with Mom and Dad, it was always the past— the same three-bedroom ranch house with its oily garage, out-of-tune Baldwin piano, and American-flag–bearing front porch. It was the same place where Adam once slept on the other side of the wall from me, the one in which I lived my entire life until leaving for college, the one that became filled with such emptiness over the years. People used to ask me why we didn't sell the house and move away after the accident, and it made me wonder, so I asked my mom.

"Because there are so many good memories here too," she told me, not missing a beat. "Because when I look into the backyard I see your brother on the swing set, I see you running around under the maple trees, and I don't want to leave those good memories behind."

For me, though, all the good stuff had been destroyed. The house was sad from then on; over the years it only got worse. I'd moved away long before I had healed, and coming back to the place that was stuck in a time warp of grief felt like salt in my wounds over and over again.

I couldn't help but rub the salt in sometimes—like I did that afternoon, when I drove into our development and decided, impulsively, to turn right a block too soon, onto the Sickels' road. I felt like a stalker, slowing my car to a crawl and holding my breath until I reached it, the fourth house on the left. It was the exact same ranch model as ours, only its asbestos shingles were painted butter yellow instead of the color of coffee ice cream. I drove by as slowly as I could without stopping and took in every detail of the property, from the white wicker loveseat on the porch to the slightly overgrown front lawn that looked pale and frozen in winter's grip. The garage door was halfway up, but all I could see in there was darkness. The curtains to Kristin's room were drawn. I thought about stopping, walking right up to the door. I couldn't picture how Mrs. Sickel's face would look—if she would have aged a lot or if she would be at all happy to see me, or if she would be stunned or even angry—and so I drove on, rounding the corner to turn onto Thornley Road.

I pulled into our driveway and felt something in me constrict, as if my whole being were preparing for an emotional assault. I thought of so many of the other times I had been in this same spot, not yet out of the safety of the car but already inside the complex bubble of home—when I returned from the hospital all those years ago, when we got home from my Bat Mitzvah, when a tipsy friend would drop me off after a keg party, when I brought Sandy here to my house for the very first time.

I had gone with my mother to the other side of town to pick Sandy up and bring her back for lunch. The get together had felt oddly formal—our first away from Miss Boyd's office—and I thought of the way she sat in the backseat of my mother's car as it idled in the driveway, rigid and unsure of herself, peering warily through her tangle of hair-sprayed bangs at our neat brick walk and at the scary-cat-and-jack-o-lantern cutout my mother had hung in the front door for Halloween. She'd stayed for just an hour or so, politely munching the turkey sandwich my mom had made her and gazing around at all the quaint details of our kitchen as if in a foreign land. Her usual badass self did not return until my mom dropped us off at the mall, when she could lead us with a confident swagger toward her friends in the pit.

Our friendship didn't last, of course. It couldn't have. Ours was one based solely upon our fresh losses, and upon our meetings with Miss Boyd. When those ended and we started high school, we boomeranged back to our predetermined crowds, occasionally stopping to chat in the hallways, and then only waving, and then, by senior year, not acknowledging each other at all. My heart would quicken a bit each time I saw her, though, and I'd watch her out of the corner of my eye as she snapped her gum and blew smoke rings with the burnouts outside of the cafeteria, or flirted or made out with the lanky, leering guys who hovered around her locker.

I would see Sandy only one final time after high school ended. It was the summer after sophomore year of college, when I was back home on the Jersey Shore, serving greasy cheese fries and burgers at a food stand on the Belmar boardwalk, trying to save money for my cross-country journey. One night I was pumping gooey orange cheese onto some piping hot fries when I heard her familiarly raspy voice. I turned around to see Sandy, bloated and drunk, with a group of older men. Her brown hair was dyed an unnatural shade of rust. I remembered hearing that she had had a baby right after high school. I put down the fries and walked to the counter.

"Hey," I called. "Sandy."

She looked up, squinting into the fluorescent lights of our little food shack until I came into focus. "Beth?" She smiled a dopey, distant grin. "Wow." The rowdy guys around her quieted, curious. But then her eyes, which had mellowed when she recognized me, quickly returned to being hard, and she was a tough girl again. "Aren't you like, in *college* or something?" She laughed, and one of the guys whispered something to her and she elbowed him in the stomach. He shoved her. I wanted to grab her, to hold her, but it was all way out of my league.

"Fuck you!" she said to him, heading away from me into

the blur of the boardwalk's post-bar crowd. Then she turned back for a second and waved. "Bye, Beth," she called. "Sorry."

~

The start of the snowfall just before dinnertime that night added to my nostalgic mood, and I used it as a reason to stay home, to give in to my old fears about going out and leaving my parents home all alone. They seemed fine by this point, but I was still unable to imagine that they were anything but wrecks underneath their facades.

"It's coming down really hard now!" I announced, sounding like a kid hoping for a snow day as I lingered near the windows at the back of the house, near where my father had gotten our fireplace roaring. He closed the book he was reading and put it down on the floor near his blue upholstered rocking chair, and my mother, who was still in the kitchen doing her post-dinner puttering, flicked off the light over the stove and came to join us, setting a small plate of sliced Entenmann's chocolate-chip nut loaf on the table we hovered around.

"Have some cake," she said, picking up a piece and taking a bite before gazing outside. "So beautiful," she said, her top lip coated with powdered sugar.

My dad had seemed lost in the view until the cake came along, then grabbed a piece and ate half of it in one bite. "Yep," he said, and put an arm around my mom.

"Adam loved watching the snow," he said then, and I knew he was about to begin some of his weepy nostalgic talk, which I still took great and constant measures to avoid. But that time I tried to bear it—mainly because I had been thinking the same thing when he said it. Adam and I had spent a lot of time watching the snow fall together; we'd hole up in the dining room, which had the largest window in the house, setting up pillows and blankets so we could really settle into the view.

"I know," I said, slowly, aware that my words were weighty, and that they would cause my parents to strain to hear the true meaning in them, as if pressing their ears against a door to hear the muffled chatter on the other side. "We used to watch it together through the big window in the dining room." Just that much put my voice on the edge of cracking, so I stopped, took a deep breath, ate some cake.

"Oh, Beth," my mom said. "I'm so sorry he's not here for you still."

And instead of huffing away after getting annoyed at her for playing God, I somehow heard what she said as a true expression of sympathy. "Me too," I told her, trying hard to swallow the dry, sugary crumbs. "And that he's not here for you, too."

My dad let out a shaky sigh. The flakes were falling in big fat clumps in the long triangle of yellow light and lay glimmering like sequins across the shallow slope of our yard. It barely resembled a hill at all, though I knew that Adam and I had spent many an afternoon sledding down it in our red plastic toboggan and shiny metal saucer. Had it flattened out? I wondered. Or had it never been steep to begin with?

I saw my mom's eyes well up and her bottom lip quiver as she shook her head slowly, staring out at the wintry yard. I let myself cry a little then too, as I leaned into her and sneaked an arm around her warm and faintly perfumed neck, settling, for just a minute, into an awkward sort of hug. Then my dad leaned his chin on my shoulder and we stood there, huddled together, just like we should have been all along.

ACKNOWLEDGMENTS

~

I WOULD like to thank the many generous people who have informed and encouraged both my writing and my healing over the years. First, thank you to the many teachers of writing workshops and classes—and all of my talented fellow students—with whom I have worked and reworked parts of this book: Richard McCann and his summer class at the Fine Arts Work Center in Provincetown; Nancy Rawlinson and her Sackett Street Writers' Workshop in Brooklyn; Precious Williams and her Mediabistro memoir workshop; Donna Minkowitz and her workshop in Park Slope; Jill Dearman and "Bang the Keys." Thank you to the places, both likely and unlikely, that sheltered me as I wrote this: our magical home in Provincetown, our beloved cave on West End Avenue, my childhood bedroom in Eatontown, the Starbucks on Broadway and West Ninety-eighth Street. For their support and wisdom I am also eternally grateful to Barbara Struble, Erin McHugh, Patrick Herold, Genine Lentine, Rabbi Sally Priesand, Janine Avril (for giving me a forum for my first public reading of this material), Lori Boyd and especially to Lynn Gold. Heartfelt thanks to the team at Harmony who made this book possible: to Shaye Areheart, for believing in this book and in me; to my editor, Julia Pastore, for her keen eye and unflappable calm; to publicity and marketing pros Campbell Wharton, Samantha Choy, and Kira Walton. Many thanks also to my kind and witty agent, Alan Nevins of Renaissance Literary and Talent. To my parents, Deborah and Martin Greenfield: Thank you for your love and undying encouragement, even for this book, which you knew would lay bare your pain. I love you. To my daughter Lula, for bringing me such joy. Finally, thank you to my partner in love and life, Kiki Herold—my fiercest advocate, my most passionate reader, and my biggest fan. I, too, am yours.

ABOUT THE AUTHOR

B ETH GREENFIELD was born and raised in Monmouth County, New Jersey. Since receiving her master's in journalism from NYU she has written about travel, entertainment, gay culture, and parenting for publications including the *New York Times*, Lonely Planet guidebooks, *Out*, *Time Out New York Kids*, and *Time Out New York*, where she is currently a staff editor. Over the years, Beth has been honored with a Front Page Award from the Newswomen's Club of New York, a nomination for a 2006 GLAAD Media Award, and a 2009 Folio Eddie for feature writing. She lives in New York City and Provincetown.